Cyber Security in AI Era:

Challenges and Opportunities

About the Author:

Izem IFEROUDJENE, is a Digital transformation expert with more than 2 decades' experience in IT and telecoms. He worked for several well-known companies in Education, Energy, Banking, Government sector and Manufacturing, such as Dessau, Samsung, Ericsson, IBM, TCS, GNL Solutions, LTI Mindtree ...,

Izem Iferoudjene, has been involved in a number of significant projects; across more than 20 countries, he contributed in building and delivering several challenging and complex digital transformation solutions, involving stakeholders from different backgrounds and nationalities.

He holds two master degrees in Computer Science and a specialization in Business strategy from the University of Virginia, Darden School of Business, he also holds more than a 100+ Certifications and diploma delivered from well-known actors such as: ISC2, EC-Council, IBM, Google, Microsoft, Cisco, Fortinet, AWS, New York State University and other institutions.

Particularly interested by cyber security Izem has a significant 15 years' experience in cybersecurity and IT project/program delivery. His main areas of interest are: Cybersecurity, Data, AI and Digital transformation.

About TCSC London Academy:

TCSC London Academy creates and provide several trainings designed to reduce the GAP between workplace market and available talent pool in a strongly competitive world. The first objective of the academy, is to equip learners with skills and knowledge to tackle the job market.

The academy provides several training in following areas:

- Cybersecurity
- Artificial intelligence AI
- Data
- UX design
- Project management
- Business strategy
- Software development
- Robotics (designed for kids and for discovery)

About Technology Consultancy and Strategy Centre:

TCSC is a comprehensive service provider that offers a wide range of solutions to meet the needs of modern businesses. The TCSC company offers services in Cyber Security, Data, AI, UX Design, Project Management, Compliance, Network and Telecoms, Business Strategy, and Training for individuals and businesses.

For more details please refer to their website: www.tcscsolutions.com

Table of Contents

About the book: This book aims to explore the evolving landscape of cybersecurity in the context of rapid advancements in artificial intelligence (AI) technology. The book highlights the intersections between AI and cybersecurity, discussing both the potential benefits and challenges that arise from their integration. you will gain insights into how AI is reshaping cybersecurity strategies, threat detection, response mechanisms, and ethical considerations.

The topics covered in this book are as following:

Chapter 1: Introduction to AI and Cybersecurity
- Overview of AI technologies and their applications
- Cybersecurity landscape and emerging threats
- Convergence of AI and cybersecurity

Chapter 2: AI for Threat Detection and Prevention
- Role of AI in identifying and mitigating cyber threats
- Machine learning and anomaly detection in cybersecurity
- Case studies of AI-powered threat detection systems

Chapter 3: AI in Intrusion Detection and Response
- Utilizing AI to detect and respond to cyber intrusions
- Real-time analysis of network traffic and behaviour
- Incorporating AI-driven incident response strategies

Chapter 4: AI-Enabled Vulnerability Management
- Automating vulnerability assessments using AI
- Predictive analytics for identifying potential vulnerabilities
- Balancing AI-driven vulnerability management with human expertise

Chapter 5: AI and Social Engineering Attacks
- AI-driven phishing and social engineering attacks
- Countermeasures for detecting and mitigating AI-generated threats
- Ethical considerations in using AI to combat social engineering attacks

Chapter 6: Ethical and Legal Implications of AI in Cybersecurity
- Addressing biases and fairness in AI cybersecurity solutions
- Ensuring transparency and accountability in AI-based decisions
- Navigating legal and regulatory challenges in AI-driven cybersecurity

Chapter 7: AI-Enhanced Security Operations Centers (SOCs)
- Role of AI in enhancing SOC capabilities
- Automation of routine tasks and threat analysis
- Benefits and limitations of AI-powered SOCs

Chapter 8: Future Trends and Challenges
- Exploring the future of AI in cybersecurity
- AI-driven adaptive attacks and defensive strategies
- Anticipating challenges and opportunities in the evolving landscape

Chapter 9: Case Studies and Practical Applications
- Analysing real-world case studies of AI-driven cybersecurity incidents
- Evaluating successful integration of AI in cybersecurity practices

Chapter 1: Introduction to AI and Cybersecurity

Section 1: Introduction to AI and its Relevance in Cybersecurity

Overview:

The Rapid Advancements in AI Technology and Integration Across Sectors:

In this section we aim to explore the rapid advancements in artificial intelligence (AI) technology and its fast integration across various sectors, including cybersecurity. We will explore the evolution of AI from its early stages to the current state of breakthroughs in machine learning and deep learning, emphasizing the significance of neural networks. The integration of AI spans diverse sectors, such as healthcare, finance, and transportation, agriculture, defence and industry. In healthcare, AI aids in medical diagnosis, treatment, and drug discovery. In finance, it enhances financial forecasting, fraud detection, and investment strategies. In transportation, AI contributes to self-driving cars, traffic optimization, and predictive maintenance.

Furthermore, this chapter underscores the critical role of AI in the cybersecurity field. It highlights AI's effectiveness in threat detection and mitigation by analyzing vast volumes of security data. AI-driven security analytics play a key role in identifying and responding to cyber threats. Additionally, AI-powered authentication methods are explored for bolstering cybersecurity efforts.

1.1. Rapid Advancements in AI Technology:

The world of technology has been witnessing rapid advancements in artificial intelligence (AI) that are transforming industries and reshaping the way we perceive and interact with machines. This module explores the dynamic landscape of AI technology and its pervasive integration across diverse sectors, with a special focus on its role in cybersecurity.

AI has come a long way since its inception, evolving from basic rule-based systems to sophisticated machine learning and deep learning algorithms. Breakthroughs in machine learning have enabled computers to learn and improve from experience, making them adept at tasks that were once considered exclusive to human intelligence. The rise of deep learning and neural networks has brought about unprecedented accuracy in image recognition, natural language processing, and pattern recognition.

1.1.1. Examples of AI Integration across Sectors:

The integration of AI spans various sectors, showcasing its versatility and adaptability to address unique challenges.

Healthcare:

AI is making significant strides in healthcare by revolutionizing medical diagnosis, treatment, and drug discovery. Machine learning algorithms can analyse medical images and predict disease outcomes, aiding doctors in making more accurate decisions. AI-powered tools are also speeding up the discovery of new drugs and therapies.

Finance:

In the financial sector, AI is enhancing decision-making processes through accurate financial forecasting and risk assessment. Fraud detection systems leverage AI algorithms to identify unusual patterns and anomalies in financial transactions. Investment strategies are being fine-tuned using AI's ability to analyse vast amounts of market data.

Transportation:

AI is transforming transportation by enabling the development of self-driving cars that use real-time data and algorithms to navigate roads safely. Traffic optimization algorithms help reduce congestion and enhance the efficiency of transportation networks. Predictive maintenance powered by AI ensures the smooth operation of vehicles and infrastructure.

1.1.2. Examples of AI Integration into Cybersecurity:

The integration of AI into the field of cybersecurity is particularly impactful, addressing the ever-evolving landscape of digital threats.

Threat Detection and Mitigation:

AI plays a crucial role in threat detection and mitigation by analysing massive volumes of security data. Machine learning algorithms can identify patterns indicative of cyberattacks, helping organizations respond proactively to potential threats.

Security Analytics:

AI-driven security analytics streamline the process of identifying and addressing security incidents. By automating the analysis of complex data sets, organizations can rapidly identify vulnerabilities and potential breaches.

Authentication and Access Control:

AI-powered authentication methods are enhancing access control mechanisms. Biometric recognition and behavioural analysis enable more secure and user-friendly authentication, reducing the risk of unauthorized access.

Conclusion:

The rapid advancements in AI technology are fuelling innovation across sectors, from healthcare and finance to transportation and cybersecurity. As AI continues to evolve, its integration into various domains is reshaping industries and leading to breakthroughs that were once considered futuristic. The world stands at the cusp of a new era, where AI's potential to drive transformation is limited only by our imagination.

Reference Links:
Advancements in AI Technology[1]
AI's Impact Across Sectors[2]
AI's Role in Cybersecurity[3]

1.2 Defining Artificial Intelligence (AI):

Introduction:

Artificial Intelligence (AI) is a groundbreaking field in computer science that aims to replicate human intelligence within machines. By harnessing the power of AI, machines can perform tasks that traditionally rely on human intelligence, pushing the boundaries of what technology can achieve.

---

[1] https://www.sciencedaily.com/news/computers_math/artificial_intelligence/

[2] https://www.forbes.com/sites/forbestechcouncil/2019/12/10/how-ai-is-impacting-the-world-across-industries/?sh=2dd1d8c812d7

[3] https://www.csoonline.com/article/3372361/the-role-of-ai-in-cybersecurity.html

1.2.1. Defining AI as Simulation of Human Intelligence:

At its core, AI involves creating algorithms and systems that mimic human cognitive functions. These systems are designed to learn, reason, problem-solve, and make decisions much like a human would. By replicating these aspects of human intelligence, machines can perform complex tasks that were previously considered the domain of human capabilities.

1.2.2. Enabling Machines to Perform Human-Like Tasks:

AI empowers machines to execute a diverse range of tasks that typically require human intelligence, including:

Natural Language Processing (NLP):

AI algorithms can analyse and understand human language, enabling machines to interpret, translate, and generate text. Chatbots and virtual assistants use NLP to engage in human-like conversations.

Computer Vision:

AI-driven computer vision systems can recognize and interpret visual data, identifying objects, faces, and patterns within images and videos. Applications range from facial recognition to self-driving cars.

Decision-Making and Problem Solving:

AI algorithms can analyse vast amounts of data to make informed decisions or solve complex problems. These capabilities find applications in financial forecasting, medical diagnosis, and more.

In conclusion, AI is revolutionizing the capabilities of machines by simulating human intelligence. This enables machines to perform tasks that once seemed beyond their reach, paving the way for transformative applications across various sectors. The journey of AI continues to push the boundaries of technology, reshaping industries and enhancing the potential of automation and innovation.

1.3 AI in Everyday Life examples:

Artificial Intelligence (AI) has rapidly integrated into our daily lives, enhancing convenience, efficiency, and personalization. This module explores various AI applications that have become integral to our routines, ranging from virtual assistants to recommendation systems and autonomous vehicles.

1.3.1. Virtual Assistants:

AI-driven virtual assistants are now ubiquitous, offering a helping hand in tasks and information retrieval.

Siri (Apple):

Siri understands natural language commands and responds with relevant information, weather updates, reminders, and more.

Google Assistant:

Google Assistant offers voice-controlled assistance, answering queries, setting alarms, and even recognizing user preferences.

Amazon Alexa:

Alexa controls smart home devices, provides news updates, and creates shopping lists through voice commands.

Reference: Virtual Assistants and Everyday AI[4]

1.3.2. Recommendation Systems:

AI-powered recommendation systems personalize our online experiences and choices.

Netflix Recommendations:

Netflix uses AI algorithms to suggest movies and TV shows based on viewing history and preferences.

Amazon Product Recommendations:

Amazon employs AI to recommend products based on purchase history and browsing behaviour, enhancing the shopping experience.

Spotify Discovery:

Spotify's AI-driven Discover Weekly playlist offers personalized music recommendations based on listening habits.

Reference: AI-Powered Recommendation Systems[5]

1.3.3. Autonomous Vehicles:

AI is transforming transportation with autonomous vehicles that can navigate without human intervention.

Tesla Autopilot:

Tesla's Autopilot uses AI to control the vehicle's movements, adjust speed, change lanes, and navigate autonomously.

Waymo (Google):

Waymo's self-driving cars rely on AI to interpret surroundings, make driving decisions, and ensure passenger safety.

Uber ATG:

Uber's Advanced Technologies Group develops AI-powered self-driving technology for ride-sharing services.

Reference: Autonomous Vehicles and AI[6]

Conclusion:

AI applications have seamlessly woven into our daily lives, offering convenience, personalization, and efficiency across various domains. Virtual assistants streamline tasks, recommendation systems personalize choices, and autonomous vehicles are reshaping transportation. As AI continues to evolve, its impact on our routines is expected to grow, offering innovative solutions to complex challenges.

---

[4] https://www.npr.org/2019/12/23/789233460/everyday-ai-virtual-assistants-like-siri-and-alexa-have-crept-into-our-lives

[5] https://www.wired.com/2017/04/the-end-of-algorithms/

[6] https://www.theverge.com/2019/8/13/20802051/autonomous-cars-self-driving-vehicles-how-they-work-level-5-avs

1.4 The Convergence of AI and Cybersecurity:

Relationship between AI and Cybersecurity: Reshaping Strategies

The dynamic landscape of cybersecurity is being transformed by the integration of artificial intelligence (AI). This module explores the symbiotic relationship between AI and cybersecurity, showcasing how AI technologies are reshaping strategies to defend against evolving digital threats.

1.4.1. Enhancing Threat Detection and Prevention:

AI's ability to analyse massive volumes of data in real-time has revolutionized threat detection.

Behaviour Analysis:

AI algorithms can detect unusual behaviour patterns across networks, identifying potential threats before they escalate.

Anomaly Detection:

AI-powered systems can detect anomalies in user behaviour or system performance, flagging suspicious activities.

Reference: AI-Driven Threat Detection[7]

1.4.2. Predictive Analysis and Risk Assessment:

AI empowers organizations to predict and mitigate risks before they materialize into threats.

Predictive Analytics:

AI systems analyse historical data to predict future attack vectors, enabling proactive measures.

Vulnerability Management:

AI algorithms identify potential vulnerabilities in software and systems, aiding in preemptive patching.

Reference: AI-Powered Risk Assessment[8]

1.4.3. Rapid Incident Response:

AI accelerates incident response times by automating tasks and providing real-time insights.

Automated Threat Containment:

AI can autonomously contain threats and halt the spread of malware within networks.

Incident Analysis:

AI-driven systems analyse incidents, extract insights, and generate actionable reports for cybersecurity teams.

Reference: AI for Incident Response[9]

1.4.4. AI-Enabled User Authentication:

AI is revolutionizing user authentication mechanisms, enhancing security while improving user experience.

Biometric Authentication:

AI-powered biometric systems analyse unique physical traits for secure user identification.

---

[7] https://www.darkreading.com/analytics/ai--the-new-darling-of-cybersecurity/a/d-id/1339445

[8] https://www.securitymagazine.com/articles/95452-ai-in-cybersecurity-the-promise-and-peril-of-a-technological-game-changer

[9] https://www.csoonline.com/article/3638612/why-ai-is-a-boost-not-a-replacement-for-cybersecurity-skill.html

Behavioural Authentication:

AI recognizes behavioural patterns, such as typing speed and mouse movements, for continuous authentication.

Reference: AI and Biometric Authentication[10]

1.4.5. Addressing Evolving Threats with AI:

Cyber threats are evolving rapidly   , and AI is being harnessed to stay ahead of adversaries.

AI-Powered Threat Intelligence:

AI processes vast threat intelligence data to identify emerging attack techniques and vulnerabilities.

AI-Generated Threats:

AI-generated cyber threats are also emerging, necessitating AI-driven defences to counteract them.

Reference: AI-Generated Cyber Threats[11]

Conclusion:

The interplay between AI and cybersecurity is reshaping strategies, providing defenders with the tools needed to combat sophisticated digital threats. From predictive analysis to rapid incident response, AI empowers organizations to proactively protect their systems and data. As cyber threats continue to evolve, AI will remain a pivotal force in ensuring the security and resilience of digital landscapes.

Reference: AI in Cybersecurity: Transforming the Landscape[12]

Section 2: Understanding AI Technologies and Their Applications

2.1 Types of AI:

Overview of Different AI Classifications: Narrow AI and General AI

Artificial Intelligence (AI) is categorized into various classifications based on its capabilities and level of human-like intelligence. This module provides an overview of two prominent classifications: Narrow AI (Weak AI) and General AI (Strong AI), highlighting their distinct characteristics and implications.

2.1.1. Narrow AI (Weak AI):

Narrow AI refers to AI systems designed to perform specific tasks within a defined domain, exhibiting intelligence only in that particular area.

1.1 Task-Focused Intelligence:

Narrow AI excels at specific tasks and functions, such as language translation, image recognition, and playing games.

---

[10] https://securityintelligence.com/articles/the-role-of-ai-in-next-gen-biometric-authentication/

[11] https://www.securitymagazine.com/articles/95311-ai-generated-malware-and-new-threat-landscape

[12] https://www.forbes.com/sites/forbestechcouncil/2020/08/24/ai-in-cybersecurity-transforming-the-landscape/?sh=1552f4c8650b

1.2 Limited Context:

These AI systems lack a broader understanding of the world and are confined to the tasks they are programmed for.

Reference: Understanding Narrow AI[13]

2.1.2. General AI (Strong AI):

General AI embodies human-like intelligence and possesses the ability to understand, learn, and apply knowledge across diverse domains.

2.1 Human-Level Intelligence:

General AI aims to replicate human cognitive functions, demonstrating the capability to reason, solve problems, and adapt to new situations.

2.2 Learning and Transferability:

General AI can apply knowledge gained from one domain to another, exhibiting versatility and adaptability akin to humans.

Reference: The Quest for General AI[14]

2.1.3. Implications of Narrow AI:

Narrow AI has transformed industries by providing efficient solutions to specific problems. It powers virtual assistants, recommendation systems, and autonomous vehicles, enhancing convenience and productivity.

3.1 Specialized Expertise:

Narrow AI excels in its designated domain but lacks the ability to generalize its knowledge to other areas.

3.2 Wide Adoption:

Narrow AI applications are prevalent across various sectors, contributing to automation and improved user experiences.

Reference: Benefits of Narrow AI[15]

2.1.4. Challenges and Aspirations of General AI:

General AI represents the aspiration of creating machines with human-like cognitive abilities, but it poses significant challenges.

4.1 Complexity and Ethical Considerations:

Creating machines that emulate human cognition involves intricate challenges related to consciousness, ethics, and decision-making.

4.2 Ethical and Societal Implications:

Achieving General AI raises ethical concerns, including issues related to control, privacy, and the potential displacement of human labor.

Reference: Challenges of Achieving General AI[16]

---

[13] https://www.bbc.com/news/technology-48195623

[14] https://venturebeat.com/2020/06/23/what-is-general-ai-and-should-you-fear-it/

[15] https://www.forbes.com/sites/forbestechcouncil/2019/12/10/how-ai-is-impacting-the-world-across-industries/?sh=2dd1d8c812d7

[16] https://www.technologyreview.com/2020/01/27/372838/the-ethical-conundrums-of-ai-without-morals/

Conclusion:

The distinction between Narrow AI and General AI lies in their capabilities and scope. While Narrow AI excels in specific tasks, General AI aims to replicate human-like intelligence across diverse domains. As technology advances, the interplay between these classifications shapes the AI landscape, impacting industries, ethics, and the potential of human-machine interaction.

2.2 Machine Learning and Deep Learning:

Introduction to machine learning (ML) and deep learning (DL) concepts.

Machine Learning (ML) and Deep Learning (DL) are two transformative branches of artificial intelligence (AI) that enable computers to learn from data and make intelligent decisions. This module provides an overview of ML and DL concepts, highlighting their significance and applications.

2.2.1. Machine Learning (ML):

Machine Learning is a subset of AI that involves developing algorithms that allow computers to learn from and make predictions or decisions based on data.

1.1 Learning from Data:

ML algorithms learn patterns from historical data to make informed decisions or predictions without being explicitly programmed.

1.2 Types of ML Algorithms:

ML encompasses various algorithms, including supervised learning, unsupervised learning, and reinforcement learning, each suited for different tasks.

Reference: Introduction to Machine Learning[17]

2.2.2. Deep Learning (DL):

Deep Learning is a subset of ML that employs artificial neural networks to model complex patterns in data.

2.1 Neural Networks:

DL utilizes neural networks with interconnected layers that mimic the structure of the human brain to extract intricate features from data.

2.2 Feature Representation:

DL excels in automatic feature extraction, enabling it to recognize subtle patterns in data, such as images, audio, and text.

Reference: Introduction to Deep Learning[18]

1.2 Language Generation:

NLP also encompasses tasks like text generation, where machines create coherent and contextually relevant language.

Reference: Introduction to NLP[19]

2.2.3. Applications of ML and DL:

Both ML and DL find applications in various domains, transforming industries and enhancing capabilities.

---

[17] https://www.ibm.com/cloud/learn/machine-learning
[18] https://towardsdatascience.com/introduction-to-deep-learning-51288c297e66
[19] https://www.ibm.com/cloud/learn/natural-language-processing

3.1 Natural Language Processing (NLP):

ML and DL power language translation, sentiment analysis, and chatbots that understand and generate human language.

3.2 Image and Video Analysis:

DL is used in image recognition, object detection, and facial recognition systems.

Reference: Applications of ML and DL[20]

2.2.4. Training and Learning Process:

Both ML and DL require training on data to learn and improve their performance.

4.1 Training Data:

Training involves exposing the algorithm to labeled data, allowing it to adjust its parameters and learn patterns.

4.2 Generalization:

Once trained, ML and DL models generalize their learning to make predictions on new, unseen data.

Reference: Understanding the Learning Process[21]

2.2.5. Impact on Industries:

ML and DL have revolutionized industries, introducing automation, efficiency, and innovative solutions.

5.1 Healthcare Diagnostics:

ML and DL aid in medical image analysis, disease diagnosis, and personalized treatment recommendations.

5.2 Autonomous Vehicles:

DL is essential for self-driving cars, enabling them to interpret surroundings and make real-time decisions.

Reference: AI's Impact Across Industries[22]

Conclusion:

Machine Learning and Deep Learning are driving the AI revolution by enabling computers to learn from data and perform complex tasks. Understanding the concepts behind these technologies is essential for unlocking their potential across industries, reshaping the way we interact with machines and data.

Explanation of Supervised, Unsupervised, and Reinforcement Learning

Machine Learning (ML) encompasses various learning paradigms that enable computers to learn from data. This module introduces three fundamental types of ML: Supervised Learning, Unsupervised Learning, and Reinforcement Learning, each catering to different learning scenarios.

2.2.6. Supervised Learning:

Supervised Learning involves training an algorithm on a labelled dataset, where inputs are associated with corresponding desired outputs.

---

[20] https://builtin.com/data-science/applications-deep-learning

[21] https://www.sas.com/en_us/insights/analytics/machine-learning.html

[22] https://www.forbes.com/sites/forbestechcouncil/2019/12/10/how-ai-is-impacting-the-world-across-industries/?sh=2dd1d8c812d7

6.1 Learning with Labelled Data:

In Supervised Learning, the algorithm learns from examples where the correct answers are provided (labels).

6.2 Classification and Regression:

Supervised Learning includes classification tasks (assigning inputs to predefined categories) and regression tasks (predicting numeric values).

Reference: Supervised Learning Explained[23]

2.2.7. Unsupervised Learning:

Unsupervised Learning involves training algorithms on data without explicit labels, allowing them to identify patterns and relationships on their own.

7.1 Clustering:

Unsupervised Learning includes clustering, where algorithms group similar data points together based on their characteristics.

7.2 Dimensionality Reduction:

Unsupervised Learning aids in dimensionality reduction, simplifying data while retaining essential information.

Reference: Unsupervised Learning Overview[24]

2.2.8. Reinforcement Learning:

Reinforcement Learning focuses on training agents to make decisions in an environment to maximize cumulative rewards.

8.1 Learning by Interaction:

Reinforcement Learning agents learn through trial and error by interacting with an environment and receiving feedback (rewards).

8.2 Sequential Decision Making:

Reinforcement Learning is suitable for tasks involving sequential decision-making, such as game playing and robotics.

Reference: Reinforcement Learning Concepts[25]

2.2.9. Applications of Each Learning Paradigm:

Each learning paradigm has distinct applications across domains.

9.1 Supervised Learning Applications:

Supervised Learning is used in image classification, sentiment analysis, and predicting housing prices.

9.2 Unsupervised Learning Applications:

Unsupervised Learning finds use in customer segmentation, recommendation systems, and anomaly detection.

9.3 Reinforcement Learning Applications:

Reinforcement Learning powers game-playing agents, self-driving cars, and robotic control.

---

[23] https://www.sas.com/en_us/insights/analytics/machine-learning.html

[24] https://www.analyticsvidhya.com/blog/2020/08/types-of-machine-learning-algorithms-and-where-to-use-them/

[25] https://towardsdatascience.com/reinforcement-learning-complete-tutorial-2021-f68a419b6fe0

Reference: Applications of Different Learning Paradigms[26]

2.2.10. Training Process and Evaluation:
Each learning paradigm involves specific training methods and evaluation criteria.

10.1 Training in Supervised Learning:
Supervised Learning requires a labelled dataset for training and is evaluated using metrics like accuracy and loss.

10.2 Training in Unsupervised Learning:
Unsupervised Learning involves training without labels and is evaluated based on cluster quality or reconstruction error.

10.3 Training in Reinforcement Learning:
Reinforcement Learning agents learn through interactions and are evaluated based on their ability to achieve goals.

Conclusion:
Understanding the nuances of Supervised, Unsupervised, and Reinforcement Learning is essential for selecting the appropriate approach for different tasks. Each learning paradigm plays a crucial role in harnessing the potential of Machine Learning across a wide range of applications.

2.3 Natural Language Processing (NLP):
Natural Language Processing (NLP) is a field of artificial intelligence that focuses on enabling computers to understand, interpret, and generate human language. This module provides an overview of NLP and highlights its diverse applications in understanding and processing human language.

2.3.1. NLP Fundamentals:
NLP involves developing algorithms and models that facilitate communication between humans and computers through natural language.

1.1 Language Understanding:
NLP algorithms aim to comprehend the semantics, syntax, and context of human language, enabling machines to understand its meaning.

2.3.2. Applications of NLP:
NLP has revolutionized various industries, enhancing communication, information retrieval, and decision-making.

2.1 Sentiment Analysis:
NLP analyses text to determine sentiment, providing insights into public opinion and customer feedback.

2.2 Language Translation:
NLP powers language translation systems that enable real-time communication across linguistic boundaries.

---

[26] https://builtin.com/data-science/supervised-vs-unsupervised-vs-reinforcement-learning

Reference: Applications of NLP[27]

2.3.3. Text Summarization:
NLP automates the extraction of essential information from large texts, creating concise summaries.

3.1 Extractive Summarization:
NLP identifies and selects important sentences or phrases from the original text to create summaries.

3.2 Abstractive Summarization:
NLP generates summaries by understanding the context and generating new sentences that capture the essence of the text.

Reference: Text Summarization Techniques[28]

2.3.4. Question Answering Systems:
NLP facilitates the development of question-answering systems that provide accurate responses to user queries.

4.1 Contextual Understanding:
NLP algorithms consider context to interpret questions and provide contextually relevant answers.

4.2 Knowledge Extraction:
NLP extracts information from texts and databases to answer questions accurately.

Reference: Building Question Answering Systems[29]

2.3.5. Chatbots and Virtual Assistants:
NLP powers chatbots and virtual assistants that engage in human-like conversations.

5.1 Natural Interaction:
NLP allows chatbots to understand and respond to user queries using natural language.

5.2 Personalization:
NLP enables virtual assistants to personalize responses based on user preferences and history.

Reference: NLP in Chatbots[30]

Conclusion:
Natural Language Processing is a transformative field that bridges the gap between human communication and machine understanding. With applications ranging from sentiment analysis to language translation and chatbots, NLP continues to redefine how humans interact with machines and information.

---

[27] https://www.sciencedirect.com/science/article/pii/S2212017318303324

[28] https://www.analyticsvidhya.com/blog/2019/06/comprehensive-guide-text-summarization-using-deep-learning-python/

[29] https://towardsdatascience.com/building-a-question-answering-system-part-1-9388aadff507

[30] https://www.analyticsvidhya.com/blog/2020/05/nlp-chatbot-using-transformer-architecture/

2.4 Computer Vision:

Computer Vision and its Role in Image and Video Analysis

Introduction: Computer Vision is a subset of artificial intelligence (AI) that focuses on enabling computers to interpret and understand visual information from the world. This module provides an overview of Computer Vision and emphasizes its significance in analysing images and videos.

2.4.1. Computer Vision Fundamentals:

Computer Vision involves developing algorithms and models that enable machines to process and understand visual data, such as images and videos.

1.1 Visual Perception:

Computer Vision aims to replicate human visual perception by interpreting patterns, shapes, and objects within images and videos.

1.2 Feature Extraction:

Computer Vision algorithms extract relevant features from visual data, such as edges, textures, and colours, to facilitate analysis.

Reference: Introduction to Computer Vision[31]

2.4.2. Applications of Computer Vision:

Computer Vision plays a key role in diverse industries, enhancing automation, safety, and decision-making.

2.1 Image Classification:

Computer Vision enables automatic categorization of images into predefined classes or categories.

2.2 Object Detection:

Computer Vision algorithms detect and locate specific objects within images or videos, aiding in applications like autonomous vehicles.

Reference: Applications of Computer Vision[32]

2.4.3. Image Segmentation:

Computer Vision segments images into meaningful regions, distinguishing between different objects or parts within an image.

3.1 Semantic Segmentation:

Computer Vision assigns specific labels to each pixel, enabling precise object separation and understanding.

3.2 Instance Segmentation:

Computer Vision differentiates between individual instances of objects within an image.

Reference: Image Segmentation Techniques[33]

2.4.4. Video Analysis and Surveillance:

Computer Vision enables the analysis of video streams for applications like surveillance, anomaly detection, and activity recognition.

---

[31] https://towardsdatascience.com/introduction-to-computer-vision-74740c5373d6

[32] https://www.forbes.com/sites/forbestechcouncil/2019/12/18/how-computer-vision-is-reshaping-businesses/?sh=1c830de9530b

[33] https://towardsdatascience.com/a-comprehensive-introduction-to-different-types-of-convolutions-in-deep-learning-669281e58215

4.1 Activity Recognition:
Computer Vision identifies and categorizes human actions and activities within video sequences.

4.2 Anomaly Detection:
Computer Vision identifies unusual or unexpected events within video streams, alerting operators to potential threats.

Reference: Video Analysis with Computer Vision[34]

2.4.5. Augmented Reality (AR) and Virtual Reality (VR):
Computer Vision is essential in AR and VR applications, overlaying digital content onto the real world.

5.1 AR Overlay:
Computer Vision aligns digital objects with the physical environment, creating interactive augmented experiences.

5.2 VR Immersion:
Computer Vision helps track user movements and interactions in virtual environments.

Reference: Computer Vision in AR and VR[35]

Conclusion:
Computer Vision is revolutionizing the way machines perceive and interpret visual information. With applications ranging from image classification to video analysis and AR/VR experiences, Computer Vision is a driving force in improving automation, safety, and enhancing human-computer interaction.

Reference: Types of AI and Their Differences[36]

Section 3: AI Applications in Cybersecurity

3.1 Threat Detection and Prevention:
In this section we will explore how AI can enhance the identification and prevention of cyber threats.

Introduction:
Artificial Intelligence (AI) has emerged as a game-changer in the field of cybersecurity, revolutionizing the identification and prevention of cyber threats. This module explores how AI technologies play a key role in bolstering cybersecurity measures.

3.1.1. AI-Powered Threat Detection:
AI technologies enhance the capability of detecting and identifying various types of cyber threats.

1.1 Anomaly Detection:
AI algorithms can detect abnormal patterns in network traffic or user behaviour, signalling potential threats like unauthorized access or data breaches.

---

[34] https://www.towardsdatascience.com/video-analysis-using-opencv-and-computer-vision-9e648b68064d

[35] https://www.techopedia.com/7-computer-vision-applications-for-virtual-and-augmented-reality/2/33614

[36] https://www.greatlearning.in/great-learnings-blog/types-of-artificial-intelligence

1.2 Behavioural Analysis:

AI learns the behaviour of users and systems to identify deviations that could indicate malicious activities.

Reference: AI-Driven Anomaly Detection[37]

3.1.2. Predictive Threat Intelligence:

AI employs predictive analytics to anticipate potential cyber threats based on historical data and ongoing trends.

2.1 Threat Hunting:

AI-enhanced systems proactively search for vulnerabilities and threats, reducing the risk of undetected attacks.

2.2 Early Warning Systems:

AI-driven predictions enable organizations to take preventive measures before threats escalate.

Reference: Predictive Threat Intelligence[38]

3.1.3. Malware Detection and Prevention:

AI techniques excel in identifying and neutralizing various forms of malware.

3.1 Signature-less Detection:

AI analyses code behaviour to identify zero-day threats, without relying solely on predefined signatures.

3.2 Sandbox Analysis:

AI-powered sandboxes can simulate and analyse malware behaviour, aiding in early detection and response.

Reference: AI in Malware Detection[39]

3.1.4. Real-time Threat Mitigation:

AI-driven systems respond to threats in real-time, minimizing damage and reducing incident response time.

4.1 Automated Incident Response:

AI can autonomously respond to threats by isolating compromised systems or blocking suspicious activities.

4.2 Adaptive Security:

AI adjusts security measures dynamically based on evolving threats and attack patterns.

Reference: AI for Real-time Threat Mitigation[40]

3.1.5. User and Entity Behaviour Analytics (UEBA):

AI-driven UEBA systems monitor user behaviour and identify deviations that could indicate insider threats.

---

[37] https://towardsdatascience.com/anomaly-detection-using-autoencoders-in-python-4c331fcf5662

[38] https://www.darkreading.com/threat-intelligence/predictive-analytics-in-cybersecurity-6-real-world-use-cases/d/d-id/1338233

[39] https://www.csoonline.com/article/3343826/ai-in-cybersecurity-features-and-vendor-options.html

[40] https://www.mcafee.com/enterprise/en-us/security-awareness/cloud-security/artificial-intelligence-automated-threat-response.html

5.1 Insider Threat Detection:

AI detects unusual user activities, potentially uncovering insider threats or compromised accounts.

5.2 Contextual Analysis:

AI analyses user behaviour in the context of their roles and responsibilities to identify anomalies.

Reference: UEBA with AI[41]

Conclusion:

The integration of AI into cybersecurity transforms the way organizations defend against cyber threats. AI's ability to rapidly detect, analyse, and respond to threats strengthens the overall security posture, making it an indispensable tool in the evolving landscape of cybersecurity.

Examples of AI-powered intrusion detection systems and antivirus software.

3.1.6 Examples of AI-Powered Intrusion Detection Systems and Antivirus Software

Introduction:

Artificial Intelligence (AI) has transformed the landscape of cybersecurity by enabling advanced intrusion detection and antivirus solutions. This module highlights notable examples of AI-powered systems that enhance security measures.

1. AI-Powered Intrusion Detection Systems:

Darktrace:

Darktrace's Enterprise Immune System employs AI algorithms to detect and respond to cyber threats in real-time. It monitors network traffic, user behaviour, and device activities to identify anomalies and potential attacks.

Reference: Darktrace AI-Powered IDS[42]

Vectra AI:

Vectra AI offers an AI-driven threat detection and response platform that uses machine learning to analyse network traffic and detect hidden threats and attacker behaviours.

Reference: Vectra AI Threat Detection[43]

2. AI-Powered Antivirus Software:

CylancePROTECT:

CylancePROTECT utilizes AI and machine learning to prevent malware and ransomware attacks. It classifies files and executables based on their behaviour, effectively stopping threats before they execute.

Reference: CylancePROTECT[44]

Norton 360 with LifeLock:

Norton's AI-enhanced antivirus suite offers proactive protection against various threats. It uses AI and machine learning to identify new and evolving malware strains.

Reference: Norton 360 with LifeLock[45]

---

[41] https://www.forcepoint.com/cyber-edu/user-entity-behaviour-analytics

[42] https://www.darktrace.com/en/technology/ai-for-ids/

[43] https://www.vectra.ai/technology

[44] https://www.cylance.com/en-us/products/protect.html

[45] https://www.norton.com/antivirus

3. Cloud-Based AI Security:

Microsoft Defender ATP:

Microsoft Defender Advanced Threat Protection (ATP) leverages AI to identify and respond to advanced threats across endpoints, networks, and email.

Reference: Microsoft Defender ATP[46]

McAfee MVISION Endpoint:

McAfee's MVISION Endpoint employs AI to protect endpoints from a wide range of threats, including malware, ransomware, and zero-day attacks.

Reference: McAfee MVISION[47]

4. Behaviour-Based Analysis:

Sophos Intercept X:

Sophos Intercept X integrates AI to analyse behaviour patterns and proactively identify malicious activities, ensuring protection against both known and unknown threats.

Reference: Sophos Intercept X[48]

ESET Smart Security Premium:

ESET's Smart Security Premium incorporates AI to analyse file behaviour and identify potentially harmful actions before they execute.

Reference: ESET Smart Security[49]

AI-driven intrusion detection systems and antivirus software have raised the bar in cybersecurity, providing organizations with advanced tools to detect, prevent, and respond to evolving cyber threats. These solutions exemplify how AI technologies play a crucial role in bolstering security measures in the digital age.

3.2 Anomaly Detection:

How machine learning algorithms identify deviations from normal patterns to detect potential cyber threats ?

Introduction:

Machine learning algorithms have revolutionized cyber threat detection by leveraging the ability to identify deviations from normal patterns. This module explains how these algorithms work to detect potential cyber threats by recognizing anomalies in data.

3.2.1. Understanding Normal Patterns:

Machine learning algorithms start by learning the normal behaviour patterns within a system, network, or user activity.

1.1 Training with Normal Data:

Algorithms are trained on a dataset containing examples of normal behaviour, capturing the baseline characteristics of the system.

---

[46] https://www.microsoft.com/en-us/microsoft-365/windows/microsoft-defender-atp

[47] https://www.mcafee.com/enterprise/en-us/products/mvision-endpoint.html

[48] https://www.sophos.com/en-us/products/intercept-x.aspx

[49] https://www.eset.com/us/home/smart-security-premium/

1.2 Feature Extraction:

Features or attributes relevant to the behaviour are extracted from the data, forming the basis for pattern recognition.

Reference: Feature Extraction Techniques[50]

3.2.2. Anomaly Detection:

Once trained on normal patterns, machine learning algorithms detect deviations or anomalies that differ from the learned baseline.

2.1 Unsupervised Learning:

Unsupervised learning algorithms, such as clustering and autoencoders, identify data points that do not conform to the established patterns.

2.2 Supervised Learning:

Supervised learning algorithms use labelled data to recognize deviations, classifying data as normal or anomalous.

Reference: Anomaly Detection Approaches[51]

3.2.3. Types of Anomalies:

Machine learning algorithms identify different types of anomalies based on their characteristics.

3.1 Point Anomalies:

Point anomalies are individual data points that significantly deviate from the normal distribution.

3.2 Contextual Anomalies:

Contextual anomalies are data points that are considered anomalous in specific contexts but not in others.

Reference: Types of Anomalies[52]

3.2.4. Feature Engineering:

Feature engineering involves selecting or creating relevant attributes that best capture deviations from normal behaviour.

4.1 Time-Series Analysis:

In time-series data, features might include temporal information to capture trends and irregularities.

4.2 Dimensionality Reduction:

Dimensionality reduction techniques reduce data complexity while preserving crucial information.

Reference: Feature Engineering Techniques

3.2.5. Model Selection:

Machine learning algorithms suited for anomaly detection include Isolation Forests, One-Class SVMs, and autoencoders.

5.1 Isolation Forests:

Isolation Forests create decision trees to isolate anomalies, making them effective for outlier detection.

---

[50] https://towardsdatascience.com/feature-extraction-techniques-d619b56e31be

[51] https://www.analyticsvidhya.com/blog/2019/02/outlier-detection-python-pyod/

[52] https://www.sciencedirect.com/science/article/pii/S2095809920300582

5.2 One-Class SVM:

One-Class Support Vector Machines create a boundary around normal data points, classifying anything outside the boundary as an anomaly.

Reference: Anomaly Detection Algorithms

Machine learning algorithms excel in identifying deviations from normal patterns, enabling accurate detection of potential cyber threats. By training on normal behaviour and recognizing anomalies, these algorithms empower cybersecurity systems to respond rapidly to suspicious activities, enhancing overall security measures.

3.3 Predictive Analysis:

how can AI predict potential security breaches based on historical data and patterns?

Introduction:

Artificial Intelligence (AI) has revolutionized the ability to predict potential security breaches by analysing historical data and patterns. This module explores how AI employs historical data to forecast and prevent security threats.

3.3.1. Historical Data Analysis:

AI leverages historical data from previous cyber incidents and security breaches.

1.1 Data Collection:

AI systems collect and store a vast amount of historical data related to cyber threats, attacks, vulnerabilities, and breach patterns.

1.2 Data Preprocessing:

Before analysis, data is cleaned, normalized, and prepared for training machine learning models.

Reference: Data Preprocessing Techniques[53] :

3.3.2. Pattern Recognition:

AI algorithms identify patterns, correlations, and trends within historical data.

2.1 Machine Learning Models:

Supervised and unsupervised machine learning models analyse data to uncover hidden patterns and anomalies.

2.2 Feature Extraction:

Relevant features are extracted from historical data, helping models identify critical attributes for prediction.

Reference: Pattern Recognition Techniques[54]

3.3.3. Predictive Analytics:

AI employs predictive analytics to forecast potential security breaches.

---

[53] https://towardsdatascience.com/data-preprocessing-techniques-for-machine-learning-65a7d5cab1d0

[54] https://www.sciencedirect.com/science/article/pii/S2095809919305717

3.1 Time-Series Analysis:
Historical data is analysed over time to detect cyclic trends, seasonality, and anomalies.

3.2 Regression Analysis:
Regression models predict future outcomes based on historical data points and relationships.

Reference: Predictive Analytics Methods[55]

3.3.4. Machine Learning Algorithms:
AI uses machine learning algorithms to predict potential security breaches.

4.1 Classification Models:
Classification models predict whether a specific event is likely to occur, such as classifying an event as a potential breach.

4.2 Anomaly Detection Models:
Anomaly detection algorithms identify unusual patterns that might indicate a security breach.

Reference: Machine Learning Algorithms for Predictive Analysis[56]

3.3.5. Continuous Learning:
AI systems continually learn from new data and adapt their predictions over time.

5.1 Model Refinement:
Models are updated with new historical data to improve accuracy and adapt to evolving threat landscapes.

5.2 Feedback Loops:
Feedback from detected incidents helps AI systems enhance their predictive capabilities.

Reference: Continuous Learning in AI Systems[57]

Conclusion:
AI's ability to predict potential security breaches based on historical data and patterns revolutionizes cybersecurity strategies. By analysing data trends, identifying patterns, and forecasting threats, AI empowers organizations to proactively implement preventive measures and mitigate potential risks.

3.4 Security Information and Event Management (SIEM) with AI:
Incorporating AI into SIEM systems for real-time analysis of security events and incidents:
The integration of Artificial Intelligence (AI) into Security Information and Event Management (SIEM) systems has transformed the way organizations handle security events and incidents. This module explains how AI enhances SIEM capabilities for real-time analysis, threat detection, and incident response.

3.4.1. SIEM and Security Event Management:
SIEM systems collect, correlate, and analyse security data from various sources to detect and respond to potential threats.

---

[55] https://towardsdatascience.com/forecasting-methods-in-machine-learning-and-neural-networks-ea63e7d06310

[56] https://www.analyticsinsight.net/top-5-machine-learning-algorithms-for-predictive-analytics/

[57] https://www.technologyreview.com/2021/06/17/1026655/ai-machine-learning-continuous-lifelong-learning/

1.1 Data Collection:
SIEM gathers logs, alerts, and data from networks, endpoints, applications, and other sources.

1.2 Correlation and Aggregation:
SIEM correlates data to identify patterns, relationships, and potential security incidents.

Reference: SIEM Overview[58]

3.4.2. Role of AI in SIEM:
AI technologies enhance SIEM systems by providing advanced analysis, pattern recognition, and automation.

2.1 Real-time Monitoring:
AI-powered SIEM systems analyse data in real-time, enabling swift detection of anomalies and threats.

2.2 Pattern Recognition:
AI algorithms identify complex patterns and trends that might indicate sophisticated attacks.

Reference: AI and SIEM[59]

3.4.3. Anomaly Detection:
AI-driven SIEM systems excel in identifying abnormal activities.

3.1 Behavioural Analytics:
AI analyses user and system behaviours to detect deviations from established norms.

3.2 Unsupervised Learning:
AI algorithms can identify unknown threats that don't match known attack patterns.

Reference: AI for Anomaly Detection[60]

3.4.4. Threat Hunting:
AI-powered SIEM enhances proactive threat hunting and investigation.

4.1 Automated Threat Detection:
AI identifies potential threats, streamlining the identification process for analysts.

4.2 Contextual Analysis:
AI correlates events with context to determine the severity and potential impact of a threat.

Reference: AI-Driven Threat Hunting[61]

3.4.5. Incident Response Automation:
AI automates incident response tasks, accelerating threat mitigation.

5.1 Workflow Orchestration:
AI-driven SIEM systems automate incident response workflows, ensuring consistent and efficient actions.

---

[58] https://searchsecurity.techtarget.com/definition/Security-Information-and-Event-Management-SIEM

[59] https://www.darkreading.com/endpoint/5-ways-ai-will-advance-the-state-of-security-information-and-event-management-siem/a/d-id/1335859

[60] https://www.techrepublic.com/article/the-6-ways-to-tackle-anomaly-detection-using-ai/

[61] https://www.splunk.com/en_us/blog/security/the-role-of-ai-and-ml-in-threat-hunting.html

5.2 Quarantine and Mitigation:

AI can automatically isolate compromised systems to prevent further damage.

Reference: Incident Response Automation with AI[62]

Conclusion:

Incorporating AI into SIEM systems empowers organizations to proactively identify and respond to security threats in real-time. By leveraging AI's capabilities in pattern recognition, anomaly detection, and automation, AI-enhanced SIEM systems significantly strengthen an organization's

3.5 Case Study: AI in Email Security:

Analysing how AI-based email security solutions detect phishing and malicious attachments.

Introduction:

Artificial Intelligence (AI) has revolutionized email security by enhancing the detection of phishing attacks and malicious attachments. This module explores the mechanisms through which AI-powered solutions analyse emails to identify and prevent phishing attempts and malware.

3.5.1. Email Content Analysis:

AI-based email security solutions analyse the content of incoming emails to identify suspicious elements.

1.1 Text Analysis:

Natural Language Processing (NLP) techniques assess email text for phishing indicators, such as urgency or requests for sensitive information.

1.2 Link and URL Analysis:

AI scans links and URLs within emails to determine if they lead to known malicious websites.

Reference: NLP for Email Security[63]

3.5.2. Image Analysis:

AI solutions can also analyse images embedded in emails for potential threats.

2.1 Visual Recognition:

AI employs image recognition to detect phishing images, logos, or attachments designed to deceive recipients.

2.2 Visual-Based URL Analysis:

AI can visually analyse URLs in images to identify potentially deceptive web addresses.

Reference: Visual-Based Email Security[64]

3.5.3. Behavioural Analysis:

AI tracks user and email behaviour to detect deviations from normal patterns.

3.1 User Behaviour Analysis:

AI learns the normal communication patterns of users and flags emails that deviate from their typical interactions.

---

[62] https://www.ibm.com/cloud/learn/incident-response-automation
[63] https://www.ncbi.nlm.nih.gov/pmc/articles/PMC6781564/
[64] https://www.mcafee.com/blogs/other-blogs/mcafee-labs/evolution-of-email-threats/

3.2 Sender Reputation Analysis:

AI evaluates the reputation of email senders to identify potential phishing sources.

Reference: Behavioural Analysis in Email Security[65]

3.5.4. Malware Detection:

AI-powered email security solutions identify and prevent malicious attachments.

4.1 File Analysis:

AI scans email attachments for malicious code, signatures, or patterns associated with malware.

4.2 Sandbox Analysis:

Attachments can be opened in a secure environment (sandbox) where AI observes their behaviour to detect potential threats.

Reference: AI-Driven Malware Detection[66]

3.5.5. Phishing Link Detection:

AI identifies links that redirect to phishing websites.

5.1 Link Behaviour Analysis:

AI emulates link clicks to analyse the behaviour of linked websites and determine if they are malicious.

5.2 Domain Reputation Analysis:

AI assesses the reputation of linked domains to identify potential phishing sources.

Reference: AI for Phishing Link Detection[67]

Conclusion:

AI-based email security solutions play a critical role in preventing phishing attacks and thwarting malicious attachments. By leveraging AI's capabilities in content analysis, image recognition, behavioural analysis, and malware detection, organizations can significantly enhance their email security measures.

Reference: AI in Cybersecurity: Applications and Use Cases[68]

Section 4: Benefits and Challenges

4.1 Benefits of AI in Cybersecurity:

Advantages of Using AI to Enhance Cybersecurity Practices

Introduction:

Artificial Intelligence (AI) has brought about a paradigm shift in the field of cybersecurity, offering numerous advantages that significantly enhance the effectiveness of cybersecurity practices. This module highlights the key benefits of utilizing AI in bolstering cybersecurity measures.

4.1.1. Advanced Threat Detection:

AI's ability to analyse vast amounts of data in real-time enables the swift identification of even the most sophisticated cyber threats.

---

[65] https://resources.infosecinstitute.com/topic/behavioural-based-email-security/

[66] https://www.symantec.com/products/advanced-threat-protection-email

[67] https://www.trendmicro.com/en_us/research/20/i/handling-phishing-urls-using-deep-learning.html

[68] https://www.csoonline.com/article/3200024/ai-in-cybersecurity-features-applications-and-challenges.html

1.1 Anomaly Detection:

AI excels in spotting abnormal activities or patterns that may indicate emerging threats, enabling early intervention.

1.2 Zero-Day Threat Detection:

AI can identify zero-day vulnerabilities and threats by detecting anomalous behaviour or malicious patterns.

Reference: AI in Threat Detection[69]

4.1.2. Enhanced Automation:

AI-powered automation streamlines security operations and reduces manual intervention.

2.1 Rapid Incident Response:

Automated AI-driven incident response accelerates threat containment and minimizes damage.

2.2 Routine Task Automation:

AI automates routine security tasks, freeing up human resources for more complex tasks.

Reference: AI-Driven Security Automation[70]

4.1.3. Continuous Monitoring:

AI enables round-the-clock monitoring and analysis, providing a proactive approach to cybersecurity.

3.1 Real-Time Analysis:

AI-driven systems analyse data in real-time, enabling the swift detection of anomalies and threats.

3.2 Predictive Analytics:

AI forecasts potential threats based on historical data, enhancing pre-emptive security measures.

Reference: AI for Continuous Monitoring[71]

4.1.4. Reduced False Positives:

AI's precision in pattern recognition and analysis minimizes false positives and alerts fatigue.

4.1 Improved Accuracy:

AI accurately distinguishes between genuine threats and benign activities, reducing unnecessary alarms.

4.2 Improved Threat Prioritization:

AI classifies threats based on severity, ensuring prompt attention to critical issues.

Reference: Reducing False Positives with AI[72]

4.1.5. Scalability and Adaptability:

AI solutions can scale effortlessly to handle growing data volumes and evolving threat landscapes.

5.1 Handling Big Data:

AI processes and analyses vast amounts of data without sacrificing accuracy.

---

[69] https://www.csoonline.com/article/3267583/the-role-of-artificial-intelligence-in-cybersecurity.html

[70] https://www.mcafee.com/blogs/enterprise/security-automation/how-security-automation-is-changing-the-cybersecurity-landscape/

[71] https://www.computerweekly.com/feature/How-AI-will-underpin-cyber-security-in-the-next-few-years

[72] https://www.csoonline.com/article/3571506/how-ai-and-machine-learning-are-reducing-false-positives-and-improving-security.html

5.2 Adapting to New Threats:

AI systems learn from new data and adapt to emerging threats, ensuring up-to-date protection.

Reference: Scalability of AI in Cybersecurity[73]

4.1.6. Efficiency and Speed:

AI-driven cybersecurity solutions excel in efficiently handling vast volumes of data and processes, enhancing overall operational efficiency.

6.1 Automated Threat Detection:

AI rapidly identifies and analyses potential threats, accelerating the detection process compared to manual efforts.

6.2 Real-Time Response:

AI responds to threats in real-time, mitigating risks rapidly and reducing the impact of attacks.

Reference: AI and Cybersecurity Efficiency[74]

4.1.7. Scalability and Adaptability:

AI's scalability enables it to handle increasing data loads and evolving cyber threats without compromising effectiveness.

7.1 Handling Data Growth:

AI seamlessly processes and analyses expanding datasets, making it ideal for the modern digital landscape.

7.2 Adaptive Defence Mechanisms:

AI systems learn from new data and adapt to emerging threats, ensuring continuous and up-to-date protection.

Reference: Scalability and Adaptability of AI[75]

4.1.8. Proactive Threat Detection:

AI's ability to recognize patterns and anomalies empowers proactive threat detection, preventing attacks before they cause harm.

8.1 Behavioural Analysis:

AI identifies deviations from normal behaviour, flagging potential threats that may go unnoticed otherwise.

8.2 Predictive Analytics:

AI forecasts potential threats based on historical data, enabling pre-emptive security measures.

Reference: AI for Proactive Threat Detection[76]

4.1.9. Reduced Human Error:

AI minimizes the influence of human error, ensuring consistent and accurate threat analysis and response.

---

[73] https://www.cio.com/article/3488653/the-role-of-ai-and-machine-learning-in-scaling-cybersecurity-solutions.html

[74] https://www.tripwire.com/state-of-security/security-data-protection/cyber-security/artificial-intelligence-ai-in-cybersecurity/

[75] https://www.cio.com/article/3488653/the-role-of-ai-and-machine-learning-in-scaling-cybersecurity-solutions.html

[76] https://www.securitymagazine.com/articles/94866-ai-and-machine-learning-in-cybersecurity-preparing-for-what-comes-next

9.1 Eliminating Fatigue:

AI doesn't suffer from alert fatigue and consistently analyses threats without being affected by stress or fatigue.

9.2 Precise Decision-Making:

AI's data-driven decisions reduce the likelihood of human errors in identifying and addressing threats.

Reference: Reducing Human Error with AI[77]

4.1.10. Comprehensive Threat Intelligence:

AI consolidates vast amounts of threat intelligence data, enabling comprehensive analysis and informed decision-making.

10.1 Data Enrichment:

AI aggregates threat intelligence from diverse sources, enhancing the accuracy and context of threat assessment.

10.2 Rapid Analysis:

AI processes and analyses complex threat data quickly, providing security teams with actionable insights.

Reference: Comprehensive Threat Intelligence with AI[78]

Conclusion:

The advantages of leveraging AI in cybersecurity are vast, encompassing advanced threat detection, automation, continuous monitoring, reduced false positives, and the ability to scale with the dynamic nature of cyber threats. By harnessing AI's capabilities, organizations can significantly fortify their cybersecurity defences and respond effectively to the ever-evolving threat landscape.

The benefits of integrating AI into cybersecurity are evident through its efficiency, speed, scalability, and adaptive defence mechanisms. By harnessing AI's capabilities, organizations can proactively address cyber threats, optimize operations, and maintain robust cybersecurity postures in the face of evolving challenges.

4.2 Challenges and Considerations:

Addressing the challenges of AI, including algorithm bias, lack of transparency, and adversarial attacks.

Introduction:

While AI offers significant potential in cybersecurity, addressing challenges like algorithm bias, lack of transparency, adversarial attacks, data privacy concerns, and false positives/negatives is essential. By implementing strategies that emphasize fairness, transparency, robustness, and collaboration between humans and AI, organizations can harness the benefits of AI while mitigating potential risks.

---

[77] https://securityintelligence.com/articles/leveraging-ai-to-reduce-human-error-in-cybersecurity/

[78] https://www.csoonline.com/article/3579273/the-role-of-ai-in-cybersecurity-where-we-are-and-what-comes-next.html

Artificial Intelligence (AI) brings significant benefits to cybersecurity, however, it also introduces challenges that need careful consideration. This module explores the key challenges associated with AI in cybersecurity and strategies to address them effectively.

4.2.1. Algorithm Bias: Challenge:

AI algorithms may inherit biases present in training data, leading to unfair or discriminatory outcomes.

1.1 Fairness and Bias Mitigation:

Biases in training data can lead to AI models that produce discriminatory or unfair outcomes. Organizations must implement techniques to identify and mitigate bias in AI models to ensure equitable cybersecurity decisions.

1.2 Fairness Audits:

Regularly audit AI models to identify and address biases that may disproportionately impact certain groups.

1.3 Ethical AI Design:

Developers should design algorithms that adhere to ethical standards and prioritize fairness in decision-making.

1.4 Diverse Training Data:

Ensure that training data represents a diverse range of demographics to minimize bias in AI decision-making.

Reference: Addressing Algorithm Bias[79]

Addressing Bias in AI[80]

4.2.2. Lack of Transparency:

AI models often operate as "black boxes," making it challenging to understand their decision-making processes.

2.1 Explainable AI (XAI):

Utilize techniques that make AI decisions interpretable and transparent to users and stakeholders.

Adopting XAI techniques helps make AI decisions transparent and understandable, increasing trust and accountability.

2.2 Interpretability Tools:

Lack of transparency in AI decision-making can hinder accountability and trust. Utilizing interpretability tools allows security professionals to analyse and interpret AI-driven insights.

Reference: Explainable AI in Cybersecurity[81]

4.2.3. Adversarial Attacks:

Adversaries can exploit vulnerabilities in AI models using adversarial attacks, tricking AI into making incorrect decisions.

---

[79] https://www.csoonline.com/article/3583980/addressing-ai-bias-8-key-components-to-watch.html

[80] https://www.securitymagazine.com/articles/95036-addressing-bias-in-ai-tools

[81] https://www.csoonline.com/article/3532108/explainable-ai-in-cybersecurity-4-key-benefits-and-challenges.html

3.1 Robustness Testing:

Regularly testing AI models against potential adversarial attacks helps identify vulnerabilities and fortify defences.

3.2 Adversarial Training:

Training AI models using adversarial techniques enhances their resilience against known attack methods.

Reference: Defending Against Adversarial Attacks[82]

4.2.4. Data Privacy Concerns:

AI models require large datasets, raising concerns about data privacy and compliance. AI in cybersecurity often requires access to sensitive data, raising concerns about user privacy and data protection

4.1 Privacy-Preserving AI:

Implementing privacy-preserving AI techniques, like federated learning, enables model training without exposing sensitive data.

4.2 Anonymization and Encryption:

Applying techniques such as data anonymization and encryption helps safeguard sensitive information.

4.3 Informed Consent:

Ensure users are aware of how their data will be used in AI-driven security processes and obtain their informed consent.

4.4 Data Minimization:

Collect and use only the minimum necessary data for AI analysis to limit potential privacy violations.

Reference: Privacy-Preserving AI[83] Ethical Data Collection[84]

4.2.5. False Positives and Negatives:

AI-powered systems may generate false positives (flagging benign actions as threats) or false negatives (failing to detect real threats).

5.1 Continuous Learning:

AI models should undergo continuous learning to reduce false positives and negatives through improved accuracy.

5.2 Human-AI Collaboration:

Incorporating human expertise in cybersecurity processes helps validate AI-generated insights and decisions.

Reference: Tackling False Positives and Negatives[85]

4.2.6. Adapting to New Threats:

Human expertise is vital for recognizing and adapting to emerging and novel cyber threats that AI models may not have encountered.

---

[82] https://www.symantec.com/content/dam/symantec/docs/white-papers/defending-against-adversarial-attacks-wp-en.pdf

[83] https://towardsdatascience.com/a-tutorial-on-federated-learning-72dd79bbf860

[84] https://www.csoonline.com/article/3584035/ethical-data-collection-what-you-need-to-know.html

[85] https://www.darkreading.com/edge/theedge/ai-in-cybersecurity-red-flags-are-waving/a/d-id/1335109

6.1 Threat Evolution:

Human analysts leverage experience to anticipate evolving threat tactics and techniques, ensuring readiness.

6.2 Zero-Day Threats:

Human intuition is crucial in detecting zero-day vulnerabilities that AI models may not have patterns for.

Reference: Human Expertise in Navigating New Threats[86]

Ethical considerations are integral when deploying AI in cybersecurity. By addressing privacy concerns, ensuring fairness and transparency, establishing accountability, maintaining human oversight, and adhering to ethical principles, organizations can harness the potential of AI while maintaining ethical integrity.

4.3 Balancing AI and Human Expertise:

importance of combining AI capabilities with human analysis and decision-making:

While Artificial Intelligence (AI) offers advanced capabilities in cybersecurity, the synergy between AI and human expertise is crucial for effective threat detection and response. This module explores the significance of combining AI with human analysis and decision-making in the domain of cybersecurity.

4.3.1. Contextual Understanding:

Human analysts provide context that AI may lack, enabling a deeper understanding of threats and their potential implications.

1.1 Complex Threats:

Human analysts can comprehend nuanced threats that may involve psychological, geopolitical, or social factors beyond AI's scope.

1.2 Behavioural Insights:

Human analysts interpret behaviours and motivations, helping identify threats that exhibit subtler patterns.

Reference: The Role of Human Intelligence in Cybersecurity[87]

4.3.2. Adapting to New Threats:

Human expertise is vital for recognizing and adapting to emerging and novel cyber threats that AI models may not have encountered.

2.1 Threat Evolution:

Human analysts leverage experience to anticipate evolving threat tactics and techniques, ensuring readiness.

2.2 Zero-Day Threats:

Human intuition is crucial in detecting zero-day vulnerabilities that AI models may not have patterns for.

Human Expertise in Navigating New Threats[88]

---

[86] https://www.tripwire.com/state-of-security/security-data-protection/cyber-security/artificial-intelligence-ai-in-cybersecurity/

[87] https://www.csoonline.com/article/3582525/the-role-of-human-intelligence-in-cybersecurity.html

[88] https://www.tripwire.com/state-of-security/security-data-protection/cyber-security/artificial-intelligence-ai-in-cybersecurity/

4.3.3. Decision Validation:

Human validation of AI-generated insights ensures accurate decision-making and reduces the risk of false positives or negatives.

3.1 Data Verification:

Human analysts verify AI findings, preventing erroneous actions based on incomplete or misinterpreted data.

3.2 Risk Assessment:

Human experts assess the potential impact of AI-detected threats and recommend suitable responses.

Reference: Human Validation in AI Decision-Making[89]

4.3.4. Complex Threat Scenarios:

Human judgment is pivotal in handling intricate scenarios that require ethical considerations, negotiation, or diplomacy.

4.1 Geopolitical Context:

Human analysts factor in geopolitical and diplomatic dynamics, guiding responses to nation-state threats.

4.2 Ethical Decisions:

In complex scenarios, human analysts weigh ethical implications, ensuring responsible cybersecurity actions.

Reference: Human Intelligence in Complex Scenarios[90]

4.3.5. AI Limitations:

Human experts identify and address limitations or anomalies in AI models, ensuring accurate and reliable results.

5.1 Identifying AI Errors:

Human analysts detect anomalies that may indicate AI model errors or malicious manipulations.

5.2 Continuous Learning:

Combining human insights with AI helps identify areas where AI models can be improved through continuous learning.

Reference: Combining Human Expertise with AI[91]

Conclusion:

The synergy between AI capabilities and human analysis is paramount in cybersecurity. Human intuition, contextual understanding, decision validation, expertise in complex scenarios, and addressing AI limitations collectively enhance the accuracy and effectiveness of cybersecurity practices.

4.4 Discussion: Future Prospects and Trends:

Future intersection of Artificial Intelligence (AI) and cybersecurity is essential for fostering critical thinking and preparing for evolving challenges. This section outlines key points to encourage an

[89] https://www.securitymagazine.com/articles/95145-validating-ai-decisions-why-this-is-essential-for-success

[90] https://www.darkreading.com/vulnerabilities---threats/cybersecuritys-human-factor-in-the-age-of-covid-19/a/d-id/1338566

[91] https://www.csoonline.com/article/3538781/human-role-in-ai-in-cybersecurity.html

engaging and insightful conversation on potential AI advancements and their implications for cybersecurity.

4.4.1. Evolution of AI in Cybersecurity:

How might AI technologies evolve in the next decade, and how can these advancements reshape cybersecurity strategies?

1.1 AI-Powered Threat Actors:

Discuss the possibility of malicious actors utilizing advanced AI tools for cyberattacks and the countermeasures needed to mitigate such threats.

1.2 AI-Generated Cyberattacks:

Explore the concept of AI autonomously generating and launching cyberattacks and the potential consequences for digital security.

Reference: The Future of AI in Cybersecurity : https://www.mitre.org/sites/default/files/publications/pr-18-2391-mitre-10th-annual-cybersecurity-symposium.pdf

4.4.2. Autonomous Defensive Measures:

How can AI-driven autonomous defensive mechanisms revolutionize incident response and threat mitigation?

2.1 Self-Healing Networks:

Discuss the idea of networks that automatically detect, isolate, and mitigate threats without human intervention.

2.2 AI-Enabled Incident Response:

Explore how AI can expedite incident response by identifying, analysing, and containing threats in real-time.

Reference: AI for Autonomous Incident Response[92]

4.4.3. Ethical Dilemmas in AI-Enhanced Security:

What ethical considerations arise when AI is entrusted with security decision-making? How can we ensure responsible AI use?

3.1 AI-Driven Targeting:

Discuss the ethical implications of AI systems making decisions about targeting individuals or organizations based on threat assessments.

3.2 Human Oversight vs. AI Autonomy:

Explore the balance between allowing AI autonomy and maintaining human oversight in critical security decisions.

Reference: Ethics and AI in Cybersecurity[93]

4.4.4. AI-Enhanced Security Skillsets: Discussion Starter:

How will the integration of AI impact the skillsets required for cybersecurity professionals in the future?

---

[92] https://www.csoonline.com/article/3401158/ai-and-machine-learning-the-ability-to-detect-and-respond-to-cyber-threats.html

[93] https://www.csoonline.com/article/3583995/ethics-and-ai-what-you-need-to-know.html

4.1 Emphasis on Data Science:

Discuss the increasing importance of data analysis and interpretation skills alongside traditional cybersecurity expertise.

4.2 Human-Machine Collaboration:

Explore how professionals will need to collaborate effectively with AI systems to ensure effective security measures.

Reference: Future Skills in AI-Driven Cybersecurity[94]

4.4.5. AI-Regulated Cyber Norms:

How might AI technologies contribute to shaping international cyber norms and regulations?

5.1 Automated Norm Enforcement:

Discuss the potential for AI systems to monitor and enforce compliance with cybersecurity norms on a global scale.

5.2 Norm Evolution with AI Progress:

Explore how the rapid advancements of AI may necessitate constant updates to cybersecurity norms and regulations.

Reference: AI and Cyber Norms[95]

Conclusion:

Engaging in discussions about future AI developments and their impact on cybersecurity encourages critical thinking, fosters awareness of emerging challenges, and helps prepare the next generation of cybersecurity professionals to navigate a technologically advanced landscape.

Reference: AI and Cybersecurity: A Double-Edged Sword[96]

---

[94] https://www.cio.com/article/3535957/5-future-cybersecurity-trends-of-the-ai-era.html

[95] https://www.belfercenter.org/sites/default/files/files/publication/CyberAIProject-Report-2019.pdf

[96] https://www.cybersecasia.net/features/ai-and-cybersecurity-a-double-edged-sword

Chapter 2: AI for Threat Detection and Prevention

2.1 Role of AI in Identifying and Mitigating Cyber Threats

2.1.1 Enhancing Threat Detection:

How AI augments traditional cybersecurity methods by analysing vast amounts of data.

In the rapidly evolving landscape of cybersecurity, the integration of Artificial Intelligence (AI) has emerged as a transformative force. AI's ability to analyse vast amounts of data has significantly enhanced traditional cybersecurity methods, enabling organizations to detect and respond to threats with greater accuracy, speed, and efficiency. This section explores how AI augments conventional cybersecurity practices by harnessing its data analytics prowess.

1. Data Overload and the Need for AI:

The digital age has ushered in an era of unprecedented data generation, making it challenging for human analysts to process and interpret the sheer volume of information. Traditional cybersecurity methods, while effective, often struggle to keep pace with the scale and complexity of modern threats. This is where AI steps in, equipped to handle massive datasets and extract meaningful insights at a speed beyond human capability.

2. Machine Learning and Pattern Recognition:

AI's strength lies in its ability to learn from historical data and identify patterns that might otherwise elude human analysts. Machine Learning algorithms excel at recognizing subtle deviations from normal behaviour, which could signal potential threats. These algorithms continuously refine their models, adapting to new attack vectors and evolving tactics employed by cybercriminals.

3. Threat Detection and Prevention:

AI-driven threat detection systems operate as digital sentinels, continuously monitoring network traffic, user behaviour, and system logs for anomalous activities. By analysing vast amounts of data in real-time, AI can rapidly flag suspicious events, such as unauthorized access attempts or unusual data transfers. This proactive approach helps prevent breaches before they escalate.

4. Predictive Analytics for Risk Mitigation:

AI's data-driven insights enable organizations to predict and mitigate risks effectively. By identifying trends and correlations within datasets, AI can forecast potential vulnerabilities and assist in developing strategies to counteract emerging threats. This predictive approach empowers cybersecurity teams to stay one step ahead of attackers.

5. Real-time Incident Response:

In the event of a cyber incident, AI accelerates incident response by rapidly analysing the nature and scope of the breach. It provides crucial context to human analysts, enabling them to make informed decisions on containment, mitigation, and recovery strategies. This collaboration between AI and human expertise optimizes response times and minimizes damage.

6. Scaling Security Operations:

Traditional cybersecurity methods often require significant manpower to monitor and analyse data. AI automates many routine tasks, allowing cybersecurity teams to focus on high-value activities that require human insight and decision-making. This scalability ensures that security operations can handle the ever-expanding threat landscape.

7. Adaptive Defence Mechanisms:

AI's adaptability enhances its value in cybersecurity. As cyber threats evolve, AI models learn from new data, allowing them to adjust and refine their detection capabilities. This adaptability empowers AI to counter sophisticated, previously unseen attacks, making it an invaluable asset in maintaining robust defences.

8. Ethical Considerations and Human Oversight:

While AI augments cybersecurity methods, human oversight remains crucial. AI is only as effective as the data it's trained on, and biases within datasets can lead to inaccurate conclusions. Human experts play a vital role in validating AI-generated insights, ensuring ethical decisions and reducing the risk of false positives.

Conclusion:

AI's capacity to analyse vast amounts of data has revolutionized traditional cybersecurity methods, propelling them into an era of greater precision and efficiency. By harnessing the power of AI-driven analytics, organizations can navigate the complex cyber landscape with a heightened ability to detect, prevent, and respond to threats, ultimately safeguarding digital assets and fostering resilience against cyber adversaries.

2.1.2 Proactive Defence:

Harnessing AI to Identify Threats Before Escalation

In the world of cybersecurity, early threat identification is key to preventing major breaches and minimizing potential damage. Artificial Intelligence (AI) has emerged as a game-changer in this arena, offering the ability to detect and neutralize threats at an early stage. This section explores the discussions surrounding the use of AI to proactively identify and mitigate threats before they escalate into significant breaches.

1. The Significance of Early Threat Detection:

Timely detection of threats is essential to thwart cyber adversaries before they gain a foothold within an organization's systems. The consequences of unchecked threats can lead to data breaches, financial losses, and reputational damage. AI's potential to identify threats in their infancy aligns with the proactive approach needed in modern cybersecurity.

2. The Power of Anomaly Detection:

AI excels at recognizing anomalies in vast datasets, which often indicate malicious activities. By establishing baselines of normal behaviour, AI algorithms can flag deviations that may signify unauthorized access, data exfiltration, or other suspicious activities. This anomaly-driven approach provides a strong foundation for early threat identification.

3. Continuous Monitoring and Real-time Analysis:

AI-driven systems operate around the clock, continuously monitoring network traffic, user behaviour, and system logs. This constant vigilance allows for the swift detection of unusual patterns or behaviours that might indicate an impending breach. The real-time analysis provided by AI ensures that threats are identified as they emerge.

4. Behavioural Analysis and Contextual Understanding:

AI can analyse user behaviour and contextual information to determine whether activities are legitimate or potentially malicious. By understanding the context of actions, AI can distinguish between normal behaviour and actions that indicate a threat. This behavioural analysis contributes to accurate threat identification.

5. Predictive Insights and Risk Mitigation:

AI's ability to analyse historical data empowers it to predict potential security breaches based on patterns and trends. This predictive capability allows organizations to proactively address vulnerabilities, shore up defences, and deploy countermeasures before threats escalate.

6. Dynamic Learning and Adaptation:

AI models continuously learn from new data, allowing them to adapt to evolving threat tactics. This dynamic learning enables AI to stay ahead of attackers by identifying and countering emerging threats, even those that have not been encountered before.

7. Reducing Alert Fatigue:

Traditional security systems often generate a high volume of alerts, overwhelming security teams and leading to alert fatigue. AI filters through these alerts, prioritizing those that require immediate attention. This ensures that security personnel focus on genuine threats rather than being inundated with false alarms.

8. Human-AI Collaboration:

While AI is a powerful ally, human expertise remains indispensable. AI-generated alerts must be validated by human analysts to ensure accuracy and context. Human analysts provide the nuanced understanding required to make informed decisions on threat severity and the appropriate response.

9. Ethical Implications and Accountability:

The use of AI in threat detection raises ethical questions about false positives, privacy, and potential biases in data analysis. Striking a balance between AI's capabilities and ethical considerations requires careful oversight and accountability.

Conclusion:

Leveraging AI to identify threats before they escalate into major breaches aligns with the proactive defence strategy required in today's cybersecurity landscape. By harnessing AI's data analysis prowess, organizations can fortify their defences, minimize potential damage, and ensure a robust cybersecurity posture that anticipates and mitigates threats at their earliest stages.

2.1.3 Real-Time Analysis:

AI's Real-Time Analysis of Network Activities and Patterns:

In the dynamic field of cybersecurity, the ability to rapidly analyse network activities and patterns is critical to staying ahead of emerging threats. Artificial Intelligence (AI) has emerged as a powerhouse in this regard, offering real-time analysis that enables organizations to detect anomalies, identify potential breaches, and respond promptly. This section shines a spotlight on AI's capability to provide real-time analysis of network activities and patterns.

1. The Need for Timely Network Analysis:

In a digital landscape teeming with potential threats, delayed detection and response can have severe consequences. Real-time analysis of network activities is imperative to identify and neutralize threats before they can escalate into breaches. AI's speed and efficiency align perfectly with the demands of swift threat identification.

2. Rapid Detection of Anomalies:

AI's proficiency in identifying deviations from established norms enables it to rapidly flag anomalies that may indicate unauthorized access, data exfiltration, or other suspicious behaviours. This anomaly detection is a cornerstone of real-time analysis, allowing threats to be identified as they emerge.

3. Continuous Monitoring and Immediate Response:

AI-driven systems continuously monitor network traffic, user behaviour, and system logs. This constant surveillance ensures that any unusual activities are rapidly captured, analysed, and responded to, reducing the time window for potential threats to exploit vulnerabilities.

4. Behavioural Profiling and Pattern Recognition:

AI excels at building behavioural profiles of users and devices within a network. By recognizing patterns in user activities, AI can detect deviations that could indicate a compromise or breach attempt. This profiling enhances the accuracy of threat identification.

5. Dynamic Learning and Adaptation:

AI models learn from new data, allowing them to adapt to evolving threats and tactics. This dynamic learning ensures that AI remains effective in detecting the latest attack vectors and techniques, even those that have not been encountered before.

6. Minimizing False Positives:

One challenge in real-time analysis is the potential for false positives, which can lead to alert fatigue. AI's data-driven approach reduces false positives by considering multiple factors and context before generating alerts, allowing security teams to focus on genuine threats.

7. Response Optimization:

AI's real-time analysis provides contextual information that enhances incident response. By offering insights into the nature and scope of threats, AI enables security teams to formulate effective strategies for containment, mitigation, and recovery.

8. Prioritizing Threats:

Not all threats are equal in terms of severity. AI's real-time analysis prioritizes threats based on their potential impact, enabling security teams to allocate resources effectively and respond to the most pressing concerns first.

9. Human-Machine Collaboration:

While AI offers rapid analysis, human expertise remains indispensable. Collaborative efforts between AI and human analysts ensure that alerts are validated, context is understood, and informed decisions are made regarding threat severity and response actions.

Conclusion:

AI's real-time analysis of network activities and patterns marks a significant advancement in cybersecurity. By offering swift and accurate threat identification, AI empowers organizations to maintain a proactive defence posture, identify emerging threats, and respond promptly to potential breaches. This capability is instrumental in safeguarding digital assets and maintaining robust cybersecurity in an ever-evolving threat landscape.

Reference: AI in Cybersecurity: Threat Detection and Prevention[97]

2.2 Machine Learning and Anomaly Detection in Cybersecurity

2.2.1 Introduction to Machine Learning (ML):

Recap of machine learning basics and its role in training AI models.

As we explore the dynamic intersection of Artificial Intelligence (AI) and cybersecurity, it's essential to revisit the foundational concept of machine learning (ML) and understand how it plays a key role in training AI models. This recap section provides a concise overview of machine learning basics and its significance in shaping AI's capabilities.

1. Machine Learning: A Brief Overview:

Machine learning is a subset of AI that empowers computers to learn from data without explicit programming. It equips machines with the ability to improve their performance over time through exposure to various datasets. Machine learning algorithms enable AI models to recognize patterns, make predictions, and perform tasks based on learned experiences.

2. The Role of Data:

At the heart of machine learning lies data. Datasets containing examples, features, and outcomes form the foundation on which AI models are built. These datasets allow algorithms to identify correlations, relationships, and trends, enabling the AI model to make informed decisions.

3. Training AI Models:

The process of training AI models involves feeding them labelled datasets, allowing algorithms to learn patterns and make predictions. During training, the model adjusts its internal parameters to minimize errors and optimize performance. This iterative process refines the model's accuracy and adaptability.

4. Supervised Learning:

Supervised learning is a fundamental machine learning approach where the model learns from labelled examples. It maps inputs to correct outputs, allowing the model to make accurate

---

[97] https://www.securityweek.com/ai-cybersecurity-threat-detection-and-prevention

predictions on new, unseen data. Supervised learning forms the basis for training AI models to recognize and classify various patterns in cybersecurity data.

5. Unsupervised Learning:

Unsupervised learning involves training AI models on unlabelled data to identify inherent structures or clusters. This approach is useful for anomaly detection and identifying previously unseen threats by recognizing deviations from normal patterns.

6. Feature Extraction and Selection:

Feature extraction involves identifying relevant attributes or features in the data that contribute to the desired outcome. Feature selection aims to choose the most informative features to enhance the model's performance and efficiency.

7. Neural Networks and Deep Learning:

Deep learning, a subset of ML, utilizes neural networks to model complex relationships in data. Neural networks consist of layers of interconnected nodes that mimic the human brain's structure. Deep learning's ability to learn hierarchical features makes it ideal for tasks such as image recognition and natural language processing.

8. Transfer Learning:

Transfer learning involves utilizing a pre-trained model on a specific task and fine-tuning it for a related task. This approach accelerates model development and improves performance with limited data.

9. Continuous Learning and Adaptation:

Machine learning enables AI models to continuously learn and adapt. As new data becomes available, models can update their parameters, improving accuracy and keeping up with evolving threat landscapes.

Conclusion:

Machine learning serves as the cornerstone of training AI models to effectively analyse cybersecurity data, recognize patterns, and make informed decisions. By harnessing the power of machine learning, AI becomes a dynamic tool that can enhance threat detection, prediction, and response capabilities, contributing to a robust and adaptive cybersecurity framework

2.2.2 Anomaly Detection:

Using Machine Learning to Identify Deviations from Normal Patterns in Network Behaviour

In the field of cybersecurity, the ability to identify anomalies and deviations from normal patterns in network behaviour is crucial for early threat detection and mitigation. Machine Learning (ML) has emerged as a powerful tool in this arena, enabling organizations to accurately pinpoint unusual activities that might indicate cyber threats. This section explores how ML is employed to identify deviations from normal patterns in network behaviour.

1. The Significance of Anomaly Detection:

Traditional rule-based approaches to cybersecurity often struggle to keep pace with the rapidly evolving tactics of cyber adversaries. Anomaly detection offers a more dynamic solution by identifying activities that deviate from established norms. These deviations could indicate malicious activities, making anomaly detection a critical component of modern cybersecurity.

2. Machine Learning's Role in Anomaly Detection:

Machine Learning excels in identifying patterns within complex and large datasets. By training models on historical data, ML algorithms learn the nuances of normal network behaviour. This learning enables them to recognize deviations that might signify potential threats.

3. Building Baselines:

To identify anomalies, ML models create baselines of normal behaviour using historical data. This baseline reflects the typical patterns of network activities, allowing the model to identify behaviours that deviate from the norm.

4. Supervised vs. Unsupervised Learning:

Both supervised and unsupervised learning approaches are used for anomaly detection. In supervised learning, models are trained on labelled data that specifies normal and anomalous behaviours. In contrast, unsupervised learning identifies anomalies without prior labelled examples by identifying deviations from the established baseline.

5. Features and Attributes:

ML models consider various features and attributes of network traffic, including traffic volume, source-destination pairs, data types, and more. These attributes contribute to the model's ability to discern between normal and abnormal patterns.

6. Adaptive Learning:

ML models are capable of adaptive learning, which means they adjust to changes in network behaviour over time. As cyber threats evolve, the model's parameters are updated to accommodate new attack vectors and tactics.

7. Complex Pattern Recognition:

ML models, especially deep learning architectures, are adept at recognizing intricate patterns that might elude traditional rule-based systems. This makes them well-suited for detecting sophisticated and evolving threats.

8. Reducing False Positives:

Anomaly detection often leads to false positives, flagging legitimate activities as anomalous. ML models work to minimize false positives by considering multiple attributes and context before raising alerts, improving the overall accuracy of threat detection.

9. Real-time Analysis:

ML-powered anomaly detection operates in real-time, allowing organizations to respond promptly to potential threats. The ability to identify and respond to anomalies as they occur is a crucial component of modern cybersecurity strategies.

Conclusion:

Machine Learning's ability to identify deviations from normal patterns in network behaviour has revolutionized cybersecurity. By continuously analysing network activities and recognizing subtle anomalies, ML-equipped systems enhance the early detection of potential threats. This proactive approach allows organizations to respond rapidly , mitigating risks and safeguarding their digital assets in an ever-evolving threat landscape.

2.2.3 Unsupervised Learning for Anomaly Detection:

How unsupervised ML techniques discover anomalies without predefined labels.

In the domain of cybersecurity, detecting anomalies and potential threats is a critical task that often involves uncovering patterns that deviate from the norm. Unsupervised Machine Learning (ML) techniques play a key role in this domain by identifying anomalies without the need for predefined labels. This section explores how unsupervised ML techniques discover anomalies through inherent patterns and behaviours in data.

1. Anomaly Detection and Unsupervised Learning:
Unsupervised ML techniques are particularly well-suited for anomaly detection scenarios where labelled data for normal and anomalous behaviours might be scarce or unreliable. Instead of relying on predefined labels, unsupervised techniques uncover irregularities by identifying patterns that differ from the general behaviour of the dataset.

2. Establishing a Baseline:
Unsupervised anomaly detection begins by establishing a baseline of normal behaviour using historical data. The model learns the typical patterns, statistical distributions, and relationships within the dataset, which serve as reference points for identifying deviations.

3. Clustering Techniques:
Clustering methods group data points based on their similarities. Anomalies are often data points that do not fit well within any cluster or form their own distinct cluster. Techniques like k-means clustering or hierarchical clustering can help pinpoint these anomalies.

4. Density-Based Approaches:
Density-based algorithms like DBSCAN (Density-Based Spatial Clustering of Applications with Noise) identify anomalies as points that have significantly lower density compared to their neighbours. Outliers with sparse or isolated occurrences are flagged as potential anomalies.

5. Distance-Based Methods:
Distance-based techniques calculate distances between data points in multi-dimensional space. Data points that are far away from the majority of other points are considered anomalies. Techniques like Local Outlier Factor (LOF) use this concept to detect outliers.

6. Isolation Forests:
Isolation Forests are tree-based algorithms that isolate anomalies by randomly selecting a feature and then randomly selecting a split value between the maximum and minimum values of that feature. The number of splits needed to isolate an instance becomes a measure of its anomaly score.

7. Autoencoders for Anomaly Detection:
Autoencoders, a type of neural network, can be trained to learn a compressed representation of input data. When presented with anomalous data, the reconstruction error of the autoencoder increases, indicating a potential anomaly.

8. Advantage of Flexibility:
Unsupervised ML techniques don't rely on predefined labels, making them adaptable to various domains and datasets. They have the ability to uncover novel or previously unseen anomalies, which is crucial in detecting emerging threats.

9. Limitations and Challenges:
While powerful, unsupervised methods can also produce false positives and require careful tuning. The lack of labelled data for training means that the definition of an anomaly might be subjective and context-dependent.

Conclusion:

Unsupervised Machine Learning techniques are invaluable for discovering anomalies in cybersecurity without the need for predefined labels. By relying on inherent patterns, relationships, and deviations within datasets, these methods enable the early identification of potential threats, contributing to a proactive and effective cybersecurity strategy.

Reference: Anomaly Detection in Network Traffic with Machine Learning[98]

2.2.4 Feature Engineering:

Overview of the process of selecting relevant features for training ML models.

In the domain of Machine Learning (ML), the process of selecting relevant features for training models is a critical step that significantly impacts the model's performance and effectiveness. This overview explores the importance of feature selection, the methods employed, and their role in optimizing ML model training.

1. The Significance of Feature Selection:

Features are the individual attributes or characteristics that define the input data for ML models. Selecting the right features is crucial as irrelevant or redundant attributes can introduce noise, hinder model performance, and increase computation costs. Feature selection aims to enhance the model's efficiency, accuracy, and generalization.

2. Data Dimensionality and Complexity:

As datasets grow in size and complexity, they often encompass numerous features, many of which might not contribute significantly to the model's predictive power. Feature selection addresses the "curse of dimensionality," where high-dimensional data can lead to overfitting or increased computational requirements.

3. Improved Model Generalization:

Feature selection enhances the model's ability to generalize to new, unseen data. By focusing on relevant features, the model can learn more meaningful patterns and relationships within the data, leading to better predictions on diverse datasets.

4. Methods of Feature Selection:

Feature selection methods can be broadly categorized into three types: filter methods, wrapper methods, and embedded methods.

Filter Methods:

These methods assess features independently of the model's predictive power. They use statistical tests, correlation analysis, or other criteria to rank or score features based on their relevance to the target variable.

Wrapper Methods:

Wrapper methods involve training and evaluating the ML model using different subsets of features. This approach gauges feature subsets' impact on model performance through cross-validation or other techniques.

Embedded Methods:

Embedded methods incorporate feature selection within the model training process itself. Algorithms like LASSO (Least Absolute Shrinkage and Selection Operator) and decision trees inherently perform feature selection during training.

5. Techniques for Selecting Features:

Several techniques aid in selecting relevant features:

Correlation Analysis:

Assessing the correlation between features and the target variable can identify strong predictors.

Mutual Information:

This measures the mutual dependence between two variables, highlighting the information a feature provides about the target variable.

Recursive Feature Elimination (RFE):

Wrapper method where less important features are recursively removed based on model performance.

Tree-Based Methods:

Decision trees and ensemble methods like Random Forests can evaluate feature importance by analysing node splits.

Regularization Techniques:

Algorithms like LASSO introduce penalties on feature coefficients, effectively performing feature selection.

6. Balancing Complexity and Interpretability:

Feature selection involves striking a balance between model complexity and interpretability. While reducing features can simplify models, it's crucial to ensure that vital information isn't discarded, especially in scenarios where feature interpretation is valuable.

7. Importance of Domain Knowledge:

Domain knowledge plays a key role in feature selection. Experts in the field can offer insights into which features are likely to be significant, aiding in informed selection decisions.

8. Continuous Evaluation:

Feature selection isn't a one-time process. As datasets evolve and new features become relevant, it's essential to regularly reassess and fine-tune feature selection strategies.

Conclusion:

Selecting relevant features for ML model training is a critical step in enhancing predictive accuracy, reducing overfitting, and optimizing computational efficiency. By carefully considering the significance of each feature and employing appropriate selection methods, practitioners can build models that extract meaningful insights from complex datasets, leading to more accurate predictions and actionable results.

2.3 Case Studies of AI-Powered Threat Detection Systems

2.3.1 Darktrace's Cyber AI:

Examination of Darktrace's AI-driven platform for autonomous threat detection.

In the landscape of cybersecurity, organizations are grappling with increasingly sophisticated and evolving threats. Darktrace's AI-driven platform represents a notable advancement in the field, employing artificial intelligence to autonomously detect and mitigate threats. This examination explores the capabilities and significance of Darktrace's platform in transforming threat detection and response.

1. The Evolution of Threat Landscape:

As cyber threats become more intricate and stealthy, traditional cybersecurity methods often struggle to keep pace. Darktrace's platform addresses this challenge by harnessing the power of AI to dynamically detect and respond to emerging threats.

2. Autonomous Threat Detection:

At the core of Darktrace's platform is its autonomous threat detection capability. The AI-powered system continuously learns the organization's network behaviour, creating a baseline of normal activities. It then identifies deviations and anomalies from this baseline, flagging potential threats for investigation.

3. Machine Learning Algorithms:

Darktrace's platform employs a range of machine learning algorithms to understand and adapt to the organization's network. These algorithms encompass unsupervised learning techniques, enabling the system to discover previously unknown threats without relying on predefined patterns or signatures.

4. Behavioural Analysis:

The platform focuses on behavioural analysis rather than relying solely on known threat indicators. By understanding the typical behaviour of users, devices, and applications, Darktrace's AI identifies deviations that might indicate unauthorized access, data exfiltration, or other malicious activities.

5. Enterprise-Wide Coverage:

Darktrace's AI-driven platform provides holistic coverage across the entire organization's digital environment. This includes on-premises networks, cloud environments, IoT devices, and even industrial control systems.

6. Real-Time Response:

Upon identifying potential threats, the platform not only alerts security teams but also offers recommendations for response actions. This real-time capability empowers organizations to rapidly mitigate threats and reduce potential damage.

7. Continuous Learning:

Darktrace's platform embraces the concept of continuous learning. As the organization's network evolves and new threats emerge, the AI system adapts and refines its threat detection capabilities, providing an ever-improving defence mechanism.

8. Autonomous Cyber AI Analyst:

One of the innovative features of the platform is the "Autonomous Cyber AI Analyst." This AI-driven component assists human analysts by providing insights, context, and recommended actions based on its analysis of threats.

9. Human-AI Collaboration:

Darktrace's approach exemplifies the collaboration between human expertise and AI capabilities. The platform's ability to augment human decision-making enhances the efficiency and effectiveness of cybersecurity operations.

10. Addressing Zero-Day Threats:

By focusing on behavioural anomalies, Darktrace's platform is well-suited for detecting zero-day threats—attacks that exploit vulnerabilities unknown to security experts.

Conclusion:

Darktrace's AI-driven platform signifies a transformative approach to cybersecurity, harnessing the power of artificial intelligence to autonomously identify and respond to evolving threats. By embracing continuous learning, real-time response, and human-AI collaboration, Darktrace's platform serves as a pivotal tool in safeguarding organizations against the dynamic and sophisticated cyber threat landscape.

Reference: Darktrace Cyber AI[99]

2.3.2 CylancePROTECT:
Case study of CylancePROTECT's AI-based approach to preventing malware and cyberattacks.

In the domain of cybersecurity, the battle against malware and cyberattacks continues to intensify. CylancePROTECT's AI-based approach represents a remarkable advancement in the field, leveraging artificial intelligence to proactively prevent threats. This case study explores the capabilities and impact of CylancePROTECT's AI-driven solution in effectively countering malware and cyberattacks.

1. Context of Modern Cyber Threats:

As cyber threats evolve to be more sophisticated and evasive, traditional signature-based approaches to cybersecurity have proven increasingly inadequate. CylancePROTECT addresses this challenge by embracing the power of AI to predict and prevent attacks before they manifest.

2. Predictive Prevention:

At the core of CylancePROTECT is its emphasis on predictive prevention. The platform utilizes machine learning algorithms to analyse vast amounts of data and identify patterns indicative of malicious behaviour. By doing so, it prevents threats from executing on endpoints, averting potential breaches.

3. AI-Powered Threat Prevention:

CylancePROTECT employs a blend of supervised and unsupervised machine learning techniques. Supervised learning involves training models on labelled data, while unsupervised learning enables the discovery of new and previously unseen threats.

---

[99] https://www.darktrace.com/en/technology/how-it-works/

4. Signatureless Approach:

A distinctive feature of CylancePROTECT is its signatureless approach. Unlike traditional antivirus solutions that rely on known signatures, this AI-driven solution can thwart novel and zero-day attacks by analysing the underlying behaviour of files and processes.

5. Prevention Over Detection:

CylancePROTECT's focus on prevention sets it apart from reactive detection-based solutions. By stopping threats before they cause harm, organizations can significantly reduce the risk of breaches and data loss.

6. Endpoint Coverage:

The platform extends its protection across a wide range of endpoints, including workstations, servers, and even IoT devices. This holistic coverage addresses the diverse threat landscape faced by modern organizations.

7. Efficient Resource Utilization:

CylancePROTECT's AI-based approach consumes fewer system resources compared to traditional antivirus solutions. This enables efficient protection without hampering device performance.

8. Continuous Learning:

Similar to other AI-driven solutions, CylancePROTECT continuously learns and adapts to evolving threats. This adaptability is crucial in countering the dynamic nature of cyberattacks.

9. Real-World Impact:

Multiple case studies demonstrate CylancePROTECT's efficacy in preventing a wide range of threats, from malware to ransomware. Its AI-driven nature allows it to detect and prevent attacks that bypass traditional defences.

10. Human Expertise and AI Synergy:

CylancePROTECT's success underscores the synergy between human expertise and AI capabilities. The platform's AI-driven prevention is enhanced by human analysis and threat intelligence.

Conclusion:

CylancePROTECT's AI-based approach marks a significant stride in the domain of cybersecurity, ushering in a new era of predictive prevention. By combining machine learning, signatureless techniques, and a focus on proactive measures, CylancePROTECT effectively thwarts malware and cyberattacks. Its ability to adapt, learn, and collaborate with human analysts underscores the potential of AI in safeguarding organizations against the evolving threat landscape.

Reference: CylancePROTECT Case Study[100]

2.3.3 Vectra Networks:

Vectra Networks': AI-powered platform for detecting and responding to cyberattacks

Organizations seek innovative solutions to detect and respond to cyberattacks effectively. Vectra Networks' AI-powered platform stands out as a remarkable tool, leveraging artificial intelligence to autonomously identify and mitigate threats. This section explores the capabilities and significance of Vectra Networks' platform in transforming the way organizations detect and respond to cyber threats.

---

[100] https://www.cylance.com/en_us/blog/protecting-endpoints-from-the-dawn-of-cybersecurity.html

1. Adapting to Advanced Threats:

Modern cyber threats are increasingly sophisticated, bypassing traditional security measures. Vectra Networks' AI-powered platform addresses this challenge by providing organizations with an advanced defence mechanism that can identify hidden threats.

2. Real-Time Threat Detection:

At the core of Vectra's platform is its real-time threat detection capability. The platform continuously monitors network traffic, analysing patterns and behaviours to identify anomalies that might indicate a cyberattack in progress.

3. AI Algorithms and Machine Learning:

Vectra Networks employs a range of AI algorithms and machine learning techniques to process large volumes of network data. These algorithms learn normal network behaviour and quickly flag deviations that may signal malicious activity.

4. Behavioural Analysis and Contextual Insights:

Unlike signature-based approaches, Vectra's platform focuses on behavioural analysis. By understanding how users, devices, and applications interact within the network, it can detect anomalies and uncover hidden threats that might go unnoticed.

5. Automated Threat Hunting:

The platform employs AI-driven threat hunting techniques, effectively acting as a digital hunter within the network. It identifies threat behaviours, maps attack paths, and provides security teams with actionable insights.

6. Real-Time Response and Mitigation:

Upon detecting a threat, Vectra's platform doesn't just alert security teams; it also offers real-time response options to mitigate the threat's impact. This proactive approach reduces the time between detection and action.

7. Focusing on Insider Threats:

Vectra's platform is particularly adept at identifying insider threats and lateral movement within the network. It highlights unusual behaviours that might indicate unauthorized access or data exfiltration.

8. Enterprise-Wide Visibility:

The platform provides comprehensive visibility across an organization's entire network, including on-premises, cloud, and hybrid environments. This holistic coverage is crucial for identifying threats that span multiple systems.

9. Human-AI Collaboration:

Vectra Networks' approach exemplifies the synergy between AI capabilities and human expertise. While the AI autonomously detects and responds to threats, human analysts provide context, analysis, and decision-making.

10. Continuous Learning and Adaptation:

As threat landscapes evolve, Vectra's platform adapts and learns from new threat intelligence, enhancing its ability to detect emerging attacks.

Conclusion:

Vectra Networks' AI-powered platform signifies a significant advancement in cybersecurity, leveraging the power of artificial intelligence to autonomously identify, analyse, and respond to cyber threats in real time. By combining behavioural analysis, threat hunting, and human-AI collaboration, Vectra's platform empowers organizations to detect and mitigate threats efficiently, ultimately enhancing their overall cybersecurity posture in an increasingly complex threat landscape.

Reference: Vectra Networks AI-Driven Cybersecurity[101]

Chapter 3: AI in Intrusion Detection and Response

3.1 Utilizing AI to Detect and Respond to Cyber Intrusions

3.1.1 AI-Enhanced Intrusion Detection:

Enhancing Intrusion Detection with AI: Analysing Patterns and Anomalies

In the domain of cybersecurity, intrusion detection stands as a critical defence against malicious activities that threaten an organization's digital assets. Artificial Intelligence (AI) has emerged as a transformative force, enhancing intrusion detection capabilities by analysing patterns and anomalies in network behaviour. This section explores how AI empowers organizations to proactively identify and respond to intrusions.

1. Traditional Intrusion Detection Challenges:
Traditional intrusion detection methods often rely on predefined signatures or patterns of known attacks. These approaches struggle to keep pace with evolving threats, zero-day vulnerabilities, and sophisticated attacks that evade known patterns.

2. AI's Pattern Recognition Power:
AI's strength lies in its ability to identify intricate patterns within vast amounts of data. Machine learning algorithms excel at recognizing both subtle and complex relationships, enabling them to uncover anomalous behaviours that might go unnoticed by conventional methods.

3. Continuous Learning and Adaptation:
AI-driven intrusion detection systems don't rely solely on historical patterns. They continuously learn from new data, adapt to changing behaviours, and evolve their understanding of what constitutes normal network activity.

4. Unsupervised Learning for Anomaly Detection:
AI techniques, particularly unsupervised learning, can identify anomalies without prior knowledge of specific threats. By learning the network's baseline behaviour, AI models can pinpoint deviations that could indicate a potential intrusion.

5. Multidimensional Analysis:
AI can analyse multiple dimensions of network data simultaneously, including traffic volume, protocols, user behaviour, and more. This holistic analysis enhances the accuracy of intrusion detection by considering a broader context.

6. Real-Time Detection and Response:
AI-powered intrusion detection operates in real time, allowing organizations to respond rapidly to emerging threats. This real-time capability minimizes the window of vulnerability during which attacks can occur.

---

[101] https://www.vectra.ai/why-vectra

7. Complex Threat Detection:

AI excels at detecting complex threats, such as advanced persistent threats (APTs), which involve subtle and prolonged malicious activities. AI models can recognize the gradual patterns associated with APTs.

8. Reducing False Positives:

AI's advanced analytics and contextual analysis help reduce false positives, which often inundate security teams in traditional systems. This efficiency enables security professionals to focus on genuine threats.

9. Scaling to Large Networks:

For organizations with extensive networks generating massive amounts of data, AI-powered intrusion detection scales effortlessly. It can process and analyse enormous volumes of data without compromising accuracy.

10. Human-Machine Synergy:

AI doesn't replace human analysts but rather enhances their abilities. Human experts provide the contextual understanding and nuanced decision-making that complements AI's pattern recognition.

Conclusion:

AI's ability to analyse patterns and anomalies revolutionizes intrusion detection by enhancing accuracy, real-time response, and the capability to detect sophisticated threats. By employing machine learning's prowess to learn from data and recognize deviations, organizations can significantly bolster their cybersecurity posture and stay ahead of emerging threats in today's dynamic threat landscape.

3.1.2 Automation of Incident Response:

Introduction to AI-driven automated incident response mechanisms.

In the domain of cybersecurity, incident response plays a key role in minimizing the impact of cyberattacks and breaches. The emergence of Artificial Intelligence (AI) has revolutionized incident response by introducing automated mechanisms that can rapidly and effectively counter threats. This introduction explores how AI-driven automated incident response mechanisms are reshaping the way organizations mitigate and recover from cybersecurity incidents.

1. The Evolution of Incident Response:

Traditional incident response methods often involve manual analysis and decision-making, which can lead to delays in identifying and containing threats. AI-driven automated incident response mechanisms address this challenge by expediting the response process.

2. Real-Time Detection and Response:

AI's real-time capabilities empower automated incident response systems to detect threats as they unfold. This immediate response minimizes the window of opportunity for attackers to cause further damage.

3. Rapid Decision-Making:

AI algorithms can rapidly process and analyse vast amounts of data to determine the nature and severity of an incident. This automated decision-making accelerates response times and reduces human error.

4. Automating Routine Tasks:

AI-driven incident response systems automate routine tasks, such as isolating compromised endpoints, blocking malicious IP addresses, and quarantining suspicious files. This frees up human analysts to focus on more complex aspects of incident management.

5. Adaptive and Learning Abilities:

AI systems continually learn from incident data and improve over time. They adapt to new threat patterns, enhancing their accuracy and effectiveness in responding to emerging threats.

6. Consistency and Scalability:

Automated incident response ensures a consistent and standardized approach to handling incidents across an organization. Furthermore, these mechanisms can scale effortlessly to manage incidents across large and complex networks.

7. Prioritization of Threats:

AI can assess the severity and potential impact of incidents, allowing organizations to prioritize responses based on risk levels. This strategic approach ensures that critical threats receive immediate attention.

8. Integration with Threat Intelligence:

AI-driven incident response mechanisms can integrate with threat intelligence feeds to provide context and enrichment for detected threats. This integration enhances understanding and response actions.

9. Reduced Dwell Time:

Dwell time, the period attackers remain undetected within a network, is significantly reduced with AI-driven automated responses. Rapid detection and containment prevent attackers from moving laterally and causing more damage.

10. Collaboration with Human Analysts:

AI doesn't replace human expertise; rather, it complements it. Automated incident response systems collaborate with human analysts, providing them with insights, recommendations, and actionable information.

Conclusion:

AI-driven automated incident response mechanisms mark a paradigm shift in cybersecurity incident management. By combining real-time detection, rapid decision-making, and automated actions, organizations can rapidly identify, contain, and mitigate threats. These mechanisms not only improve incident response times but also enhance the overall resilience of organizations in the face of evolving cyber threats.

3.1.3 AI for Behavioural Analysis:

AI's Detection of Deviations for Potential Intrusions

In the ever-evolving landscape of cybersecurity, organizations face an ongoing battle against a multitude of threats. Artificial Intelligence (AI) emerges as a powerful ally in this fight, leveraging its ability to identify deviations from normal behaviour that signal potential intrusions. This section explores how AI employs advanced techniques to recognize anomalies and pre-emptively detect cyber intrusions.

1. Understanding Normal Behaviour:

AI-driven intrusion detection starts with understanding what constitutes normal behaviour within a network. This involves collecting extensive data on user activities, application interactions, and network traffic.

2. Learning Normal Patterns:

Machine learning algorithms, particularly those employing unsupervised learning, analyse historical data to establish patterns of normal behaviour. These patterns serve as a baseline against which deviations are measured.

3. Anomaly Detection Techniques:

AI employs sophisticated anomaly detection techniques to spot deviations from the established norm. These deviations could indicate unauthorized access, malicious activities, or other anomalous behaviours.

4. Multidimensional Analysis:

AI doesn't rely solely on a single type of data but performs multidimensional analysis. This includes assessing various attributes such as time of day, user roles, resource access patterns, and more.

5. Behavioural Analysis:

AI-driven intrusion detection focuses on analysing the behaviour of users, devices, and applications. It looks for anomalies that might be indicative of cyber intrusions, such as unusual login times or sudden spikes in data transfers.

6. Contextual Analysis:

AI considers contextual information to differentiate between innocuous anomalies and potentially harmful ones. For instance, an employee accessing sensitive data after hours might raise concern, whereas accessing it during work hours might be normal.

7. Continuous Monitoring:

AI-powered systems continuously monitor network activities, enabling them to detect intrusions in real time. This minimizes the time attackers have to establish a foothold and cause damage.

8. Adaptation to Evolving Threats:

AI models are adaptive, capable of learning new behaviours and adapting to evolving threat landscapes. This adaptability ensures that the intrusion detection system remains effective even against emerging threats.

9. Reduced False Positives:

AI's contextual and behavioural analysis reduces the likelihood of false positives – instances where normal behaviour might appear anomalous. This refinement enhances the accuracy of intrusion detection.

10. Human-AI Collaboration:

AI's capabilities are bolstered by human analysis and expertise. Human analysts provide the context and nuanced understanding needed to differentiate between benign anomalies and genuine threats.

Conclusion:

AI's prowess in identifying deviations from normal behaviour revolutionizes intrusion detection by pre-emptively spotting potential cyber intrusions. Through machine learning and contextual analysis, AI-driven systems provide organizations with an enhanced ability to thwart threats before they manifest, ultimately fortifying their cybersecurity defences against the ever-evolving threat landscape.

Reference: AI in Intrusion Detection[102]

3.2 Real-Time Analysis of Network Traffic and Behaviour

3.2.1 Network Traffic Analysis:

Continuous Monitoring of Network Traffic for Unusual Patterns Using AI

In the dynamic landscape of cybersecurity, organizations face an unceasing stream of potential threats traversing their network infrastructure. Artificial Intelligence (AI) emerges as a powerful tool in this battle, offering continuous monitoring capabilities that can detect unusual patterns in network traffic. This overview explores how AI leverages its real-time analysis to identify anomalies and potential security breaches.

1. Real-Time Traffic Analysis:

AI-driven network monitoring involves the real-time analysis of network traffic as data flows between various devices, servers, and endpoints within an organization's network.

2. Data Collection and Aggregation:

AI continuously collects and aggregates data from multiple sources, including logs, packet captures, flow data, and other network telemetry sources. This data provides a comprehensive view of network activities.

3. Establishing Normal Behaviour:

Before AI can detect unusual patterns, it first establishes a baseline of normal behaviour. This involves analysing historical data to learn how devices, users, and applications typically interact within the network.

4. Machine Learning Algorithms:

AI employs machine learning algorithms, particularly those cantered on unsupervised learning, to identify deviations from the established baseline. These algorithms autonomously learn from data and adapt to evolving network behaviours.

5. Real-Time Anomaly Detection:

As network traffic flows, AI algorithms constantly compare ongoing activity against the established baseline. Any deviations from normal patterns are flagged as potential anomalies that require investigation.

6. Multidimensional Analysis:

AI's analysis extends beyond simple metrics; it considers multiple dimensions of network traffic. This includes parameters like bandwidth usage, data transfer rates, communication patterns, and more.

7. Contextual Understanding:

AI adds contextual understanding to its analysis, distinguishing between harmless anomalies and potential security threats. For instance, a sudden surge in traffic during a promotional event might be normal behaviour.

---

[102] https://www.csoonline.com/article/3234728/ai-in-intrusion-detection-what-it-means-for-you.html

8. Behavioural Correlation:

AI correlates the behaviour of different devices and users, identifying patterns that might indicate coordinated attacks or unauthorized access.

9. Real-Time Alerts and Response:

When AI detects anomalies, it triggers real-time alerts to notify security teams. This allows rapid investigation and response, minimizing the potential impact of security incidents.

10. Continuous Learning and Adaptation:

AI is not static; it continuously learns from new data and adapts to changes in network behaviour. This ensures its accuracy in identifying both existing and emerging threats.

Conclusion:

AI's ability to continuously monitor network traffic for unusual patterns represents a significant advancement in cybersecurity. By leveraging real-time analysis, multidimensional assessment, and contextual understanding, AI provides organizations with a proactive defence mechanism that can rapidly detect and respond to potential security breaches. This real-time vigilance enhances an organization's overall cybersecurity posture, helping it stay resilient against evolving threats.

3.2.2 Real-Time Threat Hunting:
how AI enables real-time threat hunting to identify active threats?

The traditional approach of waiting for threats to trigger alarms is gradually giving way to proactive threat hunting. Artificial Intelligence (AI) emerges as a game-changer in this context, enabling real-time threat hunting that actively seeks out active threats within an organization's network. This section explores how AI empowers cybersecurity professionals to identify and neutralize threats in their earliest stages.

1. Evolving from Reactive to Proactive:

Reactive approaches to threat detection wait for alarms to sound after a breach occurs. Real-time threat hunting, powered by AI, shifts the paradigm by actively searching for threats before they escalate into significant security incidents.

2. Continuous Data Analysis:

AI-driven threat hunting involves continuous analysis of vast amounts of data generated by network devices, applications, and endpoints. This real-time assessment allows for the immediate detection of suspicious activities.

3. Patterns and Anomalies:

AI leverages its pattern recognition abilities to identify subtle deviations from normal behaviour. It can discern patterns in user activities, data transfers, and communication that might indicate a potential threat.

4. Contextual Analysis:

AI adds context to its analysis, considering factors like user roles, device behaviours, and application interactions. This contextual understanding helps distinguish between innocuous activities and potentially malicious actions.

5. Threat Correlation:

AI correlates various indicators of compromise (IoCs) to identify potential relationships between seemingly unrelated events. This approach uncovers hidden attack patterns and tactics used by sophisticated threats.

6. Automation of Investigative Tasks:

AI automates time-consuming investigative tasks, such as querying logs, analysing large datasets, and correlating events across the network. This automation accelerates the threat hunting process.

7. Real-Time Alerts and Responses:

As AI detects suspicious activities, it generates real-time alerts for cybersecurity teams. These alerts provide actionable information for immediate response, minimizing the potential impact of threats.

8. Hunting for Advanced Threats:

AI is particularly adept at detecting advanced threats, such as zero-day vulnerabilities or advanced persistent threats (APTs). These threats often exhibit subtle behaviours that evade traditional detection methods.

9. Enhancing Human Expertise:

AI doesn't replace human expertise but augments it. Security analysts collaborate with AI systems, leveraging AI's insights and recommendations to make informed decisions.

10. Continuous Learning and Adaptation:

AI continually learns from new threat intelligence, evolving its understanding of emerging threats. This adaptability ensures that threat hunting capabilities remain effective over time.

Conclusion:

AI's role in enabling real-time threat hunting is revolutionizing cybersecurity practices. By leveraging AI's real-time analysis, pattern recognition, and contextual understanding, organizations can proactively identify active threats in their infancy. This approach empowers cybersecurity teams to mitigate threats before they escalate, ultimately enhancing an organization's ability to maintain a strong defence against evolving cyber threats.

3.2.3 Identifying Zero-Day Attacks:
AI's Role in Identifying Previously Unknown Threats

In the ever-evolving landscape of cybersecurity, organizations face an escalating volume of threats, many of which are previously unknown and unseen. Artificial Intelligence (AI) emerges as a crucial tool in identifying these novel threats by leveraging its advanced analytics and pattern recognition capabilities. This section explores how AI plays a key role in uncovering threats that elude traditional security measures.

1. Adapting to the Unknown:

Traditional security systems often struggle to detect threats they haven't encountered before. AI excels at adapting to the unknown by learning from data and recognizing patterns that might signify novel threats.

2. Pattern Recognition:

AI leverages its powerful pattern recognition abilities to analyse data and detect anomalous behaviours that could indicate previously unseen threats. These behaviours might include unusual data transfers, unauthorized access attempts, or suspicious application interactions.

3. Learning from Data:

Machine learning algorithms, particularly those utilizing unsupervised learning, excel at learning from data without prior labels or definitions of threats. This enables them to recognize new threat patterns that haven't been explicitly identified.

4. Identifying Emerging Threats:

AI is adept at identifying emerging threats, including zero-day vulnerabilities and advanced persistent threats (APTs). These threats often exploit new attack vectors and exhibit behaviour that hasn't been previously observed.

5. Behavioural Analysis:

AI-driven systems analyse the behaviour of users, devices, and applications to identify deviations from normal activities. This behaviour-based analysis is crucial for detecting threats that might not have recognizable signatures.

6. Contextual Understanding:

AI adds context to its analysis, considering factors such as user roles, device types, and network segments. This contextual understanding helps discern between innovative attack techniques and legitimate activities.

7. Threat Hunting Beyond Known Indicators:

AI-driven threat hunting doesn't solely rely on known indicators of compromise (IoCs). Instead, it explores relationships between data points and identifies patterns that might not match established IoCs.

8. Rapid Response to New Threats:

AI's real-time analysis allows organizations to respond rapidly to new threats. As soon as AI identifies suspicious behaviour, it triggers alerts that prompt immediate investigation and mitigation.

9. Collaboration with Human Analysts:

AI doesn't replace human analysts but collaborates with them. Human expertise adds context and nuance to AI's findings, facilitating more accurate threat assessment.

10. Continuous Adaptation:

AI systems are continuously learning from new data, which means their ability to identify unknown threats improves over time. This adaptability ensures organizations are better equipped to handle evolving threat landscapes.

Conclusion:

AI's capacity to identify previously unknown threats transforms the cybersecurity landscape. By leveraging pattern recognition, machine learning, and behavioural analysis, AI enhances an organization's ability to detect emerging threats that traditional methods might overlook. This proactive approach empowers organizations to stay one step ahead in the ongoing battle against ever-evolving cyber threats.

Reference: Real-Time Threat Detection with AI[103]

---

[103] https://www.csoonline.com/article/3324718/using-ai-to-spot-thermal-runaway-in-lithium-ion-batteries.html

3.3 Incorporating AI-Driven Incident Response Strategies

3.3.1 AI-Powered Incident Triage:

How AI assists in prioritizing and categorizing incidents for effective response.

In the domain of cybersecurity, the sheer volume of incidents can overwhelm security teams, making it challenging to allocate resources effectively. Artificial Intelligence (AI) emerges as a crucial ally in this scenario, aiding organizations in prioritizing and categorizing incidents for a more targeted and efficient response. This section explores how AI enhances incident response by leveraging data analysis and contextual understanding.

1. Data Overload and Incident Prioritization:

The increasing number of incidents, alerts, and alarms can lead to information overload for security teams. AI assists by sifting through this deluge of data and pinpointing incidents that require immediate attention.

2. Contextual Understanding:

AI doesn't just evaluate incidents in isolation; it adds context by considering factors such as the criticality of affected assets, potential impact, and the attacker's techniques.

3. Machine Learning for Classification:

Machine learning algorithms, particularly those in supervised learning, can be trained to categorize incidents based on historical data and known patterns. This classification aids in determining the severity and type of incident.

4. Behavioural Analysis:

AI examines the behaviour of incidents, users, and entities involved. This behavioural analysis helps identify incidents with abnormal patterns, which might indicate more sophisticated attacks.

5. Prioritization Based on Risk:

AI's analysis considers risk factors associated with incidents. Incidents with the potential to cause significant damage or compromise sensitive data are elevated in priority.

6. Real-Time Incident Assessment:

AI assesses incidents in real time, ensuring that emerging threats are promptly identified and prioritized. This real-time analysis minimizes response times.

7. Correlation of Indicators:

AI correlates various indicators of compromise (IoCs) and event data to identify patterns that might be indicative of larger-scale attacks. This correlation helps assign appropriate priority levels.

8. Integration with Threat Intelligence:

AI can integrate with threat intelligence feeds, enhancing its incident assessment by incorporating external context about known threats and attackers.

9. Response Time Optimization:

By categorizing and prioritizing incidents, AI enables security teams to allocate resources efficiently, ensuring that the most critical incidents receive immediate attention.

10. Human-AI Collaboration:
AI doesn't replace human judgment but collaborates with analysts. Security professionals add contextual insights and domain expertise to AI's findings, creating a well-rounded incident assessment.

Conclusion:
AI's role in prioritizing and categorizing incidents transforms incident response by streamlining resource allocation and ensuring that critical threats are addressed promptly. By leveraging contextual understanding, behavioural analysis, and machine learning, AI empowers organizations to efficiently manage incidents, enhance response times, and ultimately strengthen their overall cybersecurity posture.

3.3.2 Contextual Understanding:
How AI provides contextual information to responders for informed decision-making.

In the fast-paced world of cybersecurity, responders are often confronted with a deluge of alerts and incidents, each demanding swift and informed action. Artificial Intelligence (AI) emerges as a powerful aid in this scenario, offering contextual information that equips responders with the insights needed to make well-informed decisions. This section explores how AI enhances decision-making by providing crucial context to responders.

1. Amplifying Incident Insights:
AI doesn't just present raw data; it enriches incident information with contextual details that give responders a clearer picture of what's unfolding.

2. Understanding Incident Scope:
AI offers insights into the scope of an incident by analysing affected assets, user behaviours, and potential attack vectors. This understanding guides responders in assessing the incident's severity.

3. Correlating Data Points:
AI correlates data from various sources to identify relationships that might not be immediately apparent. This correlation uncovers potential attack patterns or tactics.

4. Threat Landscape Insights:
AI contextualizes incidents within the broader threat landscape by analysing current trends, tactics, and known attacker profiles. This knowledge helps responders tailor their approach.

5. Behaviour Analysis:
AI's analysis of user and device behaviours adds context to incidents. For instance, understanding that an employee's behaviour is anomalous can help differentiate between an insider threat and a benign incident.

6. Asset Criticality Consideration:
By assessing the criticality of affected assets, AI aids responders in prioritizing incidents based on potential impact. This prevents resource allocation for less critical incidents.

7. Real-Time Incident Updates:
AI provides real-time updates as new information becomes available. This dynamic information flow ensures that responders are armed with the most recent insights.

8. Predictive Insights:

AI's predictive capabilities offer responders insights into potential attack paths, enabling them to proactively mitigate threats before they escalate.

9. Enhanced Human Analysis:

While AI offers contextual information, it's complemented by human analysis. Responders can delve deeper into AI-provided insights to gain a comprehensive understanding of the incident.

10. Continuous Learning:

AI's learning capabilities mean that it continually improves its contextual understanding based on new data and incidents. This ensures that the context provided remains relevant and accurate.

Conclusion:

AI's provision of contextual information empowers responders with a deeper understanding of incidents, enabling them to make informed decisions amidst the complexity of the cybersecurity landscape. By offering insights into incident scope, threat trends, and behavioural patterns, AI enhances decision-making, expedites response times, and ultimately contributes to a more effective defence against evolving cyber threats.

3.3.3 Containment and Remediation:

AI's Role in Containing Threats and Guiding Remediation Actions

In the dynamic domain of cybersecurity, the ability to rapidly contain threats and initiate effective remediation actions is paramount. Artificial Intelligence (AI) emerges as a pivotal force in this scenario, offering its capabilities to assist in containing threats and providing actionable guidance for remediation. This section explores how AI empowers organizations to respond promptly and decisively to security incidents.

1. Real-Time Threat Containment:

AI's real-time analysis enables organizations to rapidly identify and contain threats as they unfold, minimizing their potential impact.

2. Behavioural Analysis:

AI examines the behaviour of threats, analysing their activities, lateral movement, and potential attack vectors. This analysis helps responders understand the scope and behaviour of threats.

3. Predictive Analysis:

AI employs predictive capabilities to anticipate the potential paths threats might take, aiding responders in taking proactive containment measures.

4. Automated Response Actions:

AI can trigger automated responses based on predefined rules and policies. For example, if a threat is detected attempting unauthorized access, AI can automatically block the attacker's access.

5. Rapid Incident Prioritization:

AI assists responders by prioritizing incidents based on factors such as threat severity, affected assets, and potential business impact. This prioritization streamlines resource allocation.

6. Guiding Remediation Steps:

AI provides actionable guidance on the steps required to remediate a threat. This guidance assists responders in containing and neutralizing threats effectively.

7. Contextual Insights:

AI offers contextual insights into the nature of threats, including their attack methods, vulnerabilities exploited, and potential ramifications. This knowledge informs appropriate response strategies.

8. Collaboration with Human Expertise:

While AI automates certain response actions, human expertise is invaluable. AI's insights are complemented by human judgment and nuanced understanding.

9. Dynamic Incident Updates:

AI continually updates responders with real-time information as threats evolve or new information surfaces. This dynamic information flow is essential for accurate decision-making.

10. Continuous Learning and Improvement:

AI systems learn from their interactions with threats and responses. This continuous learning enhances AI's ability to recommend effective containment and remediation strategies.

Conclusion:

AI's assistance in containing threats and guiding remediation actions revolutionizes incident response in cybersecurity. By leveraging real-time analysis, predictive insights, and automated responses, AI empowers organizations to rapidly and effectively neutralize threats. The collaboration between AI and human expertise ensures that responses are well-informed and aligned with an organization's specific needs, enhancing overall cybersecurity resilience.

Reference: AI-Powered Incident Response[104]

3.3.4 Case Study: IBM QRadar Advisor with Watson:

Exploring How IBM QRadar Advisor with Watson Enhances Incident Response with AI

In the fast-paced landscape of cybersecurity, the convergence of Artificial Intelligence (AI) and advanced analytics has revolutionized incident response. IBM QRadar Advisor with Watson stands as a prime example of how AI can significantly enhance incident response capabilities. This section explores the unique features and benefits of IBM QRadar Advisor with Watson in fortifying organizations against cyber threats.

1. Real-Time Data Analysis:

IBM QRadar Advisor with Watson leverages AI to analyse vast amounts of data in real time. This real-time analysis enables the platform to rapidly detect and respond to threats as they unfold.

2. Threat Hunting Enhancement:

AI empowers the platform to proactively hunt for threats beyond known indicators. It identifies patterns, behaviours, and anomalies that might signify emerging threats, including those that lack established signatures.

3. Behavioural Analysis:

The platform employs AI-driven behavioural analysis to understand normal network behaviour. When deviations occur, it can rapidly identify potential threats that might otherwise go unnoticed.

---

[104] https://www.csoonline.com/article/3234659/ai-powered-incident-response-introduction-and-considerations.html

4. Contextual Understanding:

AI enriches incident data with context by considering factors such as asset criticality, user behaviours, and historical threat intelligence. This contextual understanding enhances the accuracy of threat assessment.

5. Predictive Insights:

IBM QRadar Advisor with Watson's AI capabilities offer predictive insights, helping organizations anticipate potential threat paths and enabling proactive response measures.

6. Automated Response Recommendations:

The platform suggests automated response actions based on AI analysis. Responders can then review and execute these recommendations, streamlining incident containment.

7. Collaboration with Watson Knowledge Base:

The integration with Watson's extensive knowledge base enhances the platform's insights. It provides responders with a wealth of contextual information to inform decision-making.

8. Human-AI Partnership:

AI augments, not replaces, human expertise. The combination of AI's analytical prowess and human judgment ensures well-rounded and effective incident response.

9. Continuous Learning:

AI continually learns from new data and incidents, refining its understanding of emerging threats and evolving tactics.

10. Enhanced Incident Prioritization:

By categorizing and prioritizing incidents based on AI analysis, organizations can allocate resources more effectively and address the most critical threats first.

Conclusion:

IBM QRadar Advisor with Watson showcases the potential of AI in revolutionizing incident response. By harnessing real-time data analysis, behavioural insights, and predictive capabilities, the platform empowers organizations to proactively detect, respond to, and contain threats. This fusion of AI-driven insights and human expertise exemplifies the future of incident response, where timely and informed actions are essential to safeguarding digital assets and maintaining cybersecurity resilience.

Reference: IBM QRadar Advisor with Watson[105]

---

[105] https://www.ibm.com/cloud/learn/ibm-qradar-advisor

Chapter 4: AI-Enabled Vulnerability Management

4.1 Automating Vulnerability Assessments Using AI

4.1.1 Vulnerability Management Overview:

Introduction to Vulnerability Management: Identifying, Evaluating, and Mitigating System Vulnerabilities

In today's interconnected digital landscape, organizations face an ever-present and evolving threat landscape. Cybercriminals continuously seek to exploit vulnerabilities in systems, applications, and networks to breach security defences. To counter these threats, a systematic approach called "vulnerability management" has emerged as a critical practice. This introduction provides an overview of vulnerability management, outlining its purpose, process, and significance in maintaining robust cybersecurity.

Defining Vulnerability Management:
Vulnerability management is a proactive cybersecurity practice designed to identify, assess, prioritize, and remediate vulnerabilities present within an organization's IT environment. It encompasses a series of systematic steps aimed at minimizing an organization's attack surface by addressing weaknesses that malicious actors could exploit.

Key Components of Vulnerability Management:
- **Identification:**
  The process begins with the identification of vulnerabilities. These can range from software bugs and misconfigurations to outdated applications with known security flaws.
- **Evaluation:**
  Identified vulnerabilities are evaluated to understand their potential impact and exploitability. This step involves assessing the severity of vulnerabilities and determining their risk to the organization.
- **Prioritization:**
  Not all vulnerabilities are created equal. Effective vulnerability management involves prioritizing vulnerabilities based on their criticality, potential impact, and likelihood of exploitation.
- **Mitigation:**
  Remediation actions are taken to address identified vulnerabilities. This may involve applying patches, reconfiguring systems, updating software, or implementing security controls.
- **Verification:**
  After mitigation efforts, organizations verify whether the vulnerabilities have been successfully remediated. This step ensures that the risk associated with the vulnerability is effectively mitigated.
- **Continuous Monitoring:**

Vulnerability management is an ongoing process. As new vulnerabilities are discovered and systems change, continuous monitoring is essential to maintain an organization's security posture.

The benefits of Vulnerability Management:

- **Risk Reduction:**
  Vulnerability management is a proactive measure to minimize the risk of cyberattacks. By identifying and remediating vulnerabilities, organizations can reduce the likelihood of successful breaches.
- **Regulatory Compliance:**
  Many industries are subject to regulatory requirements that mandate vulnerability assessment and remediation. Vulnerability management helps organizations stay compliant with these regulations.
- **Timely Response:**
  Rapid identification and remediation of vulnerabilities prevent attackers from exploiting weaknesses before they are addressed.
- **Protection of Assets:**
  Effective vulnerability management safeguards an organization's digital assets, including sensitive data, intellectual property, and customer information.
- **Cost Savings:**
  Addressing vulnerabilities before they are exploited is more cost-effective than dealing with the aftermath of a breach.
- **Reputation Protection:**
  Successful cyberattacks can damage an organization's reputation. Vulnerability management contributes to maintaining customer trust and brand integrity.

Conclusion:

Vulnerability management is a crucial pillar of a comprehensive cybersecurity strategy. By systematically identifying, evaluating, and mitigating vulnerabilities, organizations can bolster their defences, reduce risk, and ensure the integrity of their digital infrastructure. In an ever-evolving threat landscape, effective vulnerability management is an essential practice for maintaining cyber resilience and safeguarding critical assets.

4.1.2 AI-Driven Vulnerability Scanning:

Automating Vulnerability Scanning with AI: Enhancing Cybersecurity Efficiency

As organizations grapple with the evolving threat landscape and the need to secure their digital assets, automation has emerged as a powerful ally in bolstering cybersecurity practices. One area where automation, specifically driven by Artificial Intelligence (AI), has made significant strides is vulnerability scanning. This section explores how AI-driven automation transforms the process of scanning systems for vulnerabilities, improving efficiency and accuracy.

Defining AI-Driven Vulnerability Scanning:

AI-driven vulnerability scanning involves the use of advanced algorithms and machine learning techniques to automate the identification and assessment of vulnerabilities present within an organization's IT infrastructure. This process streamlines the traditional manual approach, enabling rapid and comprehensive analysis of system weaknesses.

Key Aspects of AI-Driven Vulnerability Scanning:

- **Continuous Monitoring:**
  AI-powered tools can continuously scan systems, applications, and networks for vulnerabilities. This continuous monitoring ensures that new vulnerabilities are promptly identified and addressed.

- **Pattern Recognition:**
  AI algorithms excel in recognizing patterns, behaviours, and anomalies. They analyse vast datasets to identify vulnerabilities based on known patterns of exploitation.

- **Prioritization:**
  AI assesses the severity of vulnerabilities by considering factors such as exploitability, potential impact, and affected assets. This aids in prioritizing which vulnerabilities should be addressed first.

- **Real-Time Analysis:**
  AI-driven vulnerability scanners perform real-time analysis, allowing organizations to respond rapidly to emerging threats.

- **Scale and Speed:**
  Automation powered by AI enables scanning at a scale and speed that manual methods cannot achieve. This is especially valuable for organizations with extensive and dynamic IT environments.

- **False Positive Reduction:**
  AI helps in reducing false positives by cross-referencing vulnerability data with contextual information about the organization's systems and configurations.

- **Behavioural Analysis:**
  AI examines system behaviour to detect anomalies that might indicate potential vulnerabilities, including those not identified by signature-based approaches.

Advantages of AI-Driven Vulnerability Scanning:

- **Efficiency:**

AI automates the labour-intensive task of vulnerability scanning, freeing up security teams to focus on higher-level tasks.

- **Accuracy:**

AI algorithms can rapidly analyse vast amounts of data with high accuracy, reducing the chances of overlooking critical vulnerabilities.

- **Rapid Detection:**

AI's real-time analysis ensures prompt detection of vulnerabilities, reducing the window of opportunity for attackers.

- **Resource Optimization:**

AI prioritizes vulnerabilities, allowing organizations to allocate resources efficiently to address the most critical risks.

- **Adaptability:**

AI systems learn from new data and adapt to emerging threat trends, enhancing their detection capabilities over time.

AI-driven automation has revolutionized vulnerability scanning by infusing it with speed, accuracy, and adaptability. The marriage of AI's pattern recognition and machine learning with vulnerability assessment enhances an organization's ability to identify weaknesses rapidly and efficiently. As cybersecurity threats continue to evolve, the automation provided by AI-driven vulnerability scanning becomes an indispensable tool for organizations seeking to fortify their defences and maintain a robust cyber posture.

4.1.3 Continuous Monitoring:

Continuous Real-Time Vulnerability Monitoring with AI: Strengthening Cybersecurity Vigilance

In the dynamic domain of cybersecurity, the adage "constant vigilance" holds true. Organizations must remain ever-watchful for potential vulnerabilities in their IT landscape to pre-empt cyber threats. In this pursuit, Artificial Intelligence (AI) emerges as a powerful enabler of continuous real-time vulnerability monitoring. This section explores how AI empowers organizations to maintain an unceasing watch over their systems, detecting vulnerabilities as they emerge.

Understanding Continuous Real-Time Vulnerability Monitoring:

Continuous real-time vulnerability monitoring involves the use of AI-driven tools and technologies to maintain an ongoing assessment of an organization's digital infrastructure. It is a proactive approach to promptly identify, analyse, and mitigate vulnerabilities before they can be exploited by malicious actors.

Key Aspects of AI-Enabled Continuous Monitoring:

Uninterrupted Surveillance:

AI-driven solutions provide round-the-clock surveillance, ensuring that vulnerabilities are detected as soon as they emerge, regardless of time zones or working hours.

Automated Scanning:

AI automates the scanning process, eliminating the need for manual intervention in initiating vulnerability assessments.

Real-Time Detection:

AI algorithms perform real-time analysis of system behaviour and data, enabling swift detection of anomalies and potential vulnerabilities.

Immediate Alerts:

When a vulnerability is identified, AI systems trigger immediate alerts to security personnel, enabling rapid response.

Scalability:

AI's ability to process vast amounts of data makes it suitable for organizations with large and complex IT environments that require continuous monitoring.

Behavioural Analysis:

AI examines system behaviours, detecting deviations that might signify vulnerabilities or unauthorized activities.

Advantages of AI-Enabled Continuous Monitoring:
Swift Detection:

Real-time monitoring ensures vulnerabilities are identified immediately, reducing the window of opportunity for attackers.

Timely Response:

Immediate alerts empower security teams to respond promptly, mitigating vulnerabilities before they can be exploited.

Reduced Downtime:

Detecting vulnerabilities early minimizes the need for extensive downtime during patching and remediation.

Adaptability:

AI systems continuously learn from new data, adapting to evolving threat landscapes and emerging attack vectors.

Enhanced Visibility:

Continuous monitoring provides an ongoing snapshot of an organization's security posture, helping identify trends and patterns.

Conclusion:
Continuous real-time vulnerability monitoring powered by AI reshapes the cybersecurity landscape by ensuring that organizations maintain an unwavering watch over their digital assets. Through automated scanning, behavioural analysis, and immediate alerts, AI-driven solutions empower security teams to detect and respond to vulnerabilities as they emerge. In the face of ever-evolving cyber threats, the capability to monitor vulnerabilities in real-time is a crucial tool for maintaining cyber resilience and safeguarding critical assets.

Reference: AI in Vulnerability Management[106]

4.2 Predictive Analytics for Identifying Potential Vulnerabilities

4.2.1 Predictive Vulnerability Analysis:

Introduction to AI-Driven Predictive Analytics for Proactive Vulnerability Identification

In the domain of cybersecurity, the ability to foresee potential threats before they materialize as exploitations is a game-changer. This is precisely where Artificial Intelligence (AI) steps in with its predictive analytics capabilities. This introduction sheds light on how organizations are leveraging AI-driven predictive analytics to identify vulnerabilities before they are exploited, ushering in a new era of proactive cybersecurity.

The Power of Predictive Analytics:
Predictive analytics, a subset of AI, uses historical and real-time data to identify patterns, trends, and potential outcomes. In the context of cybersecurity, it empowers organizations to anticipate vulnerabilities before they become actualized threats.

---

[106] https://www.csoonline.com/article/3586651/vulnerability-management-in-the-ai-era.html

Proactive Vulnerability Identification:

Traditionally, vulnerability identification has been a reactive process, triggered by the discovery of an exploited vulnerability. However, AI-driven predictive analytics shifts this paradigm by enabling the identification of vulnerabilities before they are targeted by malicious actors.

Key Aspects of AI-Driven Predictive Analytics for Vulnerability Identification:

Data Analysis:

Predictive analytics relies on analysing vast amounts of historical and real-time data, including system behaviours, network traffic, and user activities.

Pattern Recognition:

AI algorithms identify patterns and anomalies within data, allowing them to predict potential vulnerabilities based on historical indicators.

Behavioural Insights:

Predictive analytics takes into account normal system behaviour, and deviations from this baseline can indicate potential vulnerabilities.

Risk Assessment:

AI assesses the potential risk associated with identified vulnerabilities, aiding in prioritizing remediation efforts.

Early Warning:

By identifying vulnerabilities in their early stages, organizations can take proactive measures to prevent potential breaches.

Advantages of AI-Driven Predictive Analytics for Vulnerability Identification:

Proactivity:

Organizations can address vulnerabilities before they are exploited, minimizing the window of opportunity for attackers.

Resource Optimization:

Prioritizing vulnerabilities based on predictive analytics allows organizations to allocate resources efficiently.

Time Savings:

Predictive analytics eliminates the need for manual investigation, saving valuable time during vulnerability management.

Reduced Impact:

By addressing vulnerabilities in their infancy, organizations can prevent potential data breaches and their associated consequences.

Conclusion:

AI-driven predictive analytics marks a transformative shift in cybersecurity practices, enabling organizations to foresee vulnerabilities before they are exploited. Through pattern recognition, behavioural insights, and risk assessment, predictive analytics empowers organizations to take proactive measures to safeguard their digital assets. In a landscape where rapid threats demand rapid responses, the ability to predict vulnerabilities is an invaluable tool for maintaining cybersecurity resilience and staying ahead of cyber adversaries.

4.2.2 Utilizing Historical Data:

How AI leverages historical vulnerability data to predict future threats?

Staying one step ahead of potential threats is paramount. Artificial Intelligence (AI) has emerged as a crucial ally in this endeavour by leveraging historical vulnerability data to predict and prevent future threats. This section explores how AI's ability to analyse past vulnerabilities leads to proactive threat mitigation.

Unveiling the Potential of AI-Powered Predictions:

AI's predictive capabilities are revolutionizing the way organizations approach cybersecurity. By analysing historical vulnerability data, AI can unveil patterns and trends that offer insights into the vulnerabilities of the future.

Predictive Analysis Based on Historical Vulnerability Data:

Data Accumulation:

AI aggregates and analyses a wealth of historical vulnerability data, including past breaches, exploitation patterns, and threat actors' tactics.

Pattern Identification:

Through machine learning algorithms, AI identifies recurring patterns, behaviours, and factors that have contributed to past vulnerabilities and breaches.

Risk Forecasting:

By examining the relationship between historical vulnerabilities and successful cyberattacks, AI can forecast the likelihood and potential impact of future threats.

Trend Extrapolation:

AI extends its analysis to identify emerging trends, threat vectors, and attack techniques that may evolve into vulnerabilities in the future.

Advantages of AI-Driven Predictive Analysis Using Historical Data:

Proactive Defence:

AI empowers organizations to anticipate vulnerabilities, allowing them to take pre-emptive measures before threats materialize.

Informed Decision-Making:

Predictive insights enable informed allocation of resources for vulnerability management and mitigation.

Resource Optimization:

Focusing efforts on predicted vulnerabilities optimizes resource allocation and enhances cybersecurity efficiency.

Rapid Response:

Early detection of potential vulnerabilities enables organizations to respond quickly and decisively to emerging threats.

Conclusion:
AI's ability to leverage historical vulnerability data for predictive analysis is a game-changing approach to cybersecurity. By identifying patterns, trends, and potential future threats, organizations can take proactive steps to prevent breaches and protect their digital assets. In the race against cyber adversaries, AI-driven predictions provide a vital edge, enabling organizations to stay ahead of the curve and safeguard their cyber landscape with unparalleled resilience.

4.2.3 Prioritizing Remediation:

Strategic Focus: Prioritizing Vulnerability Remediation with Predictive Analytics

Organizations are increasingly turning to Artificial Intelligence (AI) and predictive analytics to enhance their vulnerability management strategies. A key aspect of this approach is the ability to prioritize vulnerability remediation efforts effectively. This discussion explores how predictive analytics serves as a strategic compass, guiding organizations to allocate resources where they matter most.

A New Dimension to Prioritization:
Traditionally, prioritizing vulnerabilities for remediation has been a challenge. With the sheer volume of vulnerabilities and limited resources, organizations need a data-driven approach to ensure effective risk reduction. This is precisely where predictive analytics plays a transformative role.

Applying Predictive Analytics to Prioritization:
Data Analysis:

Predictive analytics leverages historical vulnerability data, threat intelligence feeds, and contextual information to analyse and evaluate the potential impact of vulnerabilities.

Risk Assessment:

AI-powered algorithms assess vulnerabilities based on factors such as exploitability, asset value, and historical attack patterns.

Probability Calculation:

Predictive analytics calculates the likelihood of a vulnerability being exploited, enabling a more accurate assessment of its risk.

Impact Estimation:

By considering potential business impact and the ease of exploitation, predictive analytics helps paint a comprehensive picture of the risks associated with each vulnerability.

Ranking and Scoring:

Predictive analytics assigns scores or ranks to vulnerabilities, aiding in creating a prioritized list for remediation efforts.

Advantages of Predictive Analytics in Vulnerability Prioritization:

Effective Resource Allocation:

Organizations can focus their limited resources on addressing the vulnerabilities that pose the highest risk, optimizing their defence efforts.

Strategic Decision-Making:

Predictive insights guide cybersecurity teams in making informed decisions about which vulnerabilities to address first.

Rapid Risk Reduction:

Prioritizing vulnerabilities based on predictive analytics reduces the time it takes to mitigate critical risks, enhancing overall cybersecurity.

Business Alignment:

Predictive analytics aligns vulnerability management with business goals and objectives, safeguarding critical assets and data.

Conclusion:

Predictive analytics breathes new life into the art of prioritizing vulnerability remediation. By merging historical vulnerability data with advanced algorithms, organizations can strategically allocate resources where they will have the most significant impact. In the intricate dance between attackers and defenders, predictive analytics empowers organizations to step confidently onto the cybersecurity stage, armed with data-backed strategies that fortify their digital defences and minimize risk exposure.

Reference: Predictive Vulnerability Management[107]

4.3 Balancing AI-Driven Vulnerability Management with Human Expertise

4.3.1 Human Validation and Context:

Human Expertise: A Crucial Validation Partner for AI-Generated Vulnerability Reports
The relationship between Artificial Intelligence (AI) and human expertise is pivotal. There's no doubt about the indispensable role human professionals play in validating AI-generated vulnerability reports, thus the need for balance between automation and human discernment.

The Dual Role of AI and Humans:
AI's prowess in rapidly analysing data and generating vulnerability reports is undeniable. However, the complexities of cybersecurity demand a human touch to validate and contextualize these reports.

Importance of Human Validation for AI-Generated Reports:
Contextual Understanding:
Human experts possess an intrinsic understanding of an organization's unique systems, processes, and business goals, enabling them to validate reports with context.

False Positives and Negatives:

---

[107] https://www.helpnetsecurity.com/2022/03/03/predictive-vulnerability-management/

While AI can reduce false positives, human expertise is vital in identifying false negatives that AI might overlook.

Triage and Prioritization:
Human validation adds an extra layer of insight, helping prioritize vulnerabilities based on business impact and organizational goals.

Zero-Day Vulnerabilities:
Novel threats and zero-day vulnerabilities often require human analysis to identify, assess, and respond effectively.

Adversarial Tactics:
Human analysts can spot sophisticated tactics employed by threat actors that might elude AI algorithms.

Human-AI Symbiosis:
Data Enhancement:

Human experts contribute to training AI models by identifying nuanced patterns and behaviours.

Decision Augmentation:

Human expertise augments AI-generated insights, leading to more informed decisions.

Contextual Intelligence:

Humans provide the crucial contextual intelligence that AI lacks, enhancing the accuracy of vulnerability assessments.

Ethical Considerations:

Human analysts ensure AI-generated reports adhere to ethical standards and norms.

Advantages of Human Validation:
Accuracy:

Human validation reduces the risk of false positives and negatives, enhancing the reliability of vulnerability reports.

Contextualization:

Human experts bring the vital context required to assess the real-world impact of vulnerabilities.

Adaptability:

Human analysts can adapt to new and emerging threat landscapes that AI might not recognize initially.

Holistic Perspective:

Combining AI's speed with human validation ensures a holistic and accurate view of vulnerabilities.

Conclusion:
While AI is a formidable ally in vulnerability assessment, the human touch remains irreplaceable. Human experts validate, contextualize, and enhance AI-generated reports, contributing invaluable

insights that lead to more informed and effective cybersecurity decisions. The synergy between AI and human expertise is the foundation of a robust cybersecurity strategy that leverages both automation and human insight to defend against evolving threats.

4.3.2 False Positives and Negatives:

We start in this section by introducing the notions of false positives and false negatives, after that wed will emphasize the role and benefits of balancing AI with Human Expertise to remediate to some well-known challenges.

1. False Positives:

1.1. Overwhelm of Alerts:

AI algorithms, when not properly tuned, can generate a high volume of alerts or notifications. False positives occur when the system incorrectly identifies a benign activity as a potential vulnerability or threat. This flood of alerts can overwhelm security teams, causing them to miss or overlook genuine threats in the noise.

1.2. Alert Fatigue:

Security analysts may become fatigued and desensitized due to the constant influx of false positive alerts. This can lead to complacency and reduced responsiveness when genuine vulnerabilities or threats are detected, putting the organization at risk.

1.3. Resource Drain:

Investigating false positives demands time and resources that could be better utilized elsewhere. Security teams may waste valuable hours chasing down non-existent threats, affecting overall operational efficiency.

2. False Negatives:

2.1. Missed Threats:

False negatives occur when AI fails to detect actual vulnerabilities or threats. This can happen for several reasons, including outdated threat intelligence, zero-day vulnerabilities, or sophisticated attack techniques that AI models haven't encountered before.

2.2. Complacency:

Relying solely on AI-driven vulnerability assessments may lead to complacency within security teams. If they trust the system too much and assume it's catching all threats, they might not remain vigilant or take proactive measures against emerging risks.

2.3. High-Risk Vulnerabilities:

False negatives can result in critical vulnerabilities going unnoticed, leaving the organization exposed to high-risk threats. These undetected vulnerabilities can be exploited by attackers, potentially leading to data breaches or system compromises.

Balancing AI with Human Expertise:

To address these challenges effectively, organizations need to strike a balance between AI-driven vulnerability assessments and human expertise:

1. Continuous Training:

AI models must be regularly updated and fine-tuned with current threat intelligence to reduce false negatives and false positives.

2. Human Oversight:

Security teams should provide oversight to AI-driven systems, verifying the accuracy of alerts and taking corrective action when necessary.

3. Contextual Analysis:

Humans can provide the contextual analysis needed to distinguish false positives from true threats, ensuring that critical vulnerabilities are addressed promptly.

4. Threat Intelligence:

Incorporating human expertise in threat intelligence gathering and analysis can help identify emerging threats that AI models might miss.

5. Automation with Caution:

While AI can automate many aspects of vulnerability management, organizations should exercise caution and avoid complete reliance on AI, ensuring that human analysts remain an integral part of the security process.

False positives and false negatives are inherent challenges in AI-driven vulnerability assessments. Achieving an effective balance between AI and human expertise is essential to harness the advantages of AI while mitigating the risks associated with these challenges. A collaborative approach that combines the strengths of AI and human analysis is key to successful vulnerability management.

4.4 Case Study: Qualys VMDR - AI-Driven Vulnerability Management:

4.4.1 Exploring how Qualys VMDR utilizes AI to provide an end-to-end vulnerability management solution.

In the quest for comprehensive vulnerability management, organizations are turning to Artificial Intelligence (AI) to bolster their defences. Qualys Vulnerability Management, Detection, and Response (VMDR) stands as a prime example of how AI-driven innovation transforms vulnerability management into a seamless end-to-end solution. This section dives into the AI-powered intricacies of Qualys VMDR and its role in safeguarding digital landscapes.

The All-Encompassing Approach of Qualys VMDR:

Qualys VMDR is more than just a vulnerability scanner; it's an integrated ecosystem that unites AI, automation, and human expertise to offer a holistic vulnerability management solution.

4.4.2 Leveraging AI for Comprehensive Vulnerability Management:

Automated Asset Discovery:
AI-driven algorithms meticulously identify and track assets, ensuring no device goes unnoticed in an organization's network.

Real-time Vulnerability Assessment:
AI continuously scans for vulnerabilities, delivering real-time insights to security teams for prompt mitigation.

Prioritization and Risk Assessment:

AI analyses vulnerabilities based on factors like exploitability, impact, and asset criticality, guiding organizations in prioritizing remediation efforts.

Patch Management:

AI-driven patch intelligence assists in identifying applicable patches and updates, streamlining the remediation process.

Threat Correlation:

AI connects vulnerability data with threat intelligence, providing context to vulnerability assessment and potential exploit risks.

4.4.3 The Human-AI Partnership:

Human Contextualization:

Human expertise contextualizes vulnerability reports, ensuring alignment with business objectives and risk tolerance.

Decision Augmentation:

AI-generated insights are enhanced by human validation, leading to informed and strategic decision-making.

4.4.4 Advantages of Qualys VMDR's AI-Driven Approach:

End-to-End Solution:

Qualys VMDR covers the entire vulnerability management lifecycle, from discovery to remediation, powered by AI.

Real-time Insights:

AI's continuous monitoring ensures real-time awareness of vulnerabilities, minimizing exposure to potential threats.

Resource Optimization:

AI-driven prioritization enables efficient allocation of resources, focusing on vulnerabilities with the highest risk.

Holistic Security:

The fusion of AI and human expertise creates a holistic security strategy that considers both automated insights and human context.

Qualys VMDR stands as a testament to the transformative potential of AI in vulnerability management. By seamlessly integrating AI-driven automation, real-time assessment, and human validation, it offers an end-to-end solution that empowers organizations to effectively mitigate vulnerabilities. In a landscape where threats evolve at lightning speed, Qualys VMDR showcases how the harmonious interplay of AI and human expertise results in a proactive and dynamic defence mechanism, securing digital assets with unparalleled efficacy

Reference: Qualys VMDR[108]

---

[108] https://www.qualys.com/vulnerability-management/vmdr/

Chapter 5: AI and Social Engineering Attacks

5.1. Analysing AI-Driven Phishing and Social Engineering Attacks

5.1.1 Introduction to Social Engineering Attacks:

Social Engineering Attacks: Exploiting Human Psychology in Cyber Intrusions

Attackers often leverage a weapon that transcends technology – human psychology. Social engineering attacks represent a cunning manipulation of human behaviour to gain unauthorized access or sensitive information.

The Deceptive Art of Social Engineering:
Social engineering attacks involve the cunning manipulation of individuals into divulging confidential information, **performing** actions, or making decisions that they otherwise wouldn't under different circumstances.

Understanding the Psychology Behind Social Engineering:
1. **Trust Exploitation:** Attackers exploit the innate human tendency to trust, often impersonating authoritative figures, coworkers, or friends to gain credibility.
2. **Urgency and Fear:** Creating a sense of urgency or fear triggers impulsive reactions, leading individuals to overlook critical thinking and act hastily.
3. **Curiosity and Greed:** Attackers capitalize on human curiosity and greed, enticing individuals to click malicious links or disclose sensitive information in exchange for promised rewards.
4. **Reciprocity:** Attackers invoke the principle of reciprocity by offering something beneficial upfront, leading individuals to feel obliged to reciprocate.
5. **Authority Obedience:** Humans have a natural inclination to obey authority figures, making them susceptible to requests or directives from seemingly credible sources.

Common Social Engineering Techniques:

- **Phishing:** Sending deceptive emails with malicious links or attachments, often masked as legitimate communications.
- **Pretexting:** Creating fabricated scenarios to manipulate individuals into sharing information or performing actions.
- **Baiting:** Luring victims with enticing offers, such as free software downloads, to infect their systems with malware.
- **Tailgating:** Gaining physical access to secure areas by following authorized personnel or posing as them.

Implications of Social Engineering Attacks:
- **Data Breaches**: Attackers gain unauthorized access to sensitive data or systems, potentially leading to data breaches.
- **Financial Loss**: Victims may unwittingly transfer funds or provide financial information to attackers.
- **Reputation Damage**: Successful attacks tarnish an individual's or organization's reputation, eroding trust.
- **Identity Theft**: Stolen personal information can lead to identity theft and subsequent misuse.

Social engineering attacks exploit the intricate nuances of human psychology to bypass technological defences. Understanding the tactics, psychology, and potential consequences of these attacks is crucial for individuals and organizations alike. By raising awareness, fostering a culture of scepticism, and providing cybersecurity education, we can fortify ourselves against the manipulation of human vulnerabilities and ensure our collective digital well-being.

5.1.2 AI-Powered Phishing:

AI's Dark Side: Enhancing Phishing Attacks through Deceptive Precision

Artificial Intelligence (AI) has emerged as a double-edged sword in the domain of cybersecurity. While it has been harnessed to bolster defences, it has also found its way into the arsenal of cybercriminals, enhancing the effectiveness of phishing attacks to unprecedented levels. This discussion explores the synergy between AI and phishing, Highlighting how AI empowers attackers to manipulate, deceive, and exploit with alarming precision.

AI-Powered Phishing: A Disturbing Evolution:

Traditionally, phishing attacks relied on mass-scale, generic campaigns to cast a wide net. The integration of AI transforms this approach into a surgical strike, targeting victims with astonishing accuracy.

The AI Advantage in Phishing:

- **Tailored Deception:** AI allows attackers to craft hyper-personalized phishing emails by analysing vast amounts of data, making the content highly relevant and convincing.
- **Contextual Baiting:** AI scans social media profiles and online activity to tailor bait that appeals to victims' interests, hobbies, and preferences.
- **Email Mimicry:** AI-powered algorithms analyse past email conversations to replicate writing styles, making malicious emails indistinguishable from legitimate ones.
- **Timing Perfection:** AI identifies optimal times for sending phishing emails based on recipients' habits, maximizing the chances of engagement.

AI's Role in Evasion Tactics:

- **Dynamic Content Generation:** AI dynamically generates content, including malicious URLs and attachments, to evade signature-based detection systems.
- **Polymorphic Attacks:** AI alters the payload's code with each attack, evading pattern recognition and bypassing traditional defences.
- **Language and Context Adaptation:** AI ensures phishing emails resonate with regional dialects, cultural nuances, and current events, increasing their authenticity.

The Escalating Threat Landscape:

- **Spear Phishing Reinvented:** AI-fuelled spear phishing emails are virtually impossible to discern from authentic communications, making them highly effective.
- **Business Email Compromise (BEC):** AI enables attackers to impersonate high-level executives with astonishing accuracy, leading to more successful BEC attacks.
- **Credential Harvesting:** AI-powered phishing emails trick victims into sharing credentials, which are then used to compromise accounts and systems.

Mitigation and Countermeasures:

- **User Education:** Raising awareness about AI-enhanced phishing is crucial, teaching individuals to scrutinize emails, links, and attachments meticulously.
- **Advanced Threat Detection:** Employing AI-driven security solutions that detect anomalies and unusual patterns in email communications.

- **Multi-Layered defence:** Combining AI with human analysis to verify suspicious emails before taking any action.

The symbiotic relationship between AI and phishing is a chilling reminder of the ever-evolving threat landscape. As AI continues to evolve, attackers wield increasingly sophisticated tools for deception. It is imperative to recognize this unsettling reality, reinforcing cybersecurity education and investing in advanced defences to safeguard against the eerie precision that AI can bring to the dark art of phishing.

5.1.3 AI in Social Engineering Techniques:

How AI is used in pretexting, baiting, tailgating, and other social engineering tactics?

The marriage of Artificial Intelligence (AI) and social engineering tactics has given rise to a new breed of cyber threats. In this section we will discuss the convergence of AI and various social engineering techniques, and how AI amplifies the effectiveness of tactics like pretexting, baiting, tailgating, and more.

AI's Role in Social Engineering Tactics:
AI offers cybercriminals a sinister advantage by enhancing the precision, scalability, and sophistication of social engineering tactics that exploit human psychology.

Pretexting Gets Personal:
AI-Powered Profiling: AI scans social media, public records, and online data to create detailed profiles, enabling attackers to fabricate convincing pretexts.

Contextual Manipulation: AI mines vast datasets to craft pretexts that align with individuals' interests, employment details, and personal situations.

Baiting Becomes Irresistible:
Tailored Lures: AI analyses user behaviour to design irresistible baits, leveraging personalized preferences to enhance the allure of malicious content.

Content Generation: AI generates clickbait headlines, fake promotional offers, and enticing content that aligns with victims' tastes.

Tailgating with AI Precision:
Behaviour Analysis: AI identifies patterns in legitimate entries to mimic them, enabling attackers to seamlessly tailgate authorized personnel.

Facial Recognition: AI-powered cameras recognize authorized personnel, enabling attackers to emulate them convincingly.

AI-Powered Deceptive Messaging:
Language Mimicry: AI studies communication patterns to replicate writing styles, tone, and even the cadence of human conversations.

Emotion Analysis: AI detects emotional cues and adapts messages to manipulate human responses, increasing the success of the attack.

The Consequences:

1. **Data Compromise:** AI-enhanced social engineering tactics lead to data breaches, unauthorized access, and potential financial loss.
2. **Identity Theft:** Attackers exploit AI-generated personas to steal identities, fabricate pretexts, and gain trust.
3. **Reputation Damage:** Successful AI-boosted attacks erode trust, tarnishing both individual and organizational reputations.

Mitigating AI-Powered Social Engineering:

Education: Training individuals to recognize AI-fuelled manipulations and deceptive tactics is paramount.

Multi-Layered Defences: Combining AI-driven threat detection tools with human intuition strengthens the defence against AI-powered social engineering.

The nexus of AI and social engineering tactics underscores the urgent need for vigilance. Cybercriminals are armed with unprecedented precision to deceive and manipulate, exploiting human vulnerabilities at an unprecedented scale. By embracing robust cybersecurity practices, fostering a culture of scepticism, and staying informed about the evolving tactics that AI empowers, individuals and organizations can mount a stronger defence against the growing threat of AI-driven social engineering.

Reference: AI-Powered Phishing Attacks[109]

5.2. Countermeasures for Detecting and Mitigating AI-Generated Threats

5.2.1 AI-Enhanced Detection Systems:

Introduction to AI-driven tools and techniques for detecting AI-generated threats.

AI-generated attack techniques.

- AI-Enhanced Phishing Attacks:

  Natural Language Generation (NLG): Attackers can use AI-powered NLG to craft convincing phishing emails and messages that mimic human communication, making them harder to detect.

  Targeted Content Generation: AI can analyse a target's online presence and generate personalized phishing content, increasing the chances of success.

- AI-Driven Social Engineering:

  Chatbots and Deepfakes: AI-driven chatbots can engage in realistic conversations with targets, tricking them into revealing sensitive information. Deepfake technology can create convincing audio and video impersonations for social engineering attacks.

  Speech Synthesis: AI-generated audio can impersonate trusted individuals or authorities, enhancing the credibility of social engineering attempts.

- Automated Password Attacks:

---

[109] https://www.darkreading.com/threat-intelligence/ai-powered-phishing-attacks-impersonate-your-coworkers/d/d-id/1340481

Credential Stuffing: AI algorithms can automate the process of trying stolen usernames and passwords across multiple sites, exploiting users who reuse passwords.

Brute Force Attacks: AI can enhance brute force attacks by optimizing password guessing strategies based on patterns in breached data.

- AI-Enhanced Malware:

Polymorphic Malware: AI can be used to continuously modify the code of malware, creating variants that evade traditional signature-based detection.

Behavioural Malware: AI can analyse target systems and adapt malware behaviour to avoid detection by mimicking legitimate processes.

- AI-Powered Reconnaissance:

Automated Scanning: AI-driven bots can scan the internet for vulnerable targets, identifying potential entry points for attacks.

Data Mining: AI can analyse massive datasets to profile organizations and individuals, aiding attackers in crafting convincing spear-phishing attacks.

- AI-Generated Vulnerability Exploits:

Automated Exploit Generation: AI can identify vulnerabilities in target systems and generate custom exploits to compromise them.

Zero-Day Exploits: AI can accelerate the discovery and exploitation of zero-day vulnerabilities, reducing the time it takes for attackers to weaponize them.

- AI-Enhanced DDoS Attacks:

Smart Botnets: AI can control botnets more intelligently, optimizing attack traffic to bypass mitigation techniques.

Pattern Recognition: AI can adapt attack patterns in real-time to avoid detection and maximize impact.

- AI-Generated False Alarms:

Adversarial Attacks: Attackers can use AI to manipulate security systems by generating adversarial examples that trigger false alarms, distracting security teams.

Challenges and Opportunities:
- **Adversarial AI:** As AI-generated threats become more sophisticated, they might employ adversarial AI to evade detection.
- **Continuous Evolution:** AI-driven tools need to evolve to keep up with the ever-changing landscape of AI-generated threats.

Collaboration between AI and Human Expertise:
- **Augmented Analysis:** AI tools provide security analysts with enhanced insights, aiding in the identification of AI-generated threats.

- **Human Contextualization:** Human experts contextualize AI-generated threat alerts, offering nuanced judgment and decision-making.

As the digital battlefield is reshaped by AI-generated threats, the domain of cybersecurity stands at a crossroads. The same AI that empowers hackers can also equip defenders with tools to uncover these threats. The ongoing arms race between innovation and security underscores the importance of embracing AI-driven detection tools while remaining vigilant against the potential challenges they bring. The journey to secure the digital landscape demands a harmonious blend of AI's power and human wisdom.

5.2.2 Behavioural Analytics:

AI Attacks Exposed: Behavioural Analytics

In the intricate dance between artificial intelligence (AI) attacks and cybersecurity, the emergence of AI-generated threats has led to an arms race of innovation and defence. At the forefront of this battle is the deployment of behavioural analytics, a potent tool that identifies unusual user behaviour, unmasking the covert presence of AI-driven attacks. We will explore in this section the dynamic interplay between AI attacks and behavioural analytics.

Behavioural Analytics:
Behavioural analytics inspects user activities, communication patterns, and system interactions to establish a baseline of normal behaviour.

Detecting the AI Footprint:
Anomalous Patterns: AI attacks, even when sophisticated, exhibit patterns that differ from legitimate human behaviour.

Speed and Scale: AI-generated attacks often manipulate data at speeds and scales that surpass human capabilities, setting off behavioural alarms.

Identifying Unconventional Actions:
Beyond Human Norms: AI attacks tend to perform tasks in a manner that diverges from typical human actions, triggering behavioural alerts.

Complex Communication: AI-generated content may use language that strays from genuine human interactions, raising suspicion.

Adaptive and Contextual Analysis:
Learning from Users: Behavioural analytics platforms adapt and learn from user interactions, becoming more adept at spotting AI-driven anomalies.

Contextual Insights: Behavioural analytics considers the context of actions, differentiating legitimate AI usage from malicious intent.

The Role of Machine Learning:
Training on AI Patterns: Machine learning algorithms are trained on AI-generated threat patterns, enabling them to detect such activities.

Real-Time Alerts: Machine learning models instantly flag deviations from expected behaviour, signalling potential AI attacks.

Adversarial AI: Attackers may employ adversarial AI techniques to mimic human behaviour, necessitating ongoing innovation in behavioural analytics.

Balancing Precision and False Positives: Striking a balance between accurate detection and minimizing false positives is a continuous challenge.

Human-AI Synergy:

Human Interpretation: Behavioural analytics serves as an early warning system, empowering human analysts to validate and respond effectively.

Investigative Depth: Human expertise contextualizes anomalies, exploring nuances that automated analytics might overlook.

In the escalating war between AI attacks and cybersecurity, behavioural analytics stands as a sentinel, unravelling the enigma of AI-generated threats. As AI attackers evolve, so must the tools that safeguard our digital landscape. By embracing the synergy of behavioural analytics and human vigilance, we fortify our defences and navigate the uncharted waters of AI-generated threats with renewed confidence.

the fusion of artificial intelligence (AI) with malicious intent has given rise to an alarming breed of threats. As AI-generated attacks become more sophisticated, they leave behind unique footprints that behavioural analytics can discern. This section explores the symbiotic relationship between AI attacks and behavioural analytics, unravelling how this powerful defence mechanism can expose unusual user behaviour triggered by AI-driven assaults.

Understanding Behavioural Analytics:

Behavioural analytics mines user data, studying patterns and actions to establish a normative baseline of behaviour.

AI's Mark on User Behaviour:

Deviation Detection: AI attacks often introduce deviations from typical user behaviour due to the algorithms' inherent distinctiveness.

Velocity and Scale: AI's ability to process vast volumes of data at incredible speeds can tip off behavioural analytics to unusual activity.

Spotting the Aberrations:

Inhuman Timing: AI attacks might execute actions at odd hours or rapid intervals, setting off alerts through behavioural analysis.

Communication Style: AI-generated content might use language patterns or topics that deviate from genuine human communication.

Adaptive Contextual Analysis:

Learning and Evolving: Behavioural analytics systems adapt through machine learning, incorporating AI attack behaviours into their detection mechanisms.

Understanding the Context: Behavioural analytics considers the broader context of user actions, distinguishing AI influence from genuine user intent.

Machine Learning's Role:

AI Attack Training: Machine learning models learn from AI-generated threat data, enabling them to identify similar patterns in the future.

Real-Time Identification: Machine learning algorithms trigger alerts in real-time, catching abnormal AI-induced behaviours rapidly .

Navigating Challenges and Opportunities:

Adversarial AI: As AI attackers employ adversarial tactics to mimic human behaviour, behavioural analytics must evolve to counter these strategies.

Precision vs. False Positives: Striking a balance between accurate detection and minimizing false alarms remains a dynamic challenge.

Human-AI Harmony:

Initial Alert: Behavioural analytics serves as an early warning system, notifying human analysts about anomalies that could indicate AI attacks.

Human Insight: Human experts bring contextual insight and critical thinking to determine whether flagged behaviour is genuinely malicious.

The complex dance between AI-generated attacks and behavioural analytics paints a vivid picture of the evolving cyber landscape. Behavioural analytics acts as a vigilant sentinel, unmasking the subtle marks left behind by AI-driven assaults. This powerful duo of technology and human intellect forms an indispensable defence against the ever-adapting domain of AI threats, steering us toward a safer digital frontier.

5.2.3 AI-Driven Threat Intelligence:
Leveraging AI in threat intelligence to identify new attack patterns.

The digital landscape is an ever-evolving battleground where cyber threats mutate and adapt, challenging conventional defence strategies. Amid this complexity, the fusion of artificial intelligence (AI) and threat intelligence offers a promising paradigm shift. Exploring the symbiotic relationship between AI-driven threat intelligence and its role in uncovering emerging attack patterns, and explaining how this synergy can revolutionize our understanding of evolving threats.

Harmonizing Threat Intelligence and AI:
Threat intelligence collates data and context to decipher risks, while AI adds an unprecedented layer of analytical prowess to this endeavour.

AI's Analytical Acumen:
Pattern Decoding: AI examines vast datasets, unearthing intricate patterns and nuanced relationships that could signify nascent attack strategies.

Rapid Processing: AI algorithms rapidly process immense data volumes, discerning subtle trends and novel attack indicators.

Revealing Uncharted Threat Patterns:
Anomaly Spotting: AI excels at detecting deviations from established norms, flagging behaviours that may hint at evolving attack methodologies.

Behavioural Shifts: AI identifies shifts in user and system behaviour, exposing tactics adversaries adopt to evade traditional defences.

Amplifying Threat Detection:

Data Fusion: AI amalgamates data from disparate sources, revealing hidden connections and offering a holistic view of an attack campaign.

Interdisciplinary Insights: AI bridges gaps between different data domains, providing insights that reveal evolving attack strategies.

Navigating Challenges and Embracing Prospects:

Data Integrity: AI-driven threat intelligence is only as robust as the quality of the data it consumes, demanding data accuracy and relevance.

Bias Mitigation: AI models must be meticulously designed to prevent biases from skewing insights derived from the data.

Human-AI Symbiosis:

Strategic Context: Human analysts inject strategic context into AI-generated findings, translating raw insights into actionable intelligence.

Informed Decisions: The blend of AI's speed and human expertise results in informed decisions about emergent threats and their implications.

The fusion of AI and threat intelligence reshapes the terrain of defence. Together, they uncover emerging attack patterns, delving into the uncharted territories where adversaries experiment and innovate. This collaboration empowers defenders with a vantage point to anticipate, dissect, and counteract evolving threats, ushering in a new era of proactive cybersecurity that adapts to the relentless evolution of malicious strategies.

Reference: AI-Enhanced Detection of Social Engineering Attacks[110]

5.3. Ethical Considerations in Using AI to Combat Social Engineering Attacks

5.3.1 The Ethics of AI Use:

Navigating AI's Role in Social Engineering defence

As the domain of cybersecurity grows more complex, the integration of artificial intelligence (AI) has become a cornerstone of defence against social engineering attacks. However, this progress raises important ethical questions that demand careful consideration. This section explores the intersection of AI and social engineering defence, shedding light on the ethical considerations that arise when harnessing AI to counter the manipulative tactics of cyber adversaries.

AI's Role in Battling Social Engineering:

AI empowers defences by analysing vast amounts of data, identifying patterns, and detecting anomalies, making it a promising tool to counteract social engineering tactics.

Ethical Quandaries in AI defence:

Privacy Intricacies: AI analyses may require access to extensive personal data, sparking concerns about privacy violations and data exploitation.

---

[110] https://www.csoonline.com/article/3514695/how-ai-is-helping-detect-social-engineering-campaigns.html

Data Collection and Consent: The acquisition of user data for AI-driven defences necessitates transparent data collection practices and informed user consent.

Balancing Protection and Profiling:
Behavioural Analysis: AI's scrutiny of user behaviours might inadvertently lead to profiling, which needs to be balanced with protection goals.

Avoiding Unintended Consequences: AI-driven defences should not inadvertently label legitimate behaviour as suspicious, respecting users' digital activities.

The Trust Factor:
Transparency: AI algorithms should be transparent, with their workings and decision-making mechanisms comprehensible to stakeholders.

Human Oversight: Human experts must maintain oversight to prevent AI from making decisions that compromise privacy or ethical boundaries.

Combatting Adversarial AI:
Adversarial Techniques: Attackers may harness AI to craft sophisticated social engineering campaigns, escalating the ethical challenges.

Defensive Innovation: Ethical AI defence requires ongoing innovation to outpace adversaries and protect users' rights.

Human-AI Synergy:
Holistic Analysis: Human judgment is critical in understanding the context of AI-generated insights, addressing nuances AI might miss.

Ethical Lens: Human analysts apply ethical considerations when interpreting AI-driven results, ensuring compliance with ethical standards.

As AI rises as a sentinel against social engineering, ethical considerations become paramount. Striking the right balance between safeguarding against manipulative tactics and upholding individual privacy and rights is a delicate endeavour. By weaving together the power of AI with ethical stewardship, we forge a path toward a more secure digital world, where innovative defence tactics complement our shared values and respect for users' autonomy.

5.3.2 Bias and Fairness:

Equity and Integrity: Ensuring Fairness in AI-Driven defence Mechanisms
In the ever-evolving landscape of cybersecurity, artificial intelligence (AI) has emerged as a potent ally in defending against a myriad of threats, including the intricate art of social engineering. The potential for bias may impact the fairness and bias, avoidance in AI-powered defences against social engineering, it is important to ensure equitable and ethical outcomes.

AI's Promising Role in Social Engineering defence:
AI's analytical capabilities empower it to analyse patterns, detect anomalies, and potentially counteract the subtleties of social engineering tactics.

Navigating Bias and Fairness:
Unconscious Biases: The data AI relies on may carry historical biases, inadvertently introducing them into defence mechanisms.

Fairness Deficit: Unchecked biases could result in discriminatory outcomes, where certain groups are unfairly targeted or excluded.

Mitigating Bias in AI-Driven defence:
Diverse Data Sources: Incorporating diverse and representative datasets can help counteract inherent biases.

Algorithmic Auditing: Regularly auditing AI algorithms can expose and rectify any emerging biases.

Ethical Implications:
Equal Treatment: AI defences must ensure equal protection for all users, irrespective of demographic factors.

Unintended Consequences: Bias in AI-driven defences could lead to misclassification of legitimate actions as suspicious, impacting user trust.

Human-Centric Oversight:
Human Analysts: Human expertise is essential to interpret AI-generated insights, identifying and addressing potential bias.

Ethical Review: Human analysts apply ethical considerations when interpreting AI-driven results, ensuring they align with fairness standards.

Combatting Adversarial Bias:
Ethical Innovation: Continuous innovation in AI defence is crucial to counter adversarial attempts to exploit biases.

Transparency and Accountability: Ensuring transparency about AI's role and limitations builds trust and accountability.

Striving for Fairness:
Ethical Frameworks: Establishing clear ethical guidelines can help AI developers steer clear of biased outcomes.

Collaborative Efforts: Stakeholders across academia, industry, and regulatory bodies must collaborate to address biases.

AI's potential in social engineering defence is vast, but the ethical imperative to ensure fairness is equally critical. Striving for unbiased, equitable outcomes ensures that AI's power is harnessed to protect all users while upholding the values of fairness and inclusivity. In the journey to secure the digital landscape, addressing bias becomes a cornerstone, as AI-driven defences work in harmony with human values to create a safer and more just online domain .

5.3.3 Transparency and Accountability:
The Significance of Transparency and Accountability in AI-Driven defence
As the practice of cybersecurity adopts the remarkable capabilities of artificial intelligence (AI), a critical concern emerges: the need for transparency and accountability in AI-driven defence strategies. This section explores the essence of transparent AI systems and the importance for accountability in defences against multifaceted threats, ensuring the ethical and effective utilization of this powerful tool.

Transparency in AI Systems:

Transparent AI systems unveil their inner workings, enabling stakeholders to comprehend how decisions are made.

The Quest for Clarity:

Trust Building: Transparent systems foster user trust by revealing the logic and rationale behind AI-generated decisions.

Exposing Bias: Transparency helps to identify and rectify potential biases, promoting fairness in AI-driven defence.

Unmasking AI Algorithms:

Open-Box Approach: Transparent AI systems operate as "open boxes," accessible for scrutiny and analysis.

Auditable Logic: Clear algorithms enable experts to audit, review, and refine the decision-making processes.

Accountability in AI-Driven defence:

Accountability ensures that the consequences of AI-driven decisions are monitored and that mechanisms exist for redressal.

Ensuring Responsible Actions:

Human Oversight: Accountability mandates human supervision to ensure AI-generated actions align with ethical norms.

Avoiding Autonomy: Defining boundaries prevents AI from taking actions that may conflict with broader security goals.

Ethical Implications:

Consequences and Liability: Accountable AI systems attribute responsibility for decisions, aiding in addressing potential consequences.

User Impact: Accountability ensures that users are protected from negative impacts arising from AI-driven defence actions.

Human-AI Synergy:

Interpretation: Human analysts interpret AI outputs, applying ethical judgment to complex situations.

Ethical Lens: Human experts apply ethical considerations to AI-generated decisions, ensuring alignment with established standards.

Strategies for Accountability:

Regulatory Frameworks: Regulatory bodies establish accountability guidelines, ensuring AI-driven defences adhere to legal and ethical standards.

Collaboration: Stakeholders across academia, industry, and policy domain s collaborate to establish accountability norms.

Transparency and accountability are cornerstones in AI-driven defence, preserving the ethical integrity of AI systems while building trust among users. Transparent AI empowers experts to scrutinize decisions, enhancing system accuracy and fairness. Accountability, on the other hand, establishes a framework to oversee AI actions, ensuring that they remain aligned with ethical and strategic goals. Together, these principles create a formidable alliance that not only safeguards the digital domain but also upholds the principles of responsible and ethical technological advancement.

Reference: Ethical Considerations in AI Cybersecurity[111]

5.4. Case Study: AI-Powered Anti-Phishing Solutions

5.4.1 Ironscales:

Case Study on Ironscales' in AI-Powered Phishing Attack Detection and Mitigation

The persistent threat of phishing attacks demands innovative defence mechanisms, and Ironscales emerges as a beacon of AI-powered defence against this pervasive menace. This case study explores the intricacies of Ironscales' AI-driven platform, showcasing how it detects and mitigates phishing attacks through the seamless integration of advanced technologies and human intelligence.

Ironscales: Revolutionizing Phishing defence with AI

Ironscales combines the prowess of artificial intelligence, machine learning, and human insight to create a comprehensive defence against phishing threats.

AI-Powered Detection:

Pattern Recognition: AI algorithms analyse vast datasets, identifying patterns that signal potential phishing attacks.

Anomaly Detection: AI excels at pinpointing anomalies in email communication, uncovering suspicious deviations from the norm.

Human-Augmented defence:

Human Verification: Suspicious emails flagged by AI undergo human verification to avoid false positives.

Collective Intelligence: Ironscales taps into the collective intelligence of human experts to enhance its detection capabilities.

Mitigating Phishing Threats:

Automated Response: AI automates the response to phishing incidents, ensuring swift action to protect users.

Quarantine and Remediation: Detected threats are quarantined and remediated, thwarting attackers' attempts.

Adaptive Learning:

Model Enhancement: Ironscales' AI continuously learns from new data, refining its detection models for evolving threats.

Rapid Adaptation: The platform adapts quickly to emerging tactics, reducing the window of vulnerability.

Results and Impact:

Reduced Response Time: Ironscales' AI drastically reduces the time taken to detect and mitigate phishing attacks.

---

[111] https://cybersecurityguide.org/ethics-in-cybersecurity/#ethics-in-ai-cybersecurity

Enhanced Accuracy: The integration of AI minimizes false positives, ensuring efficient resource utilization.

Human Touch and Technology Synergy:
Human Verification: Human analysts validate AI-generated alerts, merging human expertise with AI insights.

Continuous Improvement: Human feedback informs AI models, enhancing their accuracy and reducing human effort.

Ironscales stands as a testament to the synergy between human expertise and AI-powered defence. Through the amalgamation of cutting-edge technology and human intelligence, it offers a formidable shield against phishing attacks, an exemplar of how AI can elevate cybersecurity. Ironscales' success story underscores the immense potential of AI to transform the cybersecurity landscape, showcasing how it can empower defenders to stay one step ahead in the relentless battle against phishing threats.

Reference: Ironscales Case Study[112]

5.4.2 Cofense:

Case study: A Dive into Cofense's AI-Enabled Social Engineering Threat Solutions
In the intricate domain of cybersecurity, social engineering threats stand as formidable adversaries, necessitating innovative defences. Cofense steps into the spotlight with its AI-driven solutions that identify and neutralize social engineering threats. This section explores the intricate workings of Cofense's AI-powered platform, showcasing its prowess in safeguarding against these manipulative tactics.

Cofense: Charting a Path with AI-Powered defence
Cofense harnesses the power of artificial intelligence (AI) to create proactive defences against the multifaceted domain of social engineering threats.

AI-Powered Detection:
Behavioural Analysis: Cofense's AI dissects user behaviour to detect anomalies indicative of social engineering attacks.

Pattern Recognition: AI algorithms scrutinize vast datasets, identifying patterns synonymous with phishing and other social engineering tactics.

Human Intelligence Amplified:
Human Verification: AI-generated alerts undergo human verification, avoiding unnecessary false positives.

Collective Insights: Cofense's platform leverages human expertise to bolster AI detection capabilities.

---

[112] https://www.ironscales.com/solution

Mitigating Social Engineering Threats:

Automated Response: AI-driven mechanisms automate responses to thwart ongoing or potential attacks.

Incident Containment: Detected threats are rapidly contained and neutralized, disrupting attackers' progress.

Adaptive Learning:

Continuous Evolution: Cofense's AI adapts to new tactics by learning from real-time data, ensuring relevance against evolving threats.

Timely Updates: AI rapidly incorporates insights, minimizing the window of vulnerability for emerging attack patterns.

Outcomes and Influence:

Reduced Exposure Time: Cofense's AI-enabled solutions drastically diminish the time threats persist within the environment.

Heightened Accuracy: AI's precision reduces false positives, channelling resources effectively toward genuine threats.

Human-Machine Symbiosis:

Human Insight Integration: Human analysts' input and validation enhance AI's decision-making, optimizing detection accuracy.

Continuous Enhancement: Human feedback contributes to AI model refinements, ensuring accuracy and adaptability.

Cofense epitomizes the harmonious convergence of human intelligence and AI-powered defence. By fusing cutting-edge technology with the discernment of human experts, Cofense crafts a robust defence against social engineering threats. Its AI-driven solutions exemplify the untapped potential of AI in transforming cybersecurity, equipping organizations with an upper hand in the ceaseless struggle against social engineering adversaries.

Reference: Cofense AI-Powered Solutions[113]

---

113 https://cofense.com/products/

Chapter 6: Ethical and Legal Implications of AI in Cybersecurity

6.1. Addressing Biases and Fairness in AI Cybersecurity Solutions

6.1.1 Introduction to AI Bias and Fairness:

How biases can be introduced into AI and what's the impact on cybersecurity?

As artificial intelligence (AI) infiltrates the world of cybersecurity, an important yet often overlooked concern arises: the potential introduction of biases into AI systems. To understand biases in AI, we need to explore their origin, propagation, and their profound impact on the cybersecurity landscape.

The Seeds of Bias:

Data as Foundation: Biases in AI systems often stem from the data they are trained on, mirroring human prejudices inherent in the data.

Unintended Consequences: Biases in data can unknowingly become ingrained in AI algorithms, perpetuating skewed outcomes.

The Magnitude of Impact:

Skewed Decisions: Biased AI systems might make decisions favouring certain groups, perpetuating inequality and discrimination.

Misclassification: Bias can lead to misclassification, where genuine actions are mislabelled as threats or vice versa.

Cybersecurity's Vulnerability:

False Positives/Negatives: Biased AI can generate false positives or negatives, leading to improper threat detection or overlooking actual threats.

Resource Misallocation: Biases might lead to misallocation of resources toward perceived threats, undermining effective security strategies.

The Human Element:

Unconscious Biases: Developers' biases can inadvertently seep into AI models, further propagating pre-existing prejudices.

User Impact: Biases can affect users' trust in AI systems and result in undeserved security actions.

Strategies for Bias Mitigation:

Diverse Data: Incorporating diverse and representative datasets minimizes the risk of introducing biases.

Algorithmic Scrutiny: Regularly auditing AI algorithms helps expose and rectify emerging biases.

Ethical and Legal Dimensions:

Ethical Obligations: Developers bear a moral duty to ensure AI systems are free from biases that could harm individuals or groups.

Legal Implications: Biased AI decisions can raise legal concerns, potentially leading to liability.

Collaborative Efforts:

Multi-Stakeholder Approach: Collaborative efforts across academia, industry, and regulatory bodies are essential to address biases.

Transparency and Accountability: Openly acknowledging biases and demonstrating efforts to mitigate them build trust.

The cybersecurity landscape is marred by the potential consequences of biased AI systems. Addressing biases is not just an ethical imperative but a strategic necessity to ensure that AI-driven cybersecurity is equitable, effective, and aligned with the ethical standards upheld by society. As AI continues to revolutionize the security paradigm, vigilance against biases stands as a sentinel guarding against inadvertent harm and preserving the fairness and integrity of AI-powered defences.

6.1.2 Detecting and Mitigating Bias:

Identifying and Mitigating Biases in AI Cybersecurity Solutions

The integration of artificial intelligence (AI) into cybersecurity brings with it both revolutionary advancements and intricate challenges. One of the paramount concerns is the potential introduction of biases into AI systems. This section explores the methodologies employed to identify and mitigate biases within AI-driven cybersecurity solutions, ensuring the ethical integrity and efficacy of these cutting-edge defences.

Unmasking the Biases: Identifying Biases in AI Cybersecurity Solutions
- **Dataset Examination:** Scrutinizing the training dataset for any inherent biases that might have seeped into the AI model.
- **Disparate Impact Analysis:** Assessing whether the AI system's decisions disproportionately affect different groups.

Bias Classification and Evaluation:
- **Pre-Processing Techniques:** Employing techniques like oversampling or under-sampling to balance the dataset and reduce inherent biases.
- **Algorithmic Auditing:** Rigorously assessing AI algorithms to uncover any biases that might emerge during their decision-making process.

Human-AI Collaboration:
- **Human Review and Validation:** Involving human experts to review and validate AI-generated decisions, ensuring impartiality.
- **Diverse Development Teams:** Building diverse teams to develop AI solutions, minimizing the introduction of unintentional biases.

Mitigating Biases: Ensuring Ethical and Effective AI Solutions
- **Algorithmic Fairness**: Incorporating fairness metrics into AI model development to ensure equitable decision-making.
- **Bias-Resistant Training**: Training AI models to be robust against biases through adversarial training or re-weighting techniques.

Transparent Decision-Making:
- **Interpretability Techniques:** Employing techniques that make AI decisions more understandable, facilitating the identification of biases.
- **Bias Reporting:** Implementing mechanisms for users to report any potential biases in AI decisions.

- **Ethics Boards:** Forming ethics boards or committees to review AI models and decisions for potential biases.
- **Continuous Monitoring:** Regularly monitoring AI solutions to detect and rectify biases that might emerge post-deployment.

Education and Awareness:

- **Bias Awareness Training:** Training AI developers and stakeholders to recognize and address biases during development.
- **Community Collaboration:** Encouraging collaboration among AI practitioners to share insights and best practices for bias mitigation.

The Road to Ethical and Effective AI Cybersecurity:

Identifying and mitigating biases in AI cybersecurity solutions is a journey, not a destination. With the marriage of human expertise and cutting-edge technology, the cybersecurity community can pave the way for AI systems that not only defend against threats but do so with impartiality, ethics, and a commitment to a fair and secure digital world.

6.1.3 Fairness in Algorithmic Decisions:

Fairness: Equitable Outcomes in AI-Driven Decisions

In the era of artificial intelligence (AI), where machines wield the power to make impactful decisions, the concept of fairness takes centre stage. This section explores the ethical imperative and societal implications of ensuring equity and justice in a rapidly evolving digital landscape.

Defining Fairness: A Moral and Ethical Imperative

- **Avoiding Discrimination:** Fairness in AI decisions ensures that no individual or group is unfairly discriminated against based on protected attributes.
- **Promoting Equality:** Equitable outcomes uphold the principle of equality by treating all individuals with equal consideration.

The Human Touch: Mitigating Biases and Prejudices

- **Bias Mitigation:** Fair AI decisions counteract the biases ingrained in data, preventing unfair amplification of existing prejudices.
- **Overcoming Stereotypes:** Equitable AI decisions reject societal stereotypes and prevent their perpetuation.

Ethics and Trust: Nurturing Public Confidence in AI

- **Ethical Responsibility:** Fair outcomes in AI-driven decisions uphold the ethical duty to treat all individuals justly and equitably.
- **Trust Building:** Fair AI engenders trust among users, fostering confidence in AI-driven systems and their decisions.

Mitigating Socioeconomic Disparities: Bridging the Gap

- **Reducing Inequalities:** Fair AI can mitigate socioeconomic disparities by ensuring equal access to opportunities.
- **Addressing Bias Amplification:** Equitable AI prevents the amplification of existing disparities in resource allocation and decision-making.

- **Legal Compliance:** Fair AI decisions adhere to legal standards of non-discrimination and equal treatment.
- **Ethical Frameworks:** Ethical AI models align with established ethical principles, valuing justice and fairness.

Balancing Individual and Societal Good:

- **Maximizing Social Welfare:** Fair AI decisions strike a balance between individual rights and the greater societal good.
- **Inclusive Progress:** Equitable AI decisions drive progress that benefits all segments of society, avoiding marginalization.

Collective Responsibility

Ensuring fairness in AI-driven decisions is not just a technological challenge but a moral obligation. As AI systems continue to permeate every facet of our lives, the pursuit of fairness becomes a collaborative endeavour, involving researchers, developers, policymakers, and society at large. By weaving the thread of equity into the fabric of AI, we forge a path toward a just and harmonious digital future.

Reference: Addressing Bias and Fairness in AI[114]

6.2. Ensuring Transparency and Accountability in AI-Based Decisions

6.2.1 Importance of Transparency:

Significance of Transparency in AI Algorithms and Decision-Making

Where algorithms wield power over decisions that impact lives, the virtue of transparency emerges as a beacon of ethical and accountable practice. This section, showcases the importance of transparency in AI algorithms and decision-making, shedding light on its role in fostering trust, ethical integrity, and societal understanding.

The Pillar of Trust: Fostering User Confidence in AI

- **Cultivating Trustworthiness:** Transparency in AI decisions and algorithms nurtures trust among users, assuring them that decisions are made fairly and without hidden biases.
- **Countering Scepticism:** Transparent AI demystifies decision-making processes, countering scepticism and conspiracy theories.

Ethical Responsibility: A Duty to Disclose

- **Informed Consent:** Transparent AI ensures that users are informed about how their data is used and how decisions are reached.
- **Respecting Autonomy:** Transparency empowers users by providing them with the information needed to make informed choices.

Mitigating Bias and Unfairness: Detecting Hidden Biases

- **Bias Detection:** Transparent AI allows biases to be detected and rectified, preventing discriminatory outcomes.
- **Rooting Out Inequity:** Transparent algorithms prevent hidden biases from reinforcing existing inequalities.

---

[114] https://www.securityweek.com/addressing-ai-bias-challenge-cybersecurity

- **Traceability:** Transparent AI allows for the tracing of decisions back to their source, identifying responsibility in case of errors.
- **Auditing and Validation:** Transparent algorithms enable external audits and validations, ensuring accountability and ethical practice.

Avoiding the Black Box: Making AI Understandable

- **Interpretability:** Transparent AI is more interpretable, enabling experts and users to understand how decisions are reached.
- **Reducing Algorithmic Mystique:** Transparent AI dispels the aura of a "black box," making AI more accessible to stakeholders.

Compliance and Regulation: Navigating Legal Requirements

- **Legal Compliance:** Transparent AI algorithms align with regulations that mandate disclosure and accountability.
- **Ethics Frameworks:** Transparent AI conforms to established ethical guidelines and frameworks, ensuring ethical AI deployment.

Enabling Public Discourse: Informed Societal Discussions

- **Open Dialogue:** Transparent AI fosters informed discussions about its implications, allowing society to collectively steer its development.
- **Avoiding Moral Blind Spots:** Transparency brings ethical considerations to the forefront, preventing unforeseen ethical dilemmas.

Forging a Transparent AI Future

Transparency in AI algorithms and decision-making is not a singular endeavour but a collective commitment. It involves researchers, developers, policymakers, and the wider society. By embracing transparency as a fundamental principle, we not only unlock the potential of AI for societal progress but also safeguard its ethical integrity, ensuring that AI decisions are made in the light of accountability, fairness, and the shared values that shape our digital future.

6.2.2 Explainable AI (XAI):

Introduction to explainable AI techniques that provide insights into the decision-making process.

In the enigmatic domain of artificial intelligence (AI), where algorithms wield influence over critical decisions, the concept of explainability emerges as a guiding light. This introduction dives into explainable AI techniques, highlighting their key role in demystifying the decision-making process, fostering user trust, and advancing ethical AI practices.

The Quest for Clarity: Explainable AI

- **Demystifying Black Boxes:** Explainable AI techniques pierce through the shroud of complexity, making AI decision-making understandable.
- **User Empowerment:** Explainable AI empowers users by providing insights into how decisions are reached, facilitating informed choices.

Ethics and Accountability: building Trust

- **Building Trust:** Explainable AI cultivates trust by showing that decisions are not arbitrary but based on interpretable processes.

- **Accountability Pathways:** Explainability enables accountability, allowing for tracing decisions back to their sources.

Preventing Bias and Discrimination: Hidden Biases
- **Bias Identification:** Explainable AI exposes biases within algorithms, enabling their identification and rectification.
- **Equity Assurance:** Transparent insights from explainable AI prevent hidden biases from perpetuating social inequities.

Informed Decision-Making:
- **Human-AI Collaboration:** Explainable AI fosters collaboration between humans and AI systems by making AI decisions more understandable.
- **Supporting Experts:** Explainability equips experts with the tools to validate AI decisions and detect errors.

Navigating Complex Algorithms: Interpretability Techniques
- **Feature Importance:** Explainable AI reveals the importance of features that influence decisions, offering insights into algorithmic behaviour.
- **Visualizations:** Graphical representations provided by explainability techniques make complex AI models more comprehensible.

Ethical and Legal Compliance: Frameworks
- **Ethical Considerations:** Explainable AI aligns with ethical principles by enabling scrutiny of AI decisions for fairness and transparency.
- **Regulatory Mandates:** Explainability meets regulatory requirements that mandate transparency in AI systems.

Fostering Collaboration:
The journey into the domain of explainable AI is a collaborative voyage, involving AI practitioners, researchers, policymakers, and society at large. By embracing explainability, we not only pave the way for AI systems that are comprehensible and just but also uphold the ethical and societal principles that underpin the responsible development of AI in our rapidly evolving digital landscape.

6.2.3 Accountability in AI:
Holding AI to Account: Ensuring Responsibility for AI System Decisions

In the intricate landscape of artificial intelligence (AI), where algorithms autonomously make decisions that impact lives, the concept of accountability emerges as a cornerstone of ethical practice. This discussion explores the imperative of holding AI systems accountable for their decisions, underscoring the ethical duty and societal implications of ensuring transparency, fairness, and oversight in the domain of AI-driven decision-making.

Defining Accountability in AI: A Moral and Ethical Obligation
- **Transparent Decision Trails:** Accountability in AI entails the ability to trace decisions back to their origins, revealing the processes and data that influenced outcomes.
- **Ethical Oversight:** Accountable AI ensures that decisions adhere to established ethical guidelines, preventing harmful or biased outcomes.

- **Human Oversight:** Accountability involves human experts overseeing AI decisions, validating their fairness and correctness.
- **Human Intervention:** Accountable AI systems allow for human intervention in cases where AI decisions could lead to adverse consequences.

Ethics and Responsibility: A Duty to Society
- **Minimizing Harm:** Accountable AI aims to minimize harm to individuals, communities, and society at large by ensuring responsible decision-making.
- **Preventing Discrimination:** Accountability prevents AI systems from perpetuating discrimination or bias, ensuring equitable outcomes.

Transparency and Trust: Fostering Public Confidence
- **User Trust:** Accountable AI systems cultivate trust among users by providing insights into decision-making processes.
- **Demystification:** Accountability dispels the mystique of AI's decision-making, making it comprehensible to stakeholders.

Regulation and Oversight: Establishing Legal Frameworks
- **Regulatory Compliance:** Accountable AI aligns with regulatory requirements that mandate transparency, fairness, and ethical practice.
- **External Audits:** Accountability invites external audits to ensure that AI systems operate ethically and responsibly.

Ethical Dilemmas: Balancing Automation and Responsibility
- **Automated Decisions:** Accountable AI systems strike a balance between automation and human responsibility, preventing undue reliance on machines.
- **Moral Agency:** Accountability raises questions about the moral agency of AI systems and the consequences of their actions.

The Shared Responsibility: Society's Role in Accountability
Ensuring accountability for AI system decisions is not solely a technological challenge; it's a societal responsibility. Researchers, developers, policymakers, and citizens collectively contribute to establishing the norms, regulations, and ethical standards that govern AI accountability. By embracing accountability, we pave the way for AI systems that operate ethically, transparently, and with the greater good in mind, ushering in an era of responsible and trustworthy AI innovation.

Reference: Ensuring Transparency in AI[115]

6.3. Navigating Legal and Regulatory Challenges in AI-Driven Cybersecurity

6.3.1 Overview of Legal and Regulatory Landscape:

Introduction to the legal and regulatory considerations related to AI in cybersecurity.
In the ever-evolving landscape of artificial intelligence (AI) and cybersecurity, legal and regulatory considerations emerge as guiding beacons, shaping the ethical deployment and responsible practice of AI technologies. This introduction aims to introduce the legal and regulatory considerations related to AI in cybersecurity, highlighting their significance in upholding ethical standards, safeguarding user rights, and fostering a secure digital ecosystem.

---

[115] https://www.sciencedaily.com/releases/2020/06/200624143455.htm

- **Legal Compliance:** Legal considerations dictate that AI cybersecurity solutions must align with existing laws and regulations, ensuring adherence to ethical boundaries.
- **User Protection:** Legal frameworks require AI systems to prioritize user data protection and privacy, safeguarding sensitive information from breaches.

Cybersecurity Regulation: Ensuring Digital Safety

- **Data Breach Notification Laws:** Legal considerations mandate prompt notification of data breaches, ensuring transparency and protection for affected individuals.
- **Industry Regulations:** Specific industries, such as finance and healthcare, have sector-specific regulations that AI cybersecurity systems must adhere to.

Ethical Implications: Balancing Innovation and Responsibility

- **Ethical Algorithms:** Legal considerations encourage the development and deployment of AI algorithms that adhere to ethical principles, avoiding biases and discrimination.
- **Transparency and Accountability:** Ethical considerations in law require AI systems to be transparent, enabling accountability for their actions.

User Consent and Control: Preserving User Autonomy

- **Informed Consent:** Legal frameworks emphasize obtaining user consent for the use of AI in cybersecurity, ensuring transparency and choice.
- **User Control:** Legal considerations enable users to have control over AI-driven cybersecurity measures, allowing them to opt-out or customize their protection.

Liability and Responsibility: Attribution and Accountability

- **Attribution Challenges:** Legal considerations address the challenge of attributing cyber incidents involving AI systems, determining liability and responsibility.
- **Chain of Responsibility:** Legal frameworks dictate the allocation of responsibility among AI developers, users, and regulators in case of breaches or harm.

International Cooperation: Harmonizing Global Standards

- **Cross-Border Data Protection:** Legal considerations focus on harmonizing cross-border data protection laws, ensuring consistent user rights and cybersecurity standards.
- **Global Norms:** International agreements and treaties shape the legal landscape, establishing norms for responsible AI cybersecurity practices.

A Collaborative Endeavor: Uniting Stakeholders

Navigating the legal and regulatory considerations related to AI in cybersecurity requires collaboration among AI developers, legal experts, policymakers, and users. By embracing legal and regulatory guidelines, we pave the way for AI systems that uphold user rights, adhere to ethical principles, and contribute to a secure digital environment, ensuring that the technological advancements of AI are harnessed responsibly and ethically for the greater good.

6.3.2 GDPR and AI:

GDPR's Impact: the General Data Protection Regulation (GDPR) in AI Cybersecurity

In the dynamic landscape of artificial intelligence (AI) and cybersecurity, the General Data Protection Regulation (GDPR) stands as a pivotal landmark, shaping the ethical treatment of data and safeguarding user rights. This section explores the domain of GDPR and its profound implications for

AI in cybersecurity, highlighting its role in protecting user privacy, promoting transparency, and fostering responsible AI practices.

Upholding Data Privacy and Rights

- **Data Protection Principles:** The GDPR establishes principles that govern the processing of personal data, ensuring fair and lawful treatment.
- **User Consent:** GDPR emphasizes obtaining explicit and informed user consent for data processing, empowering individuals to control their data.

User Rights and Empowerment: GDPR's Ethical Foundations

- **Right to Access:** GDPR grants users the right to access their personal data held by AI cybersecurity systems, fostering transparency.
- **Right to Erasure:** Users have the right to request the erasure of their data, ensuring their control over their digital footprint.

Transparency and Accountability: GDPR's Pillars

- **Data Processing Transparency:** GDPR mandates clear communication of how user data is processed, promoting transparency in AI cybersecurity operations.
- **Accountability Mechanisms:** Organizations deploying AI in cybersecurity must demonstrate compliance with GDPR, fostering accountability for data handling.

Privacy by Design: Integrating Privacy in AI Systems

- **Privacy-Enhancing Measures:** GDPR requires privacy considerations to be integrated into AI cybersecurity systems from the outset, ensuring data protection by design.
- **Data Minimization:** Organizations must minimize the collection and processing of personal data, aligning with GDPR's principle of data minimization.

Cross-Border Data Transfers: GDPR's Global Reach

- **Transfer Mechanisms:** GDPR sets guidelines for transferring personal data across borders, ensuring user data is protected even in international contexts.
- **Binding Corporate Rules:** Multinational organizations can adopt Binding Corporate Rules to ensure consistent data protection practices across their subsidiaries.

Data Breach Notifications: Ensuring Prompt Action

- **Timely Reporting:** GDPR mandates the prompt reporting of data breaches to users and relevant authorities, fostering quick response to breaches.
- **User Notification:** Organizations using AI in cybersecurity must notify affected users of data breaches, enhancing user awareness and security.

The Future of Ethical AI: GDPR's Legacy

Navigating GDPR's implications for AI in cybersecurity signifies a commitment to data privacy, user empowerment, and ethical AI deployment. By adhering to GDPR's principles and incorporating privacy **considerations** into AI systems, we not only safeguard user rights but also contribute to the responsible development of AI technologies, fostering a digital landscape that respects data privacy and user autonomy.

6.3.3 Cybersecurity Regulations and Compliance:

Regulations and Compliance in AI-Driven Cybersecurity

Navigating the regulatory terrain is paramount to ensuring responsible and ethical AI-driven cybersecurity practices. Several regulations and compliance standards have impact AI-driven cybersecurity, highlighting their role in shaping ethical behaviour, safeguarding user privacy, and fostering a secure digital ecosystem.

Example of Regulations: A Framework for Ethical Conduct

- **Data Protection Laws:** Regulations such as the General Data Protection Regulation (GDPR) and the California Consumer Privacy Act (CCPA) dictate how AI-driven cybersecurity solutions handle user data, emphasizing consent and user rights.
- **Cybersecurity Regulations:** Industry-specific regulations like the NIST Cybersecurity Framework in the United States and the European Union Agency for Network and Information Security (ENISA) guidelines provide blueprints for secure AI deployment.

Example of Compliance Standards: Paving the Path to Responsibility

- **ISO/IEC 27001:** This international standard outlines best practices for information security management systems, guiding organizations in implementing robust AI-driven cybersecurity measures.
- **PCI DSS:** The Payment Card Industry Data Security Standard lays out requirements for securing payment card data, impacting AI systems that handle financial transactions.

AI Ethics and Transparency: A Growing Focus

- **EU Ethics Guidelines for Trustworthy AI:** These guidelines highlight transparency, fairness, and accountability as cornerstones of ethical AI deployment, influencing AI-driven cybersecurity practices.
- **Algorithmic Impact Assessments:** Certain regulations, like the GDPR's requirement for Data Protection Impact Assessments, drive organizations to assess the potential risks of their AI cybersecurity solutions.

Cross-Border Data Transfers: Ensuring Global Compliance

- **Cross-Border Data Transfer Regulations:** When AI-driven cybersecurity solutions operate across borders, regulations like the EU-US Privacy Shield influence data transfer practices.
- **Binding Corporate Rules:** Multinational organizations must adhere to specific data protection standards, even when transferring data between their subsidiaries, reinforcing global compliance.

Cyber Incident Reporting: Promoting Transparency

- **Mandatory Reporting Laws:** Regulations in many jurisdictions mandate organizations to report certain types of cyber incidents, enhancing transparency and response capabilities.
- **National Cybersecurity Strategies:** Many countries have developed national cybersecurity strategies that include regulations for AI cybersecurity practices, harmonizing efforts and ensuring consistency.

The Road Ahead: A Collaborative Endeavor

Adhering to regulations and compliance standards in AI-driven cybersecurity is not a solitary endeavour. It involves collaboration among AI developers, cybersecurity experts, legal professionals, and policymakers. By embracing these regulations and standards, organizations contribute to a digital landscape that prioritizes user privacy, data protection, and ethical AI practices, fostering a secure and responsible environment for innovation and progress.

6.4. Case Study: AI and Fairness in Facial Recognition

6.4.1 Amazon Recognition Controversy:

Case study: Amazon's Facial Recognition and Ethical Implications

Amazon's foray into facial recognition technology has stirred a debate that underscores the profound ethical considerations surrounding its use. This case study explores the controversy surrounding Amazon's facial recognition technology, shedding light on its implications for privacy, surveillance, bias, and the broader ethical landscape.

The Technology Unveiled: Amazon Recognition

- **Facial Recognition Capabilities:** Amazon's Recognition is designed to analyse images and video streams to identify individuals in real-time using AI-powered facial recognition algorithms.
- **Use Cases:** Amazon envisioned Recognition for a range of applications, from law enforcement and security to personal use, raising questions about its potential societal impact.

Privacy and Surveillance Concerns

- **Mass Surveillance:** Critics express concerns about the potential for mass surveillance, where the widespread use of facial recognition technology could lead to constant monitoring of individuals.
- **Erosion of Privacy:** The technology's ability to identify individuals without their knowledge or consent raises worries about individual privacy and the right to remain anonymous in public spaces.

Bias and Inaccuracy: Unintended Consequences

- **Bias in Algorithms:** Studies revealed that facial recognition algorithms, including Amazon's, have exhibited biases, leading to higher error rates for certain demographic groups, particularly people of colour.
- **Impact on Marginalized Communities:** The biases in the technology's accuracy can result in systemic discrimination against marginalized communities, perpetuating existing inequalities.

Ethical Considerations: Balancing Innovation and Responsibility

- **Transparency and Accountability:** Critics argue that Amazon's lack of transparency in Recognition's accuracy and potential biases raises concerns about accountability.
- **Dual-Use Dilemma:** The technology's dual-use nature, both for legitimate and potentially harmful purposes, prompts ethical dilemmas about its deployment.

Public Backlash and Advocacy

- **Public Pressure:** The controversy sparked public outcry, prompting advocacy groups, privacy advocates, and even Amazon employees to raise concerns about the ethical implications of the technology.

---

[116] https://www.securitymagazine.com/articles/93194-the-legal-and-regulatory-challenges-of-ai-and-cybersecurity

- **Legislative Response:** The controversy led to legislative proposals at various levels seeking to regulate and restrict the use of facial recognition technology, highlighting the need for comprehensive regulations.

Amazon's Response and Pause

- **Temporal Pause:** In response to the controversy, Amazon announced a one-year moratorium on selling Recognition to law enforcement agencies, acknowledging the need for regulatory guidelines.
- **Calls for Comprehensive Regulation:** Amazon's move underscored the necessity for comprehensive regulations that balance innovation with ethical considerations.

The Bigger Picture: Ethics in AI and Surveillance

The case of Amazon's facial recognition technology serves as a microcosm of the broader ethical considerations that arise when AI intersects with surveillance technologies. It highlights the importance of ethical development, unbiased training data, transparency, and accountability in AI systems. Ultimately, the controversy prompts critical discussions on how society can harness technological advancements while ensuring the protection of civil liberties, privacy, and societal well-being.

Reference: Amazon Recognition Controversy[117]

6.4.2 Microsoft's Approach to AI Ethics:

Microsoft's Ethical Principles and AI Development

In the dynamic landscape of artificial intelligence (AI) development, Microsoft has emerged as a frontrunner in promoting responsible and ethical AI practices. This section explores Microsoft's ethical principles and guidelines for AI development, emphasizing its commitment to transparency, fairness, inclusivity, accountability, and societal well-being.

Transparency: Shedding Light on AI Systems

- **Explainability:** Microsoft emphasizes the need for AI systems to be understandable and explainable to users, stakeholders, and the broader public.
- **Open Communication:** The company advocates transparent communication about AI capabilities, limitations, and potential biases to foster user trust.

Fairness and Inclusivity: Equal Treatment for All

- **Avoiding Bias:** Microsoft is dedicated to identifying and mitigating biases in AI systems to ensure fair and equal treatment, regardless of demographic factors.
- **Inclusive Design:** The company promotes AI systems that consider diverse user needs and avoid excluding any group due to biases or inaccuracies.

Accountability: Ownership and Responsibility

- **Human Oversight:** Microsoft emphasizes the role of human decision-making in AI systems, preventing undue delegation of decisions to algorithms.
- **Assessing Impact:** The company commits to assessing the potential societal impact of AI solutions, addressing risks and benefits comprehensively.

---

[117] https://www.cnet.com/news/amazons-facial-recognition-tech-misidentified-28-members-of-congress-aclu-says/

Robustness and Safety: Ensuring Reliable AI Systems
- **Reliability:** Microsoft focuses on building AI systems that are robust, reliable, and safe, minimizing the potential for unintended and harmful consequences.
- **Secure Development:** The company follows secure development practices to prevent malicious use and safeguard user data and privacy.

Privacy and Security: Safeguarding User Information
- **Data Privacy:** Microsoft prioritizes user privacy by collecting only necessary data, securing it, and providing users with control over their data.
- **Protection against Misuse:** The company commits to preventing AI from being used for surveillance, discrimination, or any other harmful purposes.

Human-Centred AI: Empowering Users
- **User Empowerment:** Microsoft aims to ensure that AI systems amplify human capabilities and empower users, without diminishing their autonomy.
- **User Consent:** The company emphasizes informed user consent for data collection and AI use, maintaining user agency and control.

Guidance for AI Development: The AI Principles
- **Ethical Use:** Microsoft's AI Principles guide the development of AI technologies that respect human rights, cultural diversity, and ethical norms.
- **Human Control:** The principles assert the importance of maintaining human control over AI systems and ensuring they serve human interests.

Addressing Tough Challenges: Open Discussion and Collaboration
- **AI and Societal Challenges:** Microsoft acknowledges the potential challenges AI poses to society and seeks to address them through open dialogue and collaboration.
- **Advocating Regulation:** The company actively supports the development of regulations that govern AI use, emphasizing its commitment to responsible AI deployment.

The Ongoing Journey: Ethics in AI Innovation
Microsoft's ethical principles and guidelines for AI development serve as a beacon in the ever-evolving landscape of AI technology. By championing transparency, fairness, inclusivity, and accountability, Microsoft not only shapes its own AI endeavours but also contributes to a global movement that strives to harness AI's potential while safeguarding human values and well-being.

Reference: Microsoft's AI Ethics Principles[118]

---

[118] https://www.microsoft.com/en-us/ai/ai-principles

Chapter 7: AI-Enhanced Security Operations Centres (SOCs)

7.1. Role of AI in Enhancing SOC Capabilities

7.1.1 Introduction to AI-Enhanced Security Operations Centres:

Revolutionizing Security: The Transformation of Traditional SOCs with AI

In the rapidly evolving domain of cybersecurity, the integration of artificial intelligence (AI) is revolutionizing the traditional Security Operations Centres (SOCs). This section explores how AI is transforming traditional SOCs, enhancing threat detection, response capabilities, and overall security posture, ushering in a new era of cyber defence.

Augmented Detection and Analysis: AI-Powered Threat Identification

Enhanced Threat Detection: AI algorithms analyse vast amounts of data, uncovering subtle patterns and anomalies that would evade traditional methods.

Real-time Analysis: AI systems offer real-time analysis, enabling SOCs to rapidly identify and respond to threats, reducing dwell time and potential damage.

Automated Incident Response: Rapid Reaction to Threats

Swift Response: AI-driven automation allows SOCs to respond rapidly to threats, reducing manual intervention and enhancing incident resolution time.

Efficiency: Automated processes enable SOC teams to focus on strategic tasks, allowing them to prioritize and manage multiple incidents simultaneously.

Behavioural Analysis: Understanding Patterns and Anomalies

User and Entity Behaviour Analytics (UEBA): AI models learn normal user and system behaviours, flagging deviations that indicate potential threats.

Continuous Monitoring: AI-powered behavioural analysis provides continuous monitoring, detecting suspicious activities even in dynamic environments.

Predictive Analytics: Anticipating Threats Before Impact

Predictive Threat Intelligence: AI algorithms analyse historical data and current trends to forecast potential threats, enabling proactive defences.

Preventing Breaches: Predictive analytics empowers SOCs to intervene before threats escalate into significant breaches, mitigating potential damage.

Threat Hunting: Proactive Identification of Advanced Threats

Identifying Stealthy Threats: AI assists SOC analysts in proactively hunting for advanced threats that might otherwise remain hidden.

Advanced Analytics: AI-driven threat hunting employs advanced analytics to uncover complex attack techniques and malicious activities.

Machine Learning-Assisted Analysis: Scaling Up Cybersecurity

Scalability: AI scales seamlessly, handling massive volumes of data and complex analysis, which is often unattainable with traditional methods.

Speed and Efficiency: AI enables rapid analysis and decision-making, essential in modern cyber landscapes characterized by speed and agility.

Actionable Insights: AI generates insights from data, providing SOC teams with actionable information for informed decision-making.

Reduced Alert Fatigue: AI filters out false positives, ensuring that SOC teams focus on genuine threats, reducing alert fatigue.

Challenges and Considerations: Navigating the AI Transformation

Data Quality: AI success relies on high-quality and diverse training data to avoid biases and enhance accuracy.

Human Oversight: While AI automates processes, human experts remain crucial for complex decision-making and strategic planning.

The Future of AI-Enhanced SOCs: A Synergistic Approach

The integration of AI into traditional SOCs marks a transformative journey towards more effective, efficient, and proactive cyber defence. By leveraging AI's capabilities in threat detection, incident response, and predictive analytics, organizations are better poised to tackle the dynamic and complex landscape of cyber threats. The synergy between human expertise and AI-powered technologies paves the way for a more secure digital future, where traditional SOCs evolve into intelligent hubs safeguarding critical assets from an array of evolving threats.

7.1.2 AI-Powered Threat Intelligence:

Amplifying Threat Intelligence: AI's Impact on SOC's Threat Identification

In the ever-evolving landscape of cybersecurity, artificial intelligence (AI) has emerged as a transformative force, reshaping the capabilities of Security Operations Centres (SOCs). This discussion explores how AI-driven threat intelligence enhances SOC's ability to identify, analyse, and understand threats, paving the way for a more robust and proactive defence against cyber adversaries.

a. Automated Data Collection and Analysis: A Faster, Deeper Insight

Enhanced Data Gathering: AI streamlines the collection of vast and diverse threat data from numerous sources, saving time and expanding coverage.

Deeper Contextual Analysis: AI processes data at incredible speeds, enabling the identification of connections and correlations that might be missed by manual analysis.

b. Pattern Recognition and Anomaly Detection: Unearthing Hidden Threats

Pattern Identification: AI excels at recognizing patterns across massive datasets, enabling SOC to identify known threat patterns rapidly .

Anomaly Detection: AI-powered algorithms identify deviations from normal behaviour, flagging potential threats that exhibit unusual activities.

c. Real-time Threat Monitoring: Swift Response to Emerging Threats

Continuous Surveillance: AI enables real-time monitoring of threat feeds, news, and activities, ensuring that emerging threats are identified promptly.

Early Warning: AI-driven systems issue alerts and warnings as soon as new threats are detected, allowing SOC teams to initiate proactive measures.

d. Predictive Threat Assessment: Anticipating Future Attacks

Behaviour Analysis: AI learns from historical data to predict evolving threat behaviours, offering insights into the techniques adversaries might employ.

Threat Forecasting: AI models forecast potential threats, enabling SOC to prepare defences before the attacks are launched.

e. Contextualizing Threats: Bridging the Gap in Understanding

Comprehensive Analysis: AI integrates data from various sources to provide SOC teams with a comprehensive view of threats' origin, tactics, and targets.

Contextual Understanding: AI enhances threat intelligence by contextualizing information, offering a clearer understanding of adversaries' motivations and strategies.

f. Rapid Investigation and Response: AI-Driven Triage

Automated Triage: AI performs initial triage on incoming threats, classifying them based on severity and relevance, streamlining SOC workflows.

Focus on High-Impact Threats: SOC teams can focus on the most critical threats, optimizing their resources for faster and more effective response.

g. Collaboration and Sharing: A Collective defence Approach

Threat Intelligence Sharing: AI facilitates sharing threat intelligence across organizations, enabling collective defence against common adversaries.

Global Insights: AI-driven threat intelligence platforms analyse data from diverse sources, providing SOC with global threat trends and insights.

h. Ethical Considerations and Human Oversight: Striking the Balance

Responsible Usage: While AI enhances threat intelligence, human expertise remains essential to validate AI-generated insights and decisions.

Ethical Analysis: SOC teams must consider ethical implications of AI's automated decision-making and potential biases in threat analysis.

i. Towards a Proactive defence Landscape: AI-Driven Transformation

The infusion of AI into SOC's threat intelligence marks a pivotal step towards a proactive defence landscape. By automating data collection, pattern recognition, and real-time monitoring, AI empowers SOC teams to identify and understand threats faster and more comprehensively. The amalgamation of AI-driven insights with human expertise strengthens organizations' ability to anticipate, counteract, and mitigate evolving cyber threats, ultimately bolstering their resilience against the ever-changing threat landscape.

7.1.3 AI-Driven Incident Response:

How AI automates incident response processes, reducing response times.

The dynamic and fast-paced world of cybersecurity demands swift incident response to mitigate potential threats and minimize damage. Artificial Intelligence (AI) has emerged as a powerful tool that automates incident response processes, significantly reducing response times and enhancing the effectiveness of cyber defence strategies.

1. Rapid Triage and Prioritization:

AI-driven automation aids in rapidly triaging incoming alerts based on predefined criteria. By analysing various factors such as severity, impact, and threat intelligence, AI helps categorize incidents, allowing security teams to prioritize their efforts effectively.

2. Real-time Threat Detection:

AI-powered systems continuously monitor network traffic, system logs, and other data sources. When unusual patterns or anomalies are detected, AI triggers automated alerts and responses, ensuring that potential threats are addressed in real time.

3. Automated Playbooks:

AI enables the creation and execution of automated playbooks, which outline predefined actions for specific types of incidents. This minimizes the need for manual intervention and ensures a consistent and efficient response to recurring incidents.

4. Incident Validation:

AI can assess the validity of an incident by cross-referencing multiple data points. This validation process helps prevent false positives and minimizes the time wasted on investigating non-threatening events.

5. Contextual Insights:

AI augments incident data with contextual information from various sources. This assists security analysts in quickly understanding the nature of the incident, the affected assets, and the potential impact, facilitating informed decision-making.

6. Adaptive Responses:

AI-driven incident response systems learn from past responses and adapt over time. This enables them to refine their actions and responses based on the outcomes of previous incidents, leading to improved efficiency.

7. Collaboration and Coordination:

AI assists in automating communication and coordination among different teams within an organization during incident response. By providing real-time updates and notifications, AI ensures a unified and coordinated effort.

8. Containment and Remediation:

AI can automate containment and remediation actions, isolating affected systems and stopping the spread of threats. This reduces the potential impact of incidents and prevents their escalation.

9. Regulatory Compliance:

AI-driven incident response processes can be designed to adhere to regulatory requirements and compliance standards. This ensures that response actions are aligned with legal and industry guidelines.

10. Post-Incident Analysis:

After an incident is resolved, AI can analyse the response process, identify areas for improvement, and suggest modifications to incident response plans.

11. Continuous Learning and Improvement:

AI systems continually learn from the data generated during incident response, helping organizations refine their incident response strategies and enhancing overall cybersecurity posture.

7.1.4 Challenges and Considerations:

- Ensuring that AI responses align with the organization's security policies and strategies.
- Avoiding over-automation, which may lead to incorrect decisions or escalation.
- Ensuring AI systems are regularly updated to adapt to new threats and attack techniques.

Incorporating AI into incident response processes offers organizations the advantage of speed, efficiency, and accuracy. By automating various stages of incident handling, AI reduces the time it takes to detect, analyse, respond to, and recover from security incidents. As AI-driven incident response becomes more refined and integrated, security teams can focus their efforts on strategic planning, threat hunting, and addressing more complex security challenges.

Reference: AI-Powered SOCs[119]

7.2. Automation of Routine Tasks and Threat Analysis

7.2.1 Automated Threat Detection:

Empowering Cybersecurity: AI's Role in Automating Threat Detection

Artificial Intelligence (AI) is revolutionizing the field of cybersecurity by introducing automation to the process of detecting both known and unknown threats. This transformative technology equips organizations with the ability to efficiently identify malicious activities, whether they involve established attack vectors or novel, previously unseen tactics.

1. Detecting Known Threats:

AI leverages extensive threat databases and historical attack patterns to recognize known threats promptly. Machine learning algorithms analyse signatures, indicators of compromise (IOCs), and behavioural characteristics associated with previously identified malware or attack techniques.

2. Behavioural Analysis:

AI employs behavioural analysis to identify deviations from normal system activities. By understanding baseline behaviour, AI detects anomalies that could indicate a potential known threat in progress.

3. Pattern Recognition:

Machine learning models excel at pattern recognition, allowing them to identify recurring attack tactics, techniques, and procedures (TTPs). This assists in the automated detection of threats that exhibit established patterns.

4. Automating Alerts:

AI automates the generation of alerts when it identifies known threats, notifying security teams of the intrusion or malicious activity. This ensures that timely action can be taken to mitigate the threat.

5. Identifying Unknown Threats:

AI's true potential shines in its capability to detect unknown or zero-day threats. These threats lack historical data, making traditional signature-based detection ineffective.

---

[119] https://www.securitymagazine.com/articles/95264-ai-powered-security-operations-centers-the-future-of-cybersecurity

6. Anomaly Detection:

AI-powered systems employ anomaly detection to identify activities that deviate from the norm. This includes unusual network traffic, system behaviour, or user actions that could indicate an unknown threat.

7. Predictive Analytics:

By analysing vast datasets, AI can predict potential threats based on historical data and evolving attack trends. This proactive approach aids in the detection of threats that have not been previously documented.

8. Heuristic Analysis:

AI uses heuristics to evaluate the likelihood of an activity being a threat based on its characteristics and behaviours. This helps identify previously unseen threats with similar traits to known attack methods.

9. Machine Learning in Unsupervised Mode:

AI systems in unsupervised learning mode can uncover patterns and relationships in data without requiring predefined labels. This is particularly valuable for identifying new, emerging threats.

10. Automated Threat Hunting:

AI-driven systems continuously scan data for indications of unknown threats. They proactively search for suspicious patterns that may indicate the presence of novel attack vectors.

11. Adversarial Detection:

AI can detect adversarial tactics, such as polymorphic malware or code obfuscation, even if the specific attack instance is unknown.

12. Continuous Learning:

AI models learn from every identified threat, expanding their knowledge and improving their ability to recognize both known and unknown threats over time.

Challenges and Considerations:

- Ensuring that AI models are trained on diverse and representative datasets.
- Addressing false positives and negatives in automated detection.
- Adapting AI models to evolving threat landscapes to avoid obsolescence.

AI's capacity to automate the detection of both known and unknown threats elevates cybersecurity to new heights. By combining historical data, predictive analytics, and adaptive learning, AI empowers organizations to identify threats that might otherwise go unnoticed by conventional methods. This symbiotic relationship between AI and threat detection enhances cyber resilience, enabling organizations to thwart both familiar and emerging threats, and fostering a proactive, responsive defence strategy in the digital domain .

7.2.2 Streamlining Investigations:
Explanation of how AI accelerates the investigation process by correlating and analysing data.
AI-Driven Acceleration of Investigation:

Timely and effective investigation is crucial to mitigating threats and minimizing potential damage. Artificial Intelligence (AI) has emerged as a formidable ally in this endeavour, supercharging the investigation process by rapidly correlating and analysing vast amounts of data. This section explores how AI accelerates investigations through intelligent data correlation and analysis, revolutionizing the speed and accuracy of threat detection and response.

1. Swift Data Correlation:

AI-driven tools excel at connecting disparate data points, enabling the correlation of information from various sources. This ability is essential in identifying hidden relationships between seemingly unrelated events, which could indicate potential threats.

2. Real-time Analysis:

AI conducts real-time analysis of data streams, making it possible to rapidly detect and respond to threats as they unfold. This proactive approach is essential in mitigating the impact of ongoing attacks.

3. Cross-Platform Insights:

AI leverages data from multiple platforms, applications, and sources to provide a comprehensive view of potential threats. This holistic perspective aids in identifying coordinated attacks that might otherwise be missed.

4. Behavioural Analysis:

AI employs behavioural analysis to detect anomalies and deviations from normal patterns of user and system activities. By flagging unusual behaviour, AI alerts investigators to potential threats that warrant further investigation.

5. Contextual Understanding:

AI enriches investigation by providing context to data points, aiding analysts in understanding the bigger picture. This contextual information allows for informed decision-making and accurate threat assessment.

6. Automated Data Enrichment:

AI automates the process of enriching raw data with additional information from external sources, such as threat intelligence feeds and vulnerability databases. This enrichment accelerates analysis by providing relevant context.

7. Reducing False Positives:

AI's ability to accurately correlate data helps reduce false positives, allowing investigators to focus on legitimate threats. This prevents valuable time and resources from being wasted on investigating non-threatening incidents.

8. Identifying Hidden Patterns:

AI excels at identifying subtle patterns and trends within complex datasets that might go unnoticed by human analysts. These hidden patterns can be indicative of malicious activities.

9. Rapid Response Insights:

AI provides real-time insights that aid in rapid response decision-making. This is particularly important in containing and mitigating threats before they escalate.

10. Predictive Analysis:

AI's predictive capabilities extend to investigations, where it can forecast potential threat behaviours based on historical data. This foresight enables proactive measures to be taken before threats fully manifest.

11. Machine Learning Iteration:

AI models continually learn from investigations, improving their accuracy and efficiency over time. This iterative learning process refines the system's ability to correlate and analyse data effectively.

Challenges and Considerations:

- Ensuring that AI models have access to high-quality, accurate, and relevant data.
- Avoiding biases in data that could impact the accuracy of correlations and analysis.
- Training AI models to adapt to evolving threat landscapes.

Empowering Investigators with AI

AI's role in accelerating investigations by correlating and analysing data is transformative for modern cybersecurity. By rapidly connecting the dots between disparate data points and providing context-rich insights, AI enhances investigators' ability to detect and respond to threats rapidly and accurately. The fusion of human expertise with AI-powered data analysis creates a dynamic synergy that empowers cybersecurity professionals to stay ahead of adversaries, ultimately fortifying an organization's defences and ensuring a proactive and effective approach to threat management.

7.2.3 Incident Classification and Prioritization:

How AI helps classify and prioritize incidents based on their severity:

Enhancing Cybersecurity Operations

In the fast-paced world of cybersecurity, the ability to classify and prioritize incidents efficiently is paramount. Artificial Intelligence (AI) has emerged as a game-changer in this domain, revolutionizing how cybersecurity teams manage the multitude of alerts and incidents that flood their systems. This section explores the ways AI aids in classifying and prioritizing incidents based on their severity, optimizing response efforts and mitigating potential damage.

1. Incident Triage and Categorization:

AI employs machine learning algorithms to rapidly classify incoming incidents into predefined categories. This initial categorization helps establish a baseline for further analysis.

2. Severity Assessment:

AI-driven systems assess the severity of incidents by analysing various factors, including the type of attack, affected assets, potential impact, and relevance to the organization's critical operations.

3. Contextual Analysis:

AI enriches incident data with context, such as affected systems, users, and the potential chain of events. This context aids in accurate severity assessment and appropriate prioritization.

4. Data Correlation:

AI correlates incidents with historical data and ongoing activities to identify patterns and potential connections. This assists in understanding the broader threat landscape and gauging the potential impact of incidents.

5. Prioritization Algorithms:

AI employs sophisticated algorithms to assign priority levels to incidents based on established criteria, such as the risk level, potential damage, and likelihood of successful mitigation.

6. Real-time Analysis:

AI conducts real-time analysis of incoming incidents, allowing for rapid evaluation and response. This is crucial in handling incidents that require immediate attention to prevent escalation.

7. Predictive Analytics:

AI's predictive capabilities forecast the potential impact of incidents and help predict their trajectory. This information guides prioritization efforts and resource allocation.

8. Risk Assessment:

AI evaluates the potential risk associated with each incident, factoring in the organization's vulnerabilities and threat landscape. This aids in aligning incident response with overall risk management strategies.

9. Human-AI Collaboration:

AI-generated incident severity assessments are combined with human expertise to ensure accuracy and contextual understanding. This collaboration refines AI models and enhances decision-making.

10. Mitigation Recommendations:

AI-generated prioritization often comes with mitigation recommendations tailored to the specific incident. These suggestions assist cybersecurity teams in formulating effective response strategies.

11. Reducing Alert Fatigue:

By accurately categorizing and prioritizing incidents, AI reduces the volume of false positives and helps prevent alert fatigue among security analysts.

7.3.4 Challenges and Considerations:
- Ensuring AI models consider the organization's unique context and threat landscape.
- Addressing biases that might influence AI's severity assessment.
- Ensuring continuous learning to adapt to evolving threat scenarios.

7.3.5 An Agile Approach to Incident Management

AI's contribution to incident classification and prioritization is transformative, offering cybersecurity teams the tools they need to effectively manage the flood of incidents and alerts. By employing AI's real-time analysis, predictive capabilities, and risk assessment algorithms, organizations can streamline their response efforts, allocate resources efficiently, and focus on mitigating the most critical threats first. The fusion of AI's computational prowess with human expertise forms a powerful partnership that enhances the agility and effectiveness of incident management, ultimately strengthening an organization's cyber resilience and ability to respond rapidly to emerging threats.

Reference: AI Automation in SOCs[120]

7.3. Benefits and Limitations of AI-Powered SOCs

7.3.1 Benefits of AI-Powered SOCs:

Advantages of AI-Enhanced Security Operations Centres (SOCs): Boosting Efficiency and Accuracy

In the ever-evolving landscape of cybersecurity, Security Operations Centres (SOCs) play a key role in detecting, mitigating, and responding to threats. The integration of Artificial Intelligence (AI) into SOCs has brought about transformative advancements, revolutionizing how organizations defend against cyberattacks. This section explores the advantages of AI-enhanced SOCs, highlighting how they enhance efficiency and accuracy in safeguarding digital assets.

---

[120] https://www.cio.com/article/3432929/how-ai-can-automate-soc-activities.html

1. Rapid Threat Detection:

AI-powered SOCs possess the capability to detect threats in real-time by analysing vast amounts of data quickly. This speed is crucial in identifying and responding to threats before they escalate.

2. Proactive Incident Response:

AI-driven SOCs predict potential threats and vulnerabilities based on historical data and ongoing trends. This proactive approach enables organizations to address vulnerabilities before they are exploited.

3. Automation of Routine Tasks:

AI automates routine and repetitive tasks, freeing up human analysts to focus on complex and strategic activities. This efficiency leads to better resource allocation and higher productivity.

4. Advanced Threat Analytics:

AI analyses large datasets to identify patterns, anomalies, and potential threats that might go unnoticed by human analysts. This enhanced analytics capability improves threat detection accuracy.

5. Reduced False Positives:

AI minimizes false positive alerts by learning from historical data and refining its understanding of legitimate network behaviour. This reduces alert fatigue among security analysts.

6. Enhanced Incident Investigation:

AI assists analysts by providing contextual information and correlations between events, enabling faster and more accurate incident investigation.

7. Accurate Threat Prioritization:

AI assesses the severity and potential impact of threats, allowing organizations to prioritize incidents based on risk. This ensures resources are allocated effectively.

8. Adaptive defence Strategies:

AI learns from previous incidents and adapts defence strategies accordingly. This dynamic approach evolves with the changing threat landscape.

9. Real-time Analysis:

AI processes data in real-time, enabling the detection and response to threats as they unfold. This speed is vital in preventing attacks from causing significant damage.

10. Improved Incident Resolution Time:

AI's quick identification and analysis of threats enable faster incident response and resolution, reducing the time an attacker has to operate within the network.

11. Scalability:

AI-driven SOCs can scale seamlessly to handle increasing volumes of data and threats. This scalability is essential in today's highly dynamic threat environment.

12. Data-driven Insights:

AI provides data-driven insights that guide decision-making and inform security strategies. These insights empower organizations to make informed choices based on accurate analysis.

13. Continuous Learning:

AI systems continuously learn and improve over time, adapting to new attack vectors and evolving threat tactics.

- Ensuring AI models are well-trained and remain unbiased.
- Addressing the potential for adversarial attacks against AI-driven systems.
- Balancing AI automation with human oversight for critical decision-making.

Empowering SOCs with AI:

AI-enhanced SOCs are at the forefront of the battle against cyber threats, bringing unparalleled efficiency and accuracy to cybersecurity operations. By automating routine tasks, rapidly detecting threats, and providing advanced analytics, AI not only amplifies the capabilities of security analysts but also ensures that organizations can respond to threats with the speed and precision required in today's digital landscape. The fusion of AI's computational capabilities with human expertise creates a formidable synergy that bolsters an organization's defence mechanisms, ultimately leading to increased resilience and a higher level of protection against evolving cyber threats

7.3.2 Limitations of AI in SOCs:

Navigating Challenges in AI-Enhanced Cybersecurity:

Balancing False Positives/Negatives and Human Oversight, We've already covered False Positives and false Negatives in a previous section, in this chapter we will explore the link between what we learned earlier and SOCs

While the integration of Artificial Intelligence (AI) in cybersecurity offers numerous benefits, it also comes with its fair share of challenges. Two significant challenges that organizations often face when implementing AI-driven security solutions are the occurrence of false positives and false negatives, as well as the need to maintain human oversight. This section explores these challenges in detail and discusses the importance of finding a balance between AI automation and human intervention.

1. False Positives and False Negatives:

False Positives: These occur when AI systems incorrectly identify benign activities as malicious threats. This can lead to alert fatigue among security analysts, causing them to disregard legitimate alerts due to the sheer volume of false alarms.

False Negatives: These are instances where AI systems fail to identify actual threats, allowing malicious activities to go undetected. This can result in serious breaches and significant damage to the organization's security posture.

2. The Role of Human Expertise:

While AI can process large volumes of data quickly, human expertise is crucial for understanding the context of incidents, assessing the potential impact, and making complex decisions.

3. Complex Threat Scenarios:

Sophisticated threats often involve multiple stages and evasive techniques that might elude AI systems. Human analysts are better equipped to uncover subtle, multi-vector attacks that can bypass automated systems.

4. New and Evolving Threats:

AI systems may struggle to recognize novel attack vectors or rapidly evolving threats. Human analysts possess the adaptability to respond to emerging threat patterns.

5. Lack of Contextual Understanding:

AI may interpret patterns as threats without understanding the context. Human analysts can factor in business operations and the broader threat landscape to make more accurate judgments.

6. Ethical and Legal Considerations:

The automation of security processes raises ethical questions about the potential impact on privacy and civil liberties. Human oversight is vital to ensure AI systems align with legal and ethical standards.

7. Adversarial Attacks:

Attackers may intentionally craft attacks to deceive AI systems. Human intervention is essential to recognize anomalies that deviate from established patterns.

8. Data Quality and Bias:

AI systems rely on data for training, and if this data is biased or incomplete, it can lead to skewed outcomes. Human oversight is necessary to identify and rectify biased decision-making.

9. Decision Transparency:

AI systems can sometimes make decisions that are difficult to explain or understand. Human analysts ensure transparency and accountability in the decision-making process.

10. Continuous Learning:

AI models require continuous learning to adapt to evolving threats. Human analysts play a role in refining AI algorithms based on new insights and threat intelligence.

Balancing AI Automation with Human Oversight:

The key to addressing these challenges lies in achieving a harmonious balance between AI automation and human oversight. While AI can rapidly process and analyse data, human analysts bring critical thinking, context, and the ability to make nuanced decisions. Effective strategies include:

- Regular Training and Tuning: Continuously train AI models using updated threat intelligence and real-world scenarios to improve accuracy and reduce false positives/negatives.
- Human Verification: Implement a process where human analysts review and validate AI-generated alerts before taking action, reducing the risk of overreliance on automated decisions.
- Collaborative Approach: Foster collaboration between AI systems and human analysts to leverage their respective strengths for accurate threat detection and response.

A Synergistic Approach

AI's role in cybersecurity is undoubtedly transformative, but it is not without its challenges. By embracing a synergistic approach that combines AI's computational capabilities with human intuition and expertise, organizations can create a more robust defence posture. Leveraging AI for automation while maintaining human oversight ensures that the strengths of both AI and humans are harnessed to identify and address cyber threats effectively, striking the delicate balance between speed, accuracy, and informed decision-making.

7.3.3 AI-Human Collaboration:

Synergy Between AI and Human Analysts in SOC Operations: A Powerful Collaboration

The integration of Artificial Intelligence (AI) in Security Operations Centres (SOCs) has reshaped the landscape of cybersecurity. This transformation goes beyond automation; it involves a dynamic synergy between AI-driven technologies and human analysts. This section explores the ways AI and human analysts collaborate within SOC operations to enhance threat detection, response, and overall cybersecurity effectiveness.

1. Rapid Data Processing and Analysis:

AI excels at processing massive volumes of data quickly, identifying patterns, and flagging potential threats. This capability enables SOC teams to focus on higher-level tasks rather than manual data processing.

2. Anomaly Detection and Pattern Recognition:

AI detects anomalies that may elude human analysts due to their subtlety or complexity. It identifies unusual behaviours, patterns, or deviations from the norm that might signal a cyber threat.

3. Real-time Monitoring and Detection:

AI continuously monitors network activities in real-time, identifying suspicious activities and potential threats as they occur. This proactive approach enhances response time and reduces the window of exposure to threats.

4. Contextual Insights:

AI provides contextual insights by correlating vast datasets, helping human analysts better understand the scope and potential impact of an incident. This information aids in informed decision-making.

5. Prioritization and Risk Assessment:

AI assists in categorizing and prioritizing threats based on their severity and potential impact. This helps human analysts allocate resources effectively and respond to the most critical threats first.

6. Complex Threat Analysis:

AI can analyse multifaceted attack patterns, even in cases where human analysts might struggle due to the complexity and sheer volume of data involved.

7. Reducing Alert Fatigue:

AI filters and validates alerts, reducing the number of false positives and alleviating alert fatigue among human analysts. This ensures that analysts focus on high-priority threats.

8. Adapting to New Threats:

AI models can learn from new data and adapt to evolving threat landscapes. This adaptability assists in recognizing emerging threats and attack vectors.

9. Automated Routine Tasks:

AI automates repetitive tasks, enabling human analysts to concentrate on tasks that require critical thinking and strategic decision-making.

10. Combining Human Expertise:

Human analysts bring domain expertise, intuition, and contextual understanding to the table. They can interpret complex situations, identify subtle indicators, and make nuanced judgments.

11. Decision Validation:

Human analysts validate AI-generated insights and decisions, ensuring that responses align with organizational goals and ethical considerations.

12. Adaptation to Business Context:

Human analysts understand the broader business context and operational intricacies, ensuring that security decisions are aligned with the organization's objectives.

13. Ethical and Legal Considerations:

Human analysts address ethical dilemmas and legal considerations associated with incident response, ensuring actions are compliant and ethical.

Conclusion: A Harmonious Collaboration

The synergy between AI and human analysts within SOC operations is a harmonious collaboration that maximizes the strengths of both entities. AI-driven technologies enhance efficiency, automate processes, and provide rapid analysis, while human analysts contribute their expertise, intuition, and adaptability. This partnership allows organizations to harness the full spectrum of capabilities required to effectively combat today's evolving cyber threats. The result is a dynamic defence posture that combines the speed and precision of AI with the nuanced decision-making and contextual understanding of human analysts, ultimately fortifying the organization's cybersecurity resilience.

Reference: Benefits and Challenges of AI in SOCs[121]

7.4. Case Study: IBM Watson for Cybersecurity

7.4.1 IBM Watson's Role in SOCs:

Case Study: Enhancing SOC Capabilities with IBM Watson's AI-Driven Insights

Introduction:

IBM Watson, an advanced AI platform, has played a key role in reshaping Security Operations Centres (SOCs) by providing powerful AI-driven insights that enhance threat detection, response, and overall cybersecurity effectiveness. This case study explores how IBM Watson's AI capabilities have revolutionized SOC operations through its ability to analyse vast amounts of data, identify threats, and empower human analysts to make informed decisions.

Background:

Large organizations handle massive volumes of security data daily, making it challenging for human analysts to keep pace with the rapidly evolving threat landscape. This case study highlights how IBM Watson addresses this challenge by leveraging AI to assist SOC teams in detecting and responding to threats effectively.

AI-Powered Insights:

IBM Watson employs advanced machine learning algorithms and natural language processing to analyse security data from diverse sources, including network traffic, logs, and external threat intelligence feeds. It identifies patterns, anomalies, and potential threats that might go unnoticed by traditional methods.

1. Threat Detection:

IBM Watson's AI algorithms excel at detecting subtle indicators of compromise and potential breaches. By processing real-time data and historical information, it identifies deviations from normal behaviour, pinpointing anomalies that require further investigation.

---

[121] https://www.helpnetsecurity.com/2022/02/24/ai-security-operations-centers/

2. Contextual Analysis:

The platform provides human analysts with context-rich insights by correlating data from various sources. It presents comprehensive information about the threat, the affected assets, and potential attack vectors, enabling analysts to make informed decisions quickly.

3. Prioritization:

IBM Watson's AI prioritizes alerts based on severity and potential impact, allowing SOC teams to focus on the most critical threats first. This helps allocate resources efficiently and reduce response times.

4. Threat Intelligence:

The AI-driven platform integrates threat intelligence from various sources, enriching the understanding of emerging threats and attack patterns. It offers recommendations on mitigation strategies based on the latest threat landscape.

5. Adaptive Learning:

IBM Watson continuously learns from new data, adapting its models to evolving threat trends. This ensures that the platform remains effective in identifying new attack vectors and patterns.

6. Human-AI Collaboration:

Human analysts collaborate with IBM Watson's AI-powered insights to validate alerts, review findings, and fine-tune threat models. This partnership enhances the accuracy of threat detection and response.

Benefits and Impact:

- Efficiency: IBM Watson's AI-driven insights accelerate threat detection and response, enabling analysts to address threats rapidly and reduce dwell time.
- Accuracy: The platform's AI algorithms minimize false positives, allowing analysts to focus on genuine threats, reducing alert fatigue.
- Contextual Understanding: The contextual insights provided by AI help human analysts understand the scope and potential impact of incidents, aiding in more informed decision-making.
- Scalability: The ability to analyse vast amounts of data enables organizations to scale their cybersecurity efforts without compromising effectiveness.

IBM Watson's AI-driven insights have transformed SOC operations by combining the computational power of AI with the critical thinking and decision-making skills of human analysts. This collaboration enhances threat detection, response times, and overall cybersecurity posture. By leveraging AI to analyse data, provide context, and prioritize threats, IBM Watson empowers organizations to proactively defend against evolving cyber threats, making SOC operations more efficient, effective, and adaptive.

Reference: IBM Watson for Cybersecurity : https://www.ibm.com/cloud/learn/watson-for-cybersecurity

7.4.2 Darktrace AI-Powered SOC Solutions:

Exploration of Darktrace's AI Technology in Boosting SOC Effectiveness

Introduction:

Darktrace, a leading cybersecurity company, has introduced innovative AI technology that significantly enhances the effectiveness of Security Operations Centres (SOCs). This section explores how Darktrace's AI-driven platform revolutionizes SOC operations by providing real-time threat detection, rapid response, and proactive defence mechanisms.

Darktrace's AI-Powered Platform:

Darktrace's AI technology is built on the principles of self-learning cyber AI, inspired by the human immune system's ability to detect and respond to anomalies. The platform employs unsupervised machine learning algorithms and AI-driven behavioural analysis to detect subtle deviations from normal behaviour across an organization's digital environment.

Key Features and Benefits:

1. Real-time Threat Detection:

   Darktrace's AI continuously monitors network traffic, identifying patterns and anomalies that may indicate cyber threats. It detects both known and unknown threats, including zero-day attacks and sophisticated breaches.

2. Autonomous Response:

   The platform goes beyond detection, allowing for autonomous response when unusual activities are identified. This may involve quarantining suspicious devices or segments of the network to prevent potential threats from spreading.

3. Machine Learning for Baseline Behaviour:

   Darktrace's AI establishes a baseline understanding of normal behaviour within an organization's network. Any deviations from this baseline are flagged for investigation, enabling the detection of anomalies even without predefined rules.

4. Threat Visualization:

   Darktrace's platform provides detailed visualizations of detected threats, offering contextual insights to SOC analysts. This visualization aids in understanding the scope and impact of potential incidents.

5. Threat Investigation and Prioritization:

   The platform categorizes and prioritizes threats based on their severity and potential impact. This empowers SOC teams to focus on the most critical incidents and allocate resources efficiently.

6. Adaptive Learning:

   Darktrace's AI learns from new data and adapts to evolving threat landscapes, ensuring that the platform remains effective in identifying new attack vectors.

7. Combining AI and Human Expertise:

   Darktrace emphasizes the importance of human analysts' expertise in validating and contextualizing AI-generated insights. The platform encourages a collaborative approach between AI and human analysts.

Impact and Significance:

- **Speed and Accuracy:** Darktrace's AI-driven platform provides near-instantaneous threat detection, reducing the dwell time of cyber threats within an organization's network.
- **Proactive defence:** By identifying emerging threats, even those not previously seen, the platform enables organizations to take proactive measures before incidents escalate.

- **Minimized False Positives:** The self-learning nature of the AI reduces false positives by focusing on genuine anomalies, reducing alert fatigue among SOC teams.
- **Adaptation to Evolving Threats:** Darktrace's platform evolves alongside the threat landscape, adapting to new attack methods and tactics.
- **Incident Response Efficiency:** The platform's autonomous response capabilities minimize the time between threat detection and mitigation, limiting potential damage.

Darktrace's AI technology marks a significant leap forward in enhancing SOC effectiveness. By providing real-time, AI-powered threat detection and response capabilities, the platform empowers organizations to tackle cyber threats more efficiently and proactively. Darktrace's combination of machine learning, autonomous response, and collaboration with human analysts creates a powerful synergy that strengthens an organization's cybersecurity posture and defends against a wide range of cyber threats.

Reference: Darktrace AI-Powered SOC[122]

Chapter 8: Future Trends and Challenges in AI Cybersecurity

8.1. Exploring the Future of AI in Cybersecurity

8.1.1 The Evolution of AI in Cybersecurity:

Evolution of AI's Role in Cybersecurity

---

[122] https://www.darktrace.com/en/solutions/security-operations/

Artificial Intelligence (AI) has made remarkable strides in reshaping cybersecurity practices, but its journey is far from over. As technology continues to advance, AI's role in cybersecurity is poised to evolve further, offering new possibilities and challenges.

1. Enhanced Threat Detection:
AI's ability to rapidly analyse massive datasets for anomalies will continue to be a cornerstone of cybersecurity. With more refined algorithms and improved data processing capabilities, AI will identify even more subtle deviations, aiding in early threat detection.

2. Predictive Capabilities:
As AI algorithms become more sophisticated, they'll be able to predict potential cyber threats by analysing historical data and patterns. This will empower cybersecurity teams to be proactive rather than reactive, mitigating threats before they escalate.

3. Autonomous Response:
AI will increasingly take on autonomous response capabilities, rapidly neutralizing threats without human intervention. However, balancing automated responses with human oversight to prevent false positives and unintended consequences will remain a critical challenge.

4. Behavioural Analysis and Contextual Understanding:
Future AI systems will dive deeper into behavioural analysis, not only detecting anomalies but also understanding the context behind them. This will enable AI to provide richer insights to human analysts, aiding in quicker and more informed decision-making.

5. Adversarial AI and defence:
AI-powered cybersecurity will also grapple with adversarial AI—malicious actors using AI to launch attacks. Consequently, the defensive AI will need to be capable of countering adversarial AI techniques and developing robust defence mechanisms.

6. Privacy and Ethical Considerations:
As AI analyses vast amounts of data, privacy concerns will become more pronounced. Striking a balance between effective threat detection and preserving user privacy will be a focal point, requiring robust ethical frameworks.

7. Human-AI Collaboration:
AI will increasingly act as a force multiplier for human analysts, providing them with insights, recommendations, and context. Effective collaboration between humans and AI will be essential to optimize cybersecurity operations.

8. Continuous Learning and Adaptation:
AI systems will continuously learn from new data and experiences, evolving to counter emerging threats. This adaptability will be crucial as cyber threats constantly evolve.

9. Interconnected Security:
AI's integration will extend beyond individual systems to interconnect various security layers, creating a holistic defence mechanism. AI-driven insights will help organizations visualize and respond to threats across their entire digital landscape.

10. Regulatory Frameworks:
AI's growing importance in cybersecurity will likely lead to the development of regulatory frameworks to ensure responsible AI use. Compliance with these frameworks will be essential for organizations deploying AI-based cybersecurity solutions.

The future of AI in cybersecurity holds immense potential. As AI continues to evolve, it will become an integral component of cyber defence strategies. By leveraging AI's capabilities in threat detection, prediction, response, and collaboration with human experts, organizations will be better equipped to tackle the dynamic and complex landscape of cyber threats. While exciting opportunities lie ahead, careful consideration of ethical, privacy, and regulatory aspects will be crucial to harness AI's benefits responsibly and effectively.

8.1.2 AI and Autonomous Systems:

Exploring the Potential of AI-Powered Autonomous Cybersecurity Systems

The rapid advancement of Artificial Intelligence (AI) has paved the way for revolutionary changes in the field of cybersecurity. One of the most intriguing possibilities is the development of AI-powered autonomous cybersecurity systems, capable of detecting, preventing, and mitigating cyber threats without human intervention. This section explores the potential and implications of such systems in the domain of cybersecurity.

Advantages of AI-Powered Autonomous Cybersecurity Systems:

1. **Real-Time Threat Detection:** Autonomous systems equipped with AI algorithms can continuously monitor network traffic and systems, detecting anomalies and malicious activities in real-time. This immediate threat detection minimizes the time between an attack's initiation and its containment.
2. **Speed and Accuracy:** AI systems can analyse vast amounts of data at incredible speeds, far surpassing human capabilities. This speed is crucial in identifying and responding to threats that evolve rapidly .
3. **24/7 Operations:** Human-operated security systems have limitations, including the need for breaks and sleep. AI-powered systems, on the other hand, can operate 24/7, providing round-the-clock protection against cyber threats.
4. **Adaptive defence:** Autonomous systems can adapt to changing threat landscapes by learning from new data. This adaptability ensures that the system remains effective against evolving and sophisticated threats.
5. **Reduced Human Error:** Human analysts can make errors due to fatigue, distractions, or oversight. AI systems minimize the risk of such errors and offer consistent threat analysis.
6. **Scalability:** As organizations expand their digital footprint, managing security becomes increasingly complex. AI-powered systems can scale effortlessly to cover a vast network and multitude of devices.
7. **Threat Prediction:** Autonomous systems can predict potential threats by analysing historical data and identifying patterns that could indicate impending attacks. This predictive capability allows for proactive defence strategies.
8. **Automated Incident Response:** In addition to detection, autonomous systems can autonomously respond to threats by isolating affected areas, restricting access, or applying patches to vulnerabilities.

Challenges and Considerations:

    a. **False Positives/Negatives:** Ensuring that the system doesn't generate excessive false alarms (false positives) or miss genuine threats (false negatives) is a critical challenge.

    b. **Adversarial Attacks:** Malicious actors could potentially exploit vulnerabilities in AI algorithms to launch adversarial attacks that bypass the system's defences.

    c. **Ethical Implications:** Granting AI systems the authority to make decisions about security raises ethical questions, such as accountability for errors or unintended consequences.

    d. **Transparency and Explainability:** For AI to gain trust, its decision-making processes must be transparent and explainable to human analysts.

    e. **Human Oversight:** While autonomy is advantageous, human oversight is essential to validate AI-generated insights and make critical decisions.

The potential of AI-powered autonomous cybersecurity systems is immense. They have the capacity to transform the cybersecurity landscape by providing swift, proactive, and efficient defence against a wide array of threats. As AI technology advances and the challenges are addressed, we can expect to witness the gradual integration of such systems into organizations' security strategies. The symbiotic relationship between human expertise and AI capabilities will likely be the cornerstone of successful autonomous cybersecurity systems, offering a powerful defence against ever-evolving cyber threats.

8.1.3 AI in Predictive Analysis:

Enhancing Predictive Analysis with AI for Threat Identification and Response

Predictive analysis, a cornerstone of modern cybersecurity, is poised to undergo a significant transformation with the integration of Artificial Intelligence (AI). AI's ability to process vast amounts of data, identify patterns, and make informed predictions holds the potential to revolutionize how threats are identified and responded to in cybersecurity.

1. Data-Driven Insights:
AI excels at analysing historical and real-time data to identify patterns that might not be apparent to human analysts. By ingesting a wide range of data sources – from network logs to user behaviour – AI enhances the accuracy of predictive analysis.

2. Early Threat Detection:
Traditional predictive analysis often relies on historical trends. AI, however, can detect deviations from these trends in real-time. By identifying unusual patterns, AI predicts potential threats before they escalate into major breaches.

3. Behavioural Analysis:
AI-driven predictive analysis can monitor user and network behaviour, learning what constitutes "normal." When deviations occur, the system can rapidly flag these anomalies, indicating a possible threat.

4. Contextual Understanding:
AI's ability to correlate data across various dimensions provides a more comprehensive view of the threat landscape. It considers contextual factors such as time of day, user roles, and previous incidents to refine predictions.

5. Sophisticated Threat Modelling:
AI can simulate various threat scenarios based on historical data, helping cybersecurity teams assess the potential impact and likelihood of different attacks. This assists in prioritizing responses and allocating resources effectively.

6. Adaptive Learning:

As AI continuously learns from new data, its predictive capabilities improve over time. It adapts to evolving threats and incorporates new attack techniques into its analysis.

7. Reducing False Positives:

AI's advanced pattern recognition reduces the occurrence of false positives. By analysing data comprehensively, AI can distinguish genuine threats from innocuous anomalies.

8. Accelerating Incident Response:

With early threat detection and accurate predictions, AI streamlines incident response. Cybersecurity teams can rapidly focus their efforts on addressing imminent threats, minimizing damage and downtime.

9. Threat Hunting:

AI empowers proactive threat hunting by identifying subtle indicators that might evade human detection. This shifts the focus from reactive responses to proactive defence.

10. Automated Decision Support:

AI provides human analysts with insights and recommendations, aiding in informed decision-making. This collaboration between AI and humans optimizes response strategies.

11. Continuous Monitoring:

AI's tireless monitoring ensures that threats are not missed, even during off-hours. This around-the-clock vigilance strengthens an organization's security posture.

AI's integration into predictive analysis marks a significant advancement in threat identification and response. Its ability to process vast data, detect anomalies, and predict potential threats enhances the effectiveness of cybersecurity strategies. By marrying human expertise with AI-driven insights, organizations can develop more proactive, agile, and accurate defence mechanisms. The evolution of AI-driven predictive analysis promises to play a key role in staying ahead of the ever-evolving cyber threat landscape.

Reference: The Future of AI in Cybersecurity[123]

8.2. AI-Driven Adaptive Attacks and Defensive Strategies

8.2.1 AI-Enhanced Attack Techniques:
Introduction to how attackers will increasingly utilize AI in crafting sophisticated attacks.
Introduction: The Rise of AI-Powered Sophisticated Attacks

The evolving landscape of cybersecurity is witnessing a paradigm shift as attackers increasingly harness the power of Artificial Intelligence (AI) to craft more sophisticated and potent cyberattacks. Just as organizations are leveraging AI to enhance their defence mechanisms, cybercriminals are harnessing AI's capabilities to develop stealthier, adaptive, and highly targeted attacks. This section covers the emerging trend of attackers utilizing AI to orchestrate cyber assaults that pose significant challenges to traditional security measures.

---

[123] https://www.csoonline.com/article/3503653/the-future-of-ai-in-cybersecurity.html

1. AI-Driven Automation:

Attackers are exploiting AI's automation capabilities to streamline various stages of an attack, from reconnaissance to execution. AI automates the arduous task of identifying vulnerabilities, devising attack strategies, and even customizing malware.

2. Evasion and Stealth:

AI enables attackers to create malware that can morph, evade detection, and mimic legitimate activities. These AI-generated tactics make it challenging for traditional security solutions to discern between malicious and benign actions.

3. Adaptive Attacks:

AI-powered attacks possess the ability to learn from an organization's defence mechanisms. As security measures evolve, attackers' AI algorithms can adapt to bypass these changes, rendering them ineffective.

4. Precision Targeting:

Attackers employ AI-driven analysis of vast datasets to identify high-value targets, thus increasing the success rate of their attacks. This targeting can exploit vulnerabilities unique to a particular organization.

5. Social Engineering Enhancement:

AI empowers attackers to personalize social engineering attacks by analysing vast amounts of data to craft convincing spear-phishing emails or other forms of manipulation.

6. Automated Response:

Attackers use AI to automate responses to defenders' countermeasures. This rapid adaptation makes it difficult for security teams to stay ahead.

7. Scale and Speed:

AI allows attackers to launch attacks at an unprecedented scale and speed. Automated attacks can overwhelm systems before human defenders can respond effectively.

8. Adversarial AI:

Malicious actors can deploy adversarial AI to exploit weaknesses in AI-powered security systems. This cat-and-mouse game challenges AI's ability to distinguish real threats from adversarial manipulation.

9. Camouflaged Attacks:

AI can create malware that mimics legitimate software behaviours, making detection even harder for security systems.

10. Hiding in Plain Sight:

Attackers can use AI to analyse network patterns, identifying normal traffic and mimicking it to avoid detection.

As AI technology matures, attackers' ability to harness its capabilities to create more sophisticated and evasive cyberattacks will increase. Traditional cybersecurity measures, while essential, must evolve to counter the AI-powered threats. Organizations need to recognize the potential of AI-driven attacks and invest in proactive defence strategies that combine AI-enhanced tools with human expertise. In this era of AI-driven threats, staying ahead demands continuous innovation and a holistic approach to cybersecurity.

8.2.2 AI-Driven Defensive Tactics:

Using AI to Dynamically Adapt Cybersecurity Defences Against Adaptive Attacks

In the ever-evolving landscape of cybersecurity, attackers are increasingly employing adaptive tactics to bypass traditional defences. As adversaries become more sophisticated, the need for dynamic and intelligent defence mechanisms has never been greater. This section explores how Artificial Intelligence (AI) is playing a key role in enabling cybersecurity defences to dynamically adjust and counter adaptive attacks.

1. Real-Time Threat Detection:
AI-powered systems can continuously monitor network traffic and identify anomalies that signify potential adaptive attacks. By analysing patterns and behaviours in real-time, AI can detect deviations and alert security teams promptly.

2. Behavioural Analysis:
AI examines user and system behaviours to establish baselines of normal activity. When deviations occur, such as unusual login times or unusual data transfers, AI-driven systems can flag potential threats.

3. Continuous Learning:
AI systems can learn from new data and adapt to evolving attack techniques. This ensures that defences remain up-to-date and effective against emerging threats.

4. Automated Response:
Upon detecting an adaptive attack, AI can initiate an automated response. This might include isolating compromised systems, rerouting network traffic, or deploying patches to vulnerable areas.

5. Adaptive Threat Modelling:
AI can simulate different attack scenarios based on evolving threat intelligence. This enables organizations to proactively adjust their defences against potential adaptive tactics.

6. User and Entity Behaviour Analytics (UEBA):
AI analyses user behaviour to identify suspicious activities that might indicate an adaptive attack. By identifying unusual patterns, AI can detect insider threats or compromised accounts.

7. Threat Intelligence Integration:
AI-enhanced defences can incorporate real-time threat intelligence feeds to stay updated about new attack techniques. This allows for swift adjustment of defence strategies.

8. Adaptive Authentication:
AI can assess the risk level of authentication attempts based on factors like device, location, and user behaviour. If an attempt seems anomalous, AI can prompt additional authentication steps.

9. Machine Learning Models:
Machine learning algorithms can identify subtle patterns that humans might overlook. As attackers adapt, AI algorithms can evolve alongside them, identifying new indicators of compromise.

10. Multi-Layered defence:
AI augments traditional security tools like firewalls, intrusion detection systems, and antivirus software. By continuously analysing and adapting, AI complements these measures.

In the face of adaptive attacks, traditional cybersecurity defences often fall short. AI's ability to adapt, learn, and analyse vast amounts of data in real-time provides a robust solution to counter these evolving threats. By dynamically adjusting defences based on AI-driven insights, organizations can significantly enhance their security posture. However, it's essential to strike a balance between AI automation and human oversight to ensure accurate threat detection and response. As adaptive attacks continue to evolve, the role of AI in dynamically adjusting cybersecurity defences becomes increasingly critical to maintaining a resilient and effective security strategy.

8.2.3 Cyber AI as a Decision Maker:
Exploring AI's Potential for Real-Time Attack Mitigation

In the domain of cybersecurity, the ability to respond rapidly to threats is paramount. With the increasing sophistication of cyberattacks, there's a growing need for automated and real-time decision-making to mitigate risks effectively. We will cover how Artificial Intelligence (AI) is revolutionizing the capability to make real-time decisions and take immediate actions to counteract attacks.

1. Continuous Monitoring and Analysis:
AI-powered systems can monitor vast amounts of network data in real-time. This enables them to detect anomalies, identify patterns of attack, and assess potential threats as they unfold.

2. Automated Incident Identification:
By comparing ongoing activities against predefined threat models, AI can rapidly identify deviations that match known attack patterns. This triggers immediate responses.

3. Predictive Analytics:
AI's ability to analyse historical data helps in predicting potential attack vectors and vulnerabilities. These predictive insights enable proactive measures to be taken in real-time.

4. Automated Response Orchestration:
Upon detecting an attack, AI can initiate predefined responses or orchestrations, such as blocking IP addresses, isolating compromised systems, or triggering alerts to security teams.

5. Real-Time Authentication:
AI-driven authentication systems assess the legitimacy of user activities in real-time. Suspicious behaviour can prompt immediate multi-factor authentication or account suspension.

6. Network Traffic Analysis:
AI analyses network traffic to identify unusual patterns that may indicate an ongoing attack. It can redirect or filter traffic, isolating potentially compromised sections.

7. Adaptive Threat Hunting:
AI automates threat hunting by continuously analysing data for signs of potential threats. When identified, AI can take immediate actions to neutralize or isolate them.

8. Machine Learning-Powered Decisions:
Machine learning algorithms learn from past decisions and outcomes. They can adapt their responses based on past successes, improving the efficacy of real-time actions.

9. Natural Language Processing (NLP):

NLP-powered AI can analyse and understand human-written security alerts and reports. This comprehension enables rapid response to emerging threats.

10. Automated Security Patching:

AI can identify vulnerabilities and initiate the process of applying security patches to mitigate potential exploitation in real-time.

The dynamic and rapidly evolving nature of cyber threats demands a real-time response mechanism that AI is uniquely suited to provide. AI's ability to analyse, predict, and automate actions in real-time enhances the effectiveness of cybersecurity strategies. Organizations that integrate AI-driven real-time decision-making into their defence systems are better equipped to thwart attacks before they escalate. However, while AI offers unprecedented speed and efficiency, human oversight remains essential to ensure accurate decision-making and to manage unforeseen situations. As the cybersecurity landscape evolves, harnessing AI's potential for real-time attack mitigation is pivotal in staying ahead of emerging threats and minimizing potential damage.

Reference: Adaptive Cyberattacks and AI-Driven Defences[124]

8.3. Anticipating Challenges and Opportunities in the Evolving Landscape

8.3.1 AI's Impact on the Workforce:

How AI adoption will reshape cybersecurity job roles and skill requirements?

The integration of Artificial Intelligence (AI) into cybersecurity is transforming the landscape of job roles and skill requirements within the industry. As AI technologies become more prevalent in defending against cyber threats, traditional roles are evolving, and new opportunities are emerging.

1. Automation and Routine Tasks:

AI is automating routine tasks like threat detection, analysis, and incident response. As a result, cybersecurity professionals will spend less time on repetitive activities, allowing them to focus on higher-value tasks.

2. Cyber Threat Analysts:

Analysts will leverage AI tools to identify and understand emerging threats. Their role will involve interpreting AI-generated insights, fine-tuning models, and strategizing responses.

3. AI Engineers and Data Scientists:

Demand for experts in developing, implementing, and fine-tuning AI algorithms will rise. Professionals skilled in data science, machine learning, and AI development will be essential.

4. Threat Intelligence Specialists:

Professionals in this role will need to integrate AI-driven threat intelligence platforms, ensuring they can effectively interpret and apply real-time insights in threat mitigation.

---

[124] https://www.securitymagazine.com/articles/96008-predictive-ai---anticipating-adaptive-cyberattacks

5. Ethical AI Auditors:

As AI makes decisions autonomously, experts are needed to ensure AI models are ethical, unbiased, and aligned with regulations. These auditors will hold organizations accountable for AI-driven decisions.

6. Incident Response and Remediation Experts:

AI-enabled incident response requires specialists who can interpret AI alerts, validate findings, and implement appropriate remediation measures promptly.

7. Machine Learning Security Analysts:

Professionals who understand AI's inner workings and its potential vulnerabilities will be vital. Their role includes securing AI algorithms and models against attacks.

8. Collaboration with AI:

Cybersecurity professionals will need to collaborate with AI systems, utilizing their insights to make informed decisions, adapt strategies, and manage defences effectively.

9. Understanding AI-Generated Threats:

Professionals must comprehend how adversaries use AI to launch sophisticated attacks. This understanding helps in devising countermeasures against AI-driven threats.

10. Communication and Adaptability:

As AI transforms the field, the ability to communicate AI concepts to non-technical stakeholders becomes crucial. Adaptability to rapid changes in technology is also key.

AI's impact on cybersecurity job roles is profound, enabling professionals to shift their focus from mundane tasks to strategic decision-making and innovation. Organizations will seek individuals who can integrate AI into their workflows, analyse AI-generated insights, and effectively collaborate with automated systems. Upskilling in data science, machine learning, and ethical AI considerations will be vital to thrive in this new era. While AI adoption reshapes traditional roles, the human touch remains irreplaceable in ensuring ethical use of AI, maintaining oversight, and navigating complex situations. As AI continues to evolve, cybersecurity professionals who embrace AI technologies and adapt their skillsets will be well-equipped to meet the challenges and opportunities of the future.

8.3.2 Ethical and Regulatory Considerations:
Ethical and Legal Challenges of AI in Cybersecurity

The integration of Artificial Intelligence (AI) into cybersecurity brings with it a host of ethical and legal challenges that need to be addressed. As AI technologies become more prevalent in defending against cyber threats, concerns about transparency, accountability, bias, privacy, and compliance come to the forefront. In this section we will explore the complex landscape of ethical and legal challenges associated with AI in cybersecurity.

1. Transparency and Explainability:

AI algorithms often operate as "black boxes," making it challenging to understand how decisions are reached. This lack of transparency can lead to mistrust and raises questions about the fairness of AI-driven actions.

2. Bias and Fairness:

AI algorithms can inherit biases present in training data, potentially leading to biased decisions. In cybersecurity, biased algorithms may unfairly target certain user groups, perpetuating inequalities.

3. Accountability and Responsibility:

Determining responsibility in cases of AI-generated decisions can be complex. Organizations may struggle to attribute accountability when AI systems fail or make harmful decisions.

4. Privacy and Data Protection:

AI-powered cybersecurity often involves processing vast amounts of sensitive data. Ensuring compliance with data protection regulations while using AI for analysis presents challenges in maintaining individual privacy.

5. Legal Compliance:

Using AI for threat detection and response requires adhering to legal and regulatory standards. Ambiguities in regulations regarding AI can lead to uncertainty about compliance.

6. Adversarial Attacks:

Adversaries may exploit AI vulnerabilities through adversarial attacks, fooling AI systems into making incorrect decisions. Ensuring AI defences are resilient to such attacks is crucial.

7. Ethical Decision-Making:

AI systems make decisions based on learned patterns, but ethical considerations can be complex. Determining the "right" ethical course of action can be challenging for AI systems.

8. Human Oversight:

The balance between AI automation and human oversight is critical. Ensuring that AI decisions align with human values and ethics requires continuous monitoring.

9. Cultural and Societal Impact:

AI-powered cybersecurity systems can inadvertently perpetuate existing societal biases. Deploying AI systems without considering their impact on diverse cultures can lead to unintended consequences.

10. Future Regulations and Standards:

As AI in cybersecurity evolves, regulations and standards will likely develop to address emerging ethical and legal challenges. Keeping up with evolving regulations is essential.

The ethical and legal challenges arising from the integration of AI in cybersecurity underline the need for a comprehensive framework that promotes responsible and transparent AI usage. Addressing these challenges requires collaboration among technology developers, legal experts, policymakers, and cybersecurity professionals. Ensuring AI systems are transparent, unbiased, and accountable while respecting privacy and adhering to regulations will be vital to maintain public trust and ethical integrity in the evolving landscape of AI-driven cybersecurity. Organizations must prioritize ethical considerations and legal compliance to harness the benefits of AI while mitigating potential risks.

8.3.3 Balancing Automation and Human Expertise:
Balancing AI Automation and Human Decision-Making in Cybersecurity

Striking the right balance between AI automation and human decision-making is a critical challenge in the domain of cybersecurity. While AI brings efficiency and speed, human judgment adds context and ethical considerations. Achieving this balance is essential to maximize the benefits of AI while ensuring the oversight and adaptability that humans provide.

1. Contextual Understanding:

Humans possess contextual understanding that AI may lack. They can interpret complex situations, assess the broader implications, and consider non-technical factors that AI might overlook.

2. Adaptability to New Threats:

Cyber threats constantly evolve, often requiring quick adaptations. Human analysts can understand novel attack patterns and make on-the-fly adjustments that AI algorithms might struggle with.

3. Ethical and Legal Considerations:

Humans can navigate ethical dilemmas and legal considerations that AI may not fully comprehend. Decisions related to privacy, fairness, and compliance often require human judgment.

4. Complex Decision-Making:

Certain decisions involve trade-offs and nuances that require human intuition and judgment. AI excels at data-driven decisions, but complex choices benefit from human involvement.

5. False Positives and Negatives:

AI systems can generate false positives and negatives. Human analysts can validate AI-generated alerts and prevent unnecessary actions or overlooks that might disrupt operations.

6. Unstructured Data Analysis:

AI excels at processing structured data, but unstructured data like threat narratives may require human interpretation to uncover hidden insights.

7. Crisis Management and Communication:

During cybersecurity incidents, effective communication and decision-making are crucial. Humans can lead crisis management, communication with stakeholders, and strategic decision coordination.

8. AI Oversight and Monitoring:

Humans are needed to oversee AI systems, validate their decisions, and ensure their proper functioning. This includes identifying biases or anomalies in AI outcomes.

9. Human-AI Collaboration:

Rather than a competition, the ideal approach is a collaboration between humans and AI. Humans can train AI models, fine-tune algorithms, and guide them toward ethical behaviour.

10. Learning and Improvement Loop:

Human input is essential for training and improving AI systems. Continuous feedback from human analysts helps AI algorithms become more accurate and aligned with real-world scenarios.

The key to effective cybersecurity lies in finding the equilibrium between AI automation and human decision-making. AI enhances efficiency, processes vast amounts of data, and detects patterns, but it requires human oversight for validation, context, and ethical considerations. The future of cybersecurity lies in a harmonious collaboration between AI and human experts, leveraging each other's strengths to create a robust defence against cyber threats. Organizational strategies must focus on integrating AI as an enhancer of human capabilities, valuing both the speed and accuracy of AI-driven automation and the critical thinking and adaptability of human professionals.

8.4. Case Study: AI-Driven Adaptive Attacks

8.4.1 Emotet and AI-Generated Emails:

Case Study: Emotet Malware Campaign's AI-Generated Phishing Emails

The Emotet malware campaign stands as a significant example of threat actors harnessing AI technology to elevate the effectiveness of their cyberattacks. Emotet, a versatile and notorious malware strain, employed AI-generated phishing emails to deceive users and propagate malware, illustrating the evolving landscape of cyber threats.

Background:

Emotet, initially identified in 2014 as a banking trojan, evolved into a sophisticated botnet known for delivering various payloads, including ransomware and other malware. In early 2021, security researchers discovered instances where Emotet employed AI-generated content to enhance its phishing campaigns.

AI-Generated Phishing Emails:

Emotet utilized AI to generate persuasive and contextually relevant phishing emails. This involved crafting subject lines, email bodies, and attachments that closely resembled legitimate communication, making it difficult for recipients to identify them as malicious. The AI technology enabled the malware to adapt its tactics to mimic the communication styles of genuine senders.

Key Aspects:

1. **Adaptation and Personalization:** Emotet's AI technology allowed it to personalize phishing emails based on recipient characteristics, enhancing the probability of engagement. This made the emails more convincing and harder to identify as phishing attempts.
2. **Diverse Language and Context:** The AI-driven emails spanned multiple languages and mimicked common conversation topics, making them more likely to bypass email filters and resonate with recipients.
3. **Attachment and Payload Manipulation:** Emotet leveraged AI-generated content for malicious attachments, such as infected Microsoft Office documents. The AI-generated content added a layer of sophistication to exploit potential vulnerabilities.

Impact:

The AI-generated phishing emails significantly improved Emotet's success rate in tricking users into clicking links or downloading attachments. This contributed to the propagation of the malware, leading to data breaches, financial losses, and potential network compromise.

Detection and Mitigation:

Identifying AI-generated phishing emails became challenging for traditional email security solutions due to their increased sophistication. Adaptive and AI-powered security measures were required to detect the subtle differences that set these emails apart from legitimate ones.

Lessons Learned:

1. **Adversarial Use of AI:** Emotet's case demonstrates that threat actors are integrating AI into their attacks to create more convincing and tailored phishing attempts.
2. **Evolving Threat Landscape:** The incident highlights the importance of staying updated on evolving cyber threats and adjusting cybersecurity strategies accordingly.

---

[125] https://www.forbes.com/sites/forbestechcouncil/2022/03/04/how-ai-is-changing-the-landscape-of-cybersecurity/?sh=3103a0d039de

3. **Adaptive Security Solutions:** Traditional security methods may struggle to detect AI-generated threats. Organizations need to adopt advanced AI-powered security solutions that can identify patterns unique to such attacks.

The Emotet malware campaign's use of AI-generated phishing emails underscores the relentless innovation of cybercriminals. It serves as a reminder that the cybersecurity community must remain vigilant, embracing advanced AI-powered solutions to counter evolving threats effectively. As AI continues to shape the landscape of cyberattacks, organizations need to be proactive in their defence strategies, combining human expertise and advanced technology to stay ahead of the ever-changing threat landscape.

Reference: Emotet and AI-Powered Attacks[126]

8.4.2 Microsoft's Approach to AI-Driven Security:

Exploration of Microsoft's AI-Powered Security Strategies

Microsoft, a global technology leader, has positioned itself at the forefront of using AI to enhance cybersecurity. The company's vision and strategies for AI-powered security solutions reflect its commitment to providing robust protection against evolving cyber threats. Microsoft's approach encompasses a range of technologies, services, and practices designed to empower organizations in their battle against cyberattacks.

AI Integration Across the Security Ecosystem:

Microsoft recognizes the potential of AI to transform traditional security approaches. The company strategically integrates AI across its security ecosystem, enabling intelligent threat detection, response, and prevention.

1. Threat Intelligence and Detection: Microsoft leverages AI to analyse vast amounts of data and identify subtle patterns indicative of cyber threats. Solutions like Microsoft Defender Advanced Threat Protection (ATP) use AI-driven behavioural analytics to detect and mitigate advanced threats, including zero-day attacks.

2. AI-Driven Threat Hunting: Microsoft equips security teams with AI-powered tools that facilitate proactive threat hunting. Azure Sentinel, Microsoft's cloud-native SIEM (Security Information and Event Management) solution, employs AI to uncover hidden threats across an organization's environment.

3. Predictive Analytics: AI-powered predictive analytics is a cornerstone of Microsoft's strategy. Solutions such as Microsoft 365 Defender use historical and real-time data to predict potential threats and vulnerabilities, helping organizations take proactive measures.

4. Automation and Incident Response: Microsoft emphasizes AI-driven automation in incident response. Solutions like Azure Security Center orchestrate automated responses to threats, minimizing response times and allowing human analysts to focus on more complex tasks.

5. Cloud-Native Security: Microsoft's cloud services, like Azure, provide AI-enhanced security services that protect cloud workloads. Azure Security Center uses AI to detect and respond to threats across hybrid cloud environments.

---

[126] https://www.scmagazine.com/home/security-news/emotet-is-making-a-comeback-with-phishing-emails-again/

6. Microsoft Threat Intelligence Center (MSTIC): MSTIC serves as Microsoft's hub for detecting and responding to advanced threats. It employs AI to analyse vast amounts of telemetry data, allowing the team to stay ahead of evolving threats.

Ethical AI and Inclusion:
Microsoft's AI-powered security strategies also prioritize ethical considerations. The company is dedicated to ensuring fairness, transparency, and accountability in its AI algorithms, striving to prevent biases and discrimination in security solutions.

Partnerships and Collaborations:
Microsoft collaborates with the broader cybersecurity community to enhance AI-driven security solutions. Partnerships, information sharing, and joint research efforts contribute to a more secure digital landscape.

Constant Innovation:
Microsoft maintains a proactive approach to innovation in cybersecurity. The company continues to evolve its AI-powered security offerings, adapting to emerging threats and technological advancements.

Microsoft's vision and strategies for AI-powered security solutions are rooted in harnessing the potential of AI to create more resilient and adaptive defences. By integrating AI across its security portfolio, emphasizing predictive analytics, ethical considerations, and automation, Microsoft aims to empower organizations to detect, prevent, and respond to cyber threats with greater efficiency and accuracy. The company's commitment to innovation and collaboration reinforces its role as a leader in driving AI-driven advancements in the cybersecurity landscape.

Reference: Microsoft's AI-Driven Security Approach[127]

Chapter 9: Case Studies and Practical Applications of AI in Cybersecurity

9.1. Analysing Real-World Case Studies of AI-Driven Cybersecurity Incidents

9.1.1 SolarWinds Breach:

In-Depth Analysis of the SolarWinds Breach and AI Detection
The SolarWinds breach, discovered in December 2020, was a highly sophisticated cyberattack that targeted numerous organizations, including government agencies and private companies. The breach exploited SolarWinds' Orion platform to distribute malware, leading to a massive data breach and potential compromise of sensitive information. While AI alone might not have been a panacea, it could have played a significant role in detecting and mitigating the attack by augmenting traditional security measures.

---

[127] https://www.microsoft.com/en-us/security/business/security-intelligence-report

Attack Overview:

The SolarWinds breach involved the insertion of malicious code into SolarWinds' software updates. This allowed threat actors to compromise the software supply chain, infiltrate organizations' networks, and exfiltrate data over a prolonged period. The campaign revealed a highly organized and patient adversary with a deep understanding of network operations.

AI Detection and Mitigation Possibilities:

1. Anomaly Detection: AI-powered anomaly detection could have helped identify unusual patterns of behaviour across SolarWinds' infrastructure. By leveraging AI-driven behavioural analytics, organizations might have detected suspicious activities that deviated from normal network behaviour.

2. Abnormal Data Exfiltration: AI models trained to recognize unusual data transfer patterns could have alerted security teams to large-scale data exfiltration. The breach involved extensive data transfer, which might have triggered alerts from AI-based security solutions.

3. Behaviour Analysis of Compromised Accounts: AI could have been employed to analyse the behaviour of compromised accounts, detecting irregularities and unauthorized activities. This might have enabled organizations to isolate compromised accounts rapidly .

4. Threat Hunting with AI: AI-driven threat hunting could have assisted security teams in proactively seeking out indicators of compromise that were difficult to identify using conventional methods.

5. Rapid Incident Response: AI-powered incident response automation could have accelerated the detection-to-response time, isolating compromised systems and preventing the lateral movement of attackers.

6. Identifying Supply Chain Anomalies: AI systems could have been trained to identify anomalies within software supply chains, recognizing unexpected changes in code, signatures, or behaviours that could indicate tampering.

7. Real-Time Network Monitoring: AI-enhanced network monitoring tools could have provided real-time visibility into network activities, detecting unusual traffic flows associated with the breach.

8. Recognizing Sophisticated Techniques: AI could have been trained to recognize sophisticated attack techniques, such as code signing abuse and evasive manoeuvres, improving the chances of early detection.

Challenges and Considerations:

1. Data Privacy and Model Bias: AI models must handle sensitive data responsibly, and potential biases in models need to be addressed to avoid incorrect detections or overlooking certain attack vectors.

2. Complexity of Attack Vectors: The SolarWinds breach involved several layers of complexity. While AI can assist, its effectiveness depends on the comprehensiveness of training data and attack scenarios.

3. Continuous Learning and Adaptation: AI models must continually learn and adapt to evolving attack techniques. Threat actors can adjust tactics, rendering AI models ineffective without ongoing training.

Conclusion:

The SolarWinds breach demonstrated the need for advanced security measures capable of countering sophisticated attacks. While AI detection and mitigation could have potentially improved detection speed and accuracy, no single solution can provide complete security. AI's role is most effective when combined with human expertise, proactive threat hunting, continuous monitoring, and collaborative threat intelligence sharing. The breach underscored the importance of a multi-layered defence strategy, where AI enhances the capabilities of security professionals to respond to evolving cyber threats.

Reference: SolarWinds Hack[128]

9.1.2 NotPetya Ransomware Attack:

Examination of the NotPetya Attack and AI's Potential Role in Prevention
The NotPetya attack, which occurred in 2017, was one of the most devastating and widespread cyberattacks in history. It highlighted the urgency for advanced cybersecurity measures, including the potential role of AI in preventing similar attacks from spreading and causing massive damage.

Attack Overview:

NotPetya, a type of ransomware, targeted organizations globally by exploiting the Ukrainian tax software MEDoc. The attack rapidly spread using multiple vectors, encrypting victims' files and demanding a ransom for decryption. However, NotPetya was not a traditional ransomware; its primary goal seemed to be causing disruption rather than financial gain.

AI's Potential Role:

1. Behaviour-Based Anomaly Detection: AI-driven behaviour analysis could have identified the anomalous behaviour exhibited by NotPetya. The malware spread quickly through lateral movement, a pattern that AI models could have recognized as unusual and flagged for investigation.

2. Rapid Threat Hunting: AI-powered threat hunting tools could have quickly identified signs of compromise and suspicious activities associated with the NotPetya attack, allowing security teams to respond promptly.

3. Dynamic Malware Detection: AI can analyse malware behaviour and patterns to detect variants of known malware. AI models trained on the behaviour of NotPetya could have identified similar strains early, preventing their spread.

4. Predictive Analytics: Predictive analytics powered by AI could have forecasted the potential impact of NotPetya-like attacks based on historical data, enabling organizations to take proactive measures.

5. Network Segmentation and Isolation: AI-driven network segmentation tools could have isolated infected systems and prevented the lateral movement of the malware, limiting its spread.

6. Zero-Day Exploit Detection: AI models can analyse and predict the exploitation of zero-day vulnerabilities. NotPetya exploited known vulnerabilities, but AI could have helped detect attempts to exploit new, unknown vulnerabilities.

---

[128] https://www.csoonline.com/article/3601124/the-solarwinds-hack-how-cybercriminals-infiltrated-the-highest-levels-of-the-us-government.html

Challenges and Considerations:

1. Adaptability to New Threats: AI models need constant training and updating to adapt to new attack techniques and strains of malware. The evolving nature of cyber threats requires ongoing efforts to ensure AI's effectiveness.

2. False Positives/Negatives: AI systems can produce false positives or negatives, leading to incorrect detections or missed threats. Proper tuning and calibration are essential to minimize these issues.

3. Ethical Considerations: Using AI for cybersecurity must consider ethical concerns, such as privacy implications and potential unintended consequences of automated responses.

4. Collaboration with Human Expertise: AI should complement, not replace, human expertise. Effective AI-enhanced cybersecurity requires collaboration between AI systems and skilled security professionals.

The NotPetya attack highlighted the need for advanced, proactive cybersecurity solutions. While AI holds promise in preventing the spread of such attacks, it must be viewed as part of a broader cybersecurity strategy that includes human analysis, threat intelligence sharing, and continuous monitoring. AI's ability to detect anomalies, identify malware patterns, and predict potential threats can significantly enhance an organization's defences against fast-spreading and destructive cyberattacks. However, ongoing investment in AI development, training, and collaboration remains essential to effectively combatting evolving threats like NotPetya.

Reference: NotPetya Ransomware Attack[129]

9.1.3 Deepfake Attacks:

The Rise of Deepfake Attacks and AI Detection and Countermeasures
The rise of deepfake attacks, which involve the manipulation of audio, video, or text to create highly convincing yet fabricated content, presents significant challenges in various domains, including politics, media, and cybersecurity. These attacks leverage AI to generate content that is nearly indistinguishable from authentic information, raising concerns about misinformation, impersonation, and potential security breaches. However, AI itself can play a crucial role in detecting and combating deepfake attacks.

The Challenge of Deepfakes:
Deepfake technology has advanced to a point where it can convincingly mimic the voice and appearance of individuals, leading to the potential for cyberattacks that exploit trust and deceive recipients. Attackers can use deepfakes to impersonate executives, manipulate video evidence, and spread false information, causing reputational damage and compromising sensitive data.

AI's Role in Detection and Countermeasures:
1. Content Verification: AI algorithms can analyse videos, audios, and images to detect subtle discrepancies that indicate manipulation. Machine learning models trained on a diverse dataset of authentic and manipulated content can identify anomalies in facial expressions, lip-syncing, and voice patterns.

---

[129] https://www.zdnet.com/article/notpetya-an-inside-look-at-the-most-devastating-ransomware-outbreak-in-history/

2. Digital Forensics: AI-enabled digital forensics tools can analyse metadata, timestamps, and source information to verify the authenticity of media content. This approach helps detect discrepancies and inconsistencies in the creation and distribution of deepfakes.

3. Deepfake Detection Models: AI-driven detection models, often utilizing deep learning techniques, can differentiate between authentic and manipulated content by identifying artifacts introduced during the generation process. These models can analyse visual and auditory cues, identifying signs of manipulation that the human eye might miss.

4. Multimodal Analysis: AI can integrate data from various sources, such as video, audio, and textual information, to conduct multimodal analysis. This approach enhances the accuracy of deepfake detection by cross-referencing different modalities for inconsistencies.

5. Deepfake Attribution: AI can be used to trace the origin of deepfake content by analysing digital fingerprints, watermarks, and other hidden indicators within the media. This attribution can assist in identifying the culprits behind deepfake attacks.

6. Continuous Learning: AI models can continuously learn and adapt to new deepfake techniques, ensuring that detection mechanisms remain effective as attackers refine their methods.

Challenges and Considerations:

1. Evolving Deepfake Techniques: As deepfake technology evolves, attackers can develop more sophisticated methods to create convincing forgeries. AI detection methods must evolve in parallel to stay ahead of these advancements.

2. Adversarial Attacks: Attackers may use AI to develop adversarial attacks that are specifically designed to evade detection algorithms. This requires constant innovation in detection methods to stay ahead of such tactics.

3. Ethical Concerns: Using AI for deepfake detection raises ethical considerations, such as privacy and consent. Balancing the need for security with respecting individuals' rights is crucial.

4. False Positives/Negatives: AI detection systems can produce false positives, flagging authentic content as manipulated, or false negatives, missing actual deepfakes. Striking the right balance is vital to maintain user trust.

The rise of deepfake attacks underscores the urgency of developing AI-driven solutions for detection and prevention. AI's ability to analyse and identify subtle discrepancies in multimedia content can be harnessed to safeguard against the spread of misinformation and impersonation. While deepfake technology presents challenges, the application of AI in detection and countermeasures represents a crucial step in mitigating the potential risks posed by these sophisticated attacks. Effective defence against deepfakes requires ongoing collaboration between AI experts, cybersecurity professionals, and relevant stakeholders to stay ahead of this evolving threat landscape.

Reference: Deepfake Threat[130]

---

[130] https://www.nytimes.com/2022/02/25/technology/deepfake-technology.html

9.2. Evaluating Successful Integration of AI in Cybersecurity Practices

9.2.1 IBM Watson for Cybersecurity:

Case Study: Successful Integration of IBM Watson's AI Technology in Cybersecurity Operations

Introduction: IBM Watson, an AI-powered cognitive computing platform, has been at the forefront of innovative solutions in various industries, including cybersecurity. This case study explores the successful integration of IBM Watson's AI technology in cybersecurity operations and how it has transformed the way organizations detect, analyse, and respond to cyber threats.

Background: IBM Watson is renowned for its ability to process vast amounts of data, learn from it, and make informed decisions. When applied to cybersecurity, this technology enhances threat detection, incident response, and overall security posture.

Integration Process:

1. Threat Intelligence: IBM Watson ingests and analyses a wide range of threat intelligence data, including malware samples, indicators of compromise (IoCs), and vulnerabilities. This data is processed to identify patterns, trends, and emerging threats.

2. Anomaly Detection: Watson's AI capabilities enable it to identify anomalies and deviations from baseline behaviour across network traffic, user activities, and system performance. This proactive approach helps identify potential threats before they escalate.

3. Incident Response Automation: IBM Watson's AI can automate incident response processes by suggesting appropriate actions based on historical data and the context of the ongoing incident. This reduces response times and minimizes manual intervention.

4. Natural Language Processing (NLP): Watson's NLP capabilities allow it to analyse and understand unstructured data, such as security reports and user logs. This enhances the platform's ability to extract valuable insights from a variety of sources.

5. Threat Hunting: IBM Watson assists security analysts in threat hunting by correlating data from disparate sources and identifying connections that might be missed by human analysts alone.

Benefits and Outcomes:

1. Enhanced Detection Accuracy: The integration of IBM Watson's AI technology has significantly improved the accuracy of threat detection. Its ability to analyse vast datasets and identify subtle patterns enables organizations to detect both known and unknown threats.

2. Faster Incident Response: By automating incident response processes, IBM Watson enables organizations to respond rapidly to security incidents. This reduces the potential impact of cyberattacks and minimizes downtime.

3. Improved Threat Intelligence: Watson's analysis of threat intelligence data provides organizations with actionable insights, helping them stay ahead of emerging threats and vulnerabilities.

4. Adaptive Learning: IBM Watson continually learns from new data and evolving threat landscapes, allowing it to adapt and refine its detection and response capabilities over time.

5. Human-AI Collaboration: The platform fosters collaboration between human analysts and AI. It assists analysts by providing context-rich insights and recommendations, enhancing their decision-making process.

The successful integration of IBM Watson's AI technology in cybersecurity operations showcases the transformative potential of AI in enhancing threat detection, incident response, and overall security posture. By leveraging Watson's advanced capabilities, organizations can bolster their cyber defence strategies, effectively manage threats, and adapt to the ever-evolving cybersecurity landscape. This case study serves as an example of how AI-driven solutions can revolutionize the way organizations approach cybersecurity challenges, providing them with the tools to proactively address threats and protect their digital assets.

Reference: IBM Watson for Cybersecurity[131]

9.2.2 McAfee's AI-Driven Security Solutions:

Exploration of McAfee's Comprehensive Approach to Cybersecurity Leveraging AI

Introduction: McAfee, a leading cybersecurity company, has been at the forefront of integrating artificial intelligence (AI) into its solutions to provide a comprehensive and proactive approach to cybersecurity. This section explores how McAfee leverages AI to address various aspects of cybersecurity and protect organizations from evolving threats.

AI-Driven Threat Detection:

McAfee's AI-powered threat detection systems analyse large volumes of data, including network traffic, user behaviour, and threat intelligence feeds. By using machine learning algorithms, these systems can identify anomalies, patterns, and indicators of compromise that might be missed by traditional signature-based methods.

Behavioural Analytics:

McAfee's AI solutions utilize behavioural analytics to establish baselines of normal user and system behaviour. Deviations from these baselines are flagged as potential security incidents. This approach helps detect unauthorized access, insider threats, and other unusual activities that might indicate a breach.

Predictive Analysis:

McAfee harnesses the power of predictive analytics to anticipate and prevent cyber threats. By analysing historical data and identifying trends, the AI algorithms can predict potential attack vectors and vulnerabilities that attackers might exploit.

Automation and Orchestration:

McAfee's AI-driven automation and orchestration capabilities streamline incident response processes. When a threat is detected, AI can automatically trigger predefined response actions, reducing the time it takes to mitigate the impact of an attack.

Vulnerability Management:

McAfee's AI-enhanced vulnerability management solutions automate vulnerability assessments by scanning systems, identifying potential weaknesses, and prioritizing remediation efforts based on risk and impact.

Cloud Security:

AI plays a crucial role in McAfee's cloud security offerings. It continuously monitors cloud environments for unauthorized access, data breaches, and configuration errors, helping organizations maintain a strong security posture in dynamic cloud environments.

---

[131] https://www.ibm.com/cloud/learn/watson-for-cybersecurity

Threat Intelligence Sharing:

McAfee leverages AI to analyse and share threat intelligence across its customer base. This collective intelligence allows organizations to benefit from real-time insights into emerging threats and attack trends.

Advantages:

1. **Proactive Threat Detection:** By using AI, McAfee enhances its ability to detect threats in real-time and even predict potential attacks, allowing organizations to take preventive measures.
2. **Rapid Incident Response:** AI-powered automation speeds up incident response processes, minimizing the impact of breaches and reducing the time needed for containment.
3. **Scalability:** AI-driven solutions can handle vast amounts of data and adapt to the growing volume of cyber threats, providing scalable protection for organizations of all sizes.
4. **Adaptive Learning:** McAfee's AI systems continually learn from new data, improving their accuracy and effectiveness over time.
5. **Improved Decision-Making:** By providing security analysts with context-rich insights, AI helps them make informed decisions and prioritize actions.

McAfee's comprehensive approach to cybersecurity, fuelled by AI technologies, demonstrates the company's commitment to staying ahead of the evolving threat landscape. By leveraging AI-driven threat detection, predictive analysis, automation, and other innovative techniques, McAfee offers organizations a powerful defence against cyber threats. This approach underscores the importance of AI in bolstering cybersecurity strategies and highlights the transformative impact of AI on the industry as a whole.

Reference: McAfee AI-Driven Security[132]

9.2.3 Google's Chronicle Backstory:

Analysis of Google's Chronicle Backstory and AI-driven Data Analysis

Introduction: Google's Chronicle Backstory is a cybersecurity platform that demonstrates the application of artificial intelligence (AI) to analyse massive data sets for threat detection, incident investigation, and proactive security measures. This analysis explores how Chronicle Backstory utilizes AI to process vast amounts of security telemetry data and derive actionable insights.

AI-Powered Data Analysis:

Chronicle Backstory employs AI algorithms to analyse enormous volumes of security-related data collected from various sources, including endpoints, networks, and cloud environments. The platform's AI-driven analysis focuses on identifying patterns, anomalies, and indicators of compromise that might indicate malicious activity.

Behavioural Analytics:

One of the key aspects of Chronicle Backstory's AI approach is its behavioural analytics capabilities. AI algorithms establish baselines of normal behaviour across an organization's digital environment. Deviations from these baselines are flagged as potential threats, helping security teams detect breaches and unauthorized activities.

---

[132] https://www.mcafee.com/enterprise/en-us/security-awareness/artificial-intelligence.html

Threat Hunting and Investigation:

AI-driven analytics in Chronicle Backstory enable security professionals to proactively search for threats and investigate incidents. By sifting through historical data and identifying subtle indicators, the platform assists in understanding attack timelines and tactics used by adversaries.

Threat Intelligence Sharing:

Chronicle Backstory's AI capabilities extend to aggregating and correlating global threat intelligence. This shared intelligence helps organizations stay informed about emerging threats and attack patterns, contributing to collective defence.

Advantages of AI-Driven Data Analysis:

1. Scalability: Chronicle Backstory's AI-powered approach enables the analysis of vast data sets at scale, a critical capability in the modern threat landscape.

2. Real-Time Insights: AI algorithms can process data in real-time, providing security teams with timely insights into ongoing attacks and vulnerabilities.

3. Pattern Recognition: AI excels at recognizing patterns and anomalies that might be missed by traditional methods, enabling the detection of sophisticated threats.

4. Enhanced Efficiency: By automating data analysis, AI reduces the manual effort required for threat hunting, freeing up security professionals for more strategic tasks.

5. Proactive defence: AI's ability to predict and identify threats before they manifest as breaches allows organizations to adopt a proactive security stance.

Google's Chronicle Backstory showcases the transformative potential of AI in cybersecurity by applying advanced analytics to vast data sets. The platform's AI-driven data analysis capabilities empower organizations to detect, investigate, and mitigate cyber threats effectively. As the cybersecurity landscape evolves, AI's role in processing and deriving insights from large data volumes becomes increasingly vital. Chronicle Backstory's innovative approach exemplifies the power of AI in transforming cybersecurity operations and exemplifies the future of threat detection and incident response.

Conclusion:

In the era of Artificial intelligence, we are witnessing rapid advancement in both sides; the attackers are getting smarter benefitting from AI based tools, and the defenders trying to counter the new generation attacks and using AI capabilities to reduce the impact and probability of such threats.

This book tries to highlight main intersection fields between Cybersecurity and AI, it aims also to reduce the GAP between technology advancements and global understanding of challenges and opportunities introduced by these new technologies.

If you liked this book, please refer one of our other publications:

- Cyber security : a strategic approach
- International Cyber Conflicts : Challenges and Impacts

Appendix: Acronyms and Definitions

A

Access Control List (ACL)

Access Control List, or ACL, is a security feature that defines which users or groups have permission to access specific resources on a computer or network.

Advanced Persistent Threat (APT)

An Advanced Persistent Threat, or APT, is a sophisticated type of cyber-attack that targets a specific organization or individual over an extended period of time, with the intention of stealing sensitive data or intellectual property.

Adware

Adware is a type of software that displays unwanted advertisements on a user's computer, often bundled with other programs or downloaded without the user's knowledge.

Ammy Admin

Ammy Admin is a remote desktop software that enables users to remotely connect to and control another computer over the internet.

Antivirus

Antivirus software is a program designed to detect, prevent, and remove malicious software, such as viruses, worms, and Trojan horses, from a computer.

Authentication

Authentication is the process of verifying the identity of a user or device, usually through a username and password, biometric information, or a security token.

Authorization

Authorization is the process of granting or denying access to a resource or system based on a user's identity, role, or other criteria.

Attack Surface

An Attack Surface is the total number of vulnerabilities and entry points that an attacker can use to exploit a system or network.

Asset

An Asset is any resource, system, or data that has value to an organization and needs to be protected.

Application Security

Application Security refers to the process of designing, testing, and implementing security measures to protect software applications from unauthorized access, modification, or destruction.

Advanced Encryption Standard (AES):

Advanced Encryption Standard (AES) is a symmetric encryption algorithm used to protect sensitive data by transforming it into a format that is unreadable without the correct decryption key.

Application Programming Interface (API)

An Application Programming Interface, or API, is a set of protocols and standards that allow different software applications to communicate with each other.

Access Point

An Access Point is a device that enables wireless devices to connect to a wired network.

Attack Vector

An Attack Vector is the path or means by which an attacker gains unauthorized access to a system or network.

Air Gap

An Air Gap is a security measure that physically separates a computer or network from the internet or any other unsecured network to prevent unauthorized access or data transfer.

Authentication Factor

Authentication Factor refers to the means by which a user proves their identity, typically through something they know (e.g., a password), something they have (e.g., a security token), or something they are (e.g., biometric information).

Adversary

Adversary refers to an individual, group, or organization that launches cyber-attacks against another party or entity.

Audit Trail

Audit Trail is a record of events that allows administrators to trace and examine activities and changes on a system or network.

APT Framework

APT Framework is a structured approach used to identify, prevent, and respond to Advanced Persistent Threats.

Application Whitelisting

Application Whitelisting is a security measure that allows only approved applications to run on a system, preventing the execution of malware and other unauthorized software.

Access Management

Access Management refers to the process of controlling who has access to specific resources or systems within an organization.

Authorization Token

Authorization Token is a piece of data that verifies a user's permission to access a particular resource or system.

Attack Tree

Attack Tree is a visual representation of a systematic process used to evaluate the potential vulnerabilities and attack scenarios for a system or network.

Attack Map

Attack Map is a graphical representation of a cyber-attack in real-time, displaying the source and destination of the attack, the attack type, and the potential impact.

Anonymity

Anonymity refers to the state of being anonymous or unidentifiable, typically used to protect user privacy and prevent tracking or surveillance.

Artificial Intelligence (AI)

Artificial Intelligence (AI) refers to the simulation of human intelligence in machines, including tasks such as natural language processing, learning, and problem-solving.

Algorithm

Algorithm is a set of rules or instructions used to perform a specific task or solve a problem.

Aircrack-ng

Aircrack-ng is a suite of software tools used to crack Wi-Fi passwords and monitor wireless networks.

Anti-spyware

Anti-spyware is software designed to detect and remove spyware, which is malicious software used to collect data from a computer or network without the user's knowledge or consent.

Asset Management

Asset Management is the process of tracking and managing an organization's physical and digital assets, including hardware, software, and data.

Asymmetric Encryption

Asymmetric Encryption is a type of encryption that uses two separate keys, a public key for encryption and a private key for decryption, to securely transmit information over a network.

Application Security Testing

Application Security Testing is the process of identifying and mitigating vulnerabilities and weaknesses in software applications to prevent cyber-attacks.

Attribute-based Access Control (ABAC)

Attribute-based Access Control (ABAC) is a security model that uses attributes or characteristics of a user or resource to determine access permissions.

Address Resolution Protocol (ARP)

Address Resolution Protocol (ARP) is a protocol used to map a network address (such as an IP address) to a physical address (such as a MAC address) on a local network.

Access Point Name (APN)

Access Point Name (APN) is a unique identifier used by mobile devices to connect to a mobile network.

B

Botnet

A Botnet is a network of compromised computers or devices that can be remotely controlled by an attacker to perform malicious activities, such as launching distributed denial of service (DDoS) attacks.

Brute Force Attack

A Brute Force Attack is a method of cracking passwords or encryption by attempting all possible combinations until the correct one is found.

Backup

Backup refers to the process of copying and storing data in a secure location to protect against data loss due to hardware failure, human error, or cyber-attacks.

Browser Hijacking

Browser Hijacking is a type of cyber-attack that takes control of a user's web browser, often redirecting the user to malicious websites or installing unwanted software.

Bot

A Bot, short for robot, is a software application designed to perform automated tasks over the internet, often used for malicious purposes such as spamming, phishing, or DDoS attacks.

Black Hat Hacker

A Black Hat Hacker is a malicious hacker who uses their skills to gain unauthorized access to systems, steal data, or cause damage to networks or devices.

Bricking

Bricking refers to the intentional or unintentional act of rendering a device or system unusable, often through software manipulation or modification.

Bluetooth Hacking

Bluetooth Hacking is a type of cyber-attack that exploits vulnerabilities in Bluetooth-enabled devices to gain unauthorized access or steal sensitive information.

Biometric Authentication

Biometric Authentication is a security method that uses unique physical or behavioural characteristics of an individual, such as fingerprints, facial recognition, or voice recognition, to verify their identity.

Binary Code

Binary Code is a system of representing data and instructions using only two digits, usually 0 and 1, which are interpreted by computers and other electronic devices.

Business Continuity Planning (BCP)

Business Continuity Planning (BCP) is a process of developing and implementing strategies and procedures to ensure that essential business functions can continue during and after a disaster or other disruptive event.

Bot Herder

A Bot Herder is a person who creates or controls a Botnet, often for malicious purposes such as launching cyber-attacks or stealing sensitive information.

Backdoor

A Backdoor is a hidden entry point in a computer system or software application that allows unauthorized access to the system or application.

Banner Grabbing

Banner Grabbing is a technique used to gather information about a target computer system or network by retrieving the banner or header information from a service or application running on the system.

Bluejacking

Bluejacking is a type of cyber-attack that sends unsolicited messages or data to Bluetooth-enabled devices, often to promote a product or service.

Blacklist

A Blacklist is a list of IP addresses, domain names, or other identifiers that are blocked or restricted from accessing a network or system, usually due to a history of malicious or suspicious activity.

Behavioural Analytics

Behavioural Analytics is a process of analysing user behaviour and activity patterns to identify and prevent cyber threats, such as insider attacks or account takeovers.

Block Cipher

A Block Cipher is a type of encryption that operates on fixed-size blocks of data, typically using a secret key to transform the data into ciphertext.

Blockchain Security

Blockchain Security refers to the measures and techniques used to protect the integrity, confidentiality, and availability of data stored on a blockchain, a distributed and decentralized ledger technology.

Boot Sector Virus

A Boot Sector Virus is a type of virus that infects the boot sector of a storage device, such as a hard drive or floppy disk, and spreads to other devices or systems through file sharing or other means.

Branded Spear Phishing

Branded Spear Phishing is a type of targeted phishing attack that uses the branding and logos of a well-known company or organization to trick users into revealing sensitive information or downloading malware.

Browser Extension Security

Browser Extension Security refers to the measures and best practices used to ensure the security and privacy of browser extensions, which are small software programs that add functionality to web browsers.

Business Email Compromise (BEC)

Business Email Compromise (BEC) is a type of cyber-attack that uses social engineering and phishing techniques to impersonate an executive or employee in a company and fraudulently obtain money or sensitive information.

Binary Exploitation

Binary Exploitation is a type of cyber-attack that targets vulnerabilities in compiled binary code to execute malicious code, gain unauthorized access, or steal sensitive data.

Beaconing

Beaconing is a technique used by malware to periodically send small amounts of data to a command and control (C2) server, indicating that the malware is still active and awaiting further instructions.

Business Impact Analysis (BIA)

Business Impact Analysis (BIA) is a process of identifying and analysing the potential impacts of a disruption to business operations, such as a cyber-attack or natural disaster, to prioritize recovery efforts.

Blind SQL Injection

Blind SQL Injection is a type of cyber-attack that exploits vulnerabilities in web applications to inject malicious SQL code into a database, often without the attacker having direct access to the database.

Binary Tree

A Binary Tree is a data structure used in computer science and mathematics to represent hierarchical relationships between elements, typically used for searching and sorting algorithms.

Browser Isolation

Browser Isolation is a security technique that isolates web browsers from the underlying operating system and network, typically using virtualization or sandboxing, to prevent web-based cyber-attacks.

Bot Imitation

Bot Imitation is a technique used by attackers to mimic the behaviour of a legitimate user or bot to bypass security measures, such as CAPTCHA or IP blocking.

Big Data Analytics

Big Data Analytics is a process of analysing and extracting insights from large and complex datasets using advanced algorithms and tools, often used for cybersecurity to detect and prevent cyber threats.

Behavioural Biometrics

Behavioural Biometrics is a type of biometric authentication that uses unique behavioural patterns of an individual, such as mouse movements, keystrokes, or swipes, to verify their identity.

Bootkit

A Bootkit is a type of malware that infects the master boot record (MBR) or boot sector of a storage device, allowing the attacker to control the boot process and evade detection by traditional security measures.

Blind Spot

A Blind Spot is an area of a computer system or network that is not monitored or protected by security measures, leaving it vulnerable to cyber-attacks.

Botmaster

A Botmaster is a person who creates or controls a Botnet, often for malicious purposes such as launching cyber-attacks or stealing sensitive information.

Browser Sandbox

A Browser Sandbox is a virtual environment that isolates web browsers from the underlying operating system and network, often used for testing or secure browsing.

Blockchain Mining

Blockchain Mining is the process of verifying and adding transactions to a blockchain ledger, typically using specialized computer hardware and software to solve complex mathematical puzzles.

Beacon Frequency

Beacon Frequency refers to the rate at which a malware beacon sends data to a command and control (C2) server, often used to evade detection by security measures.

Behavioural Detection

Behavioural Detection is a method of detecting cyber threats based on unusual or suspicious behaviour patterns, often using machine learning or artificial intelligence algorithms.

Bit

A Bit, short for binary digit, is the smallest unit of digital information, typically represented by a 0 or 1.

Business Process Compromise (BPC)

Business Process Compromise (BPC) is a type of cyber-attack that targets the business processes and operations of a company, often using social engineering or spear phishing techniques.

Blacklist Filter

A Blacklist Filter is a security measure that blocks or restricts access to specific IP addresses, domain names, or other identifiers that are known to be malicious or suspicious.

Binary Analysis

Binary Analysis is the process of analysing and understanding the behaviour and vulnerabilities of compiled binary code, typically used for reverse engineering or vulnerability assessment.

Bitlocker

Bitlocker is a built-in encryption feature in Microsoft Windows operating systems, designed to encrypt and protect data on hard drives and other storage devices.

Bloatware

Bloatware is a type of software that is pre-installed on a computer or mobile device, often causing performance issues or security vulnerabilities.

Bot Controller

A Bot Controller is a person or group that controls a Botnet, often using command and control (C2) servers to issue instructions and collect information.

Blockchain Node

A Blockchain Node is a computer or device that participates in a blockchain network, typically used to validate and record transactions and maintain the integrity of the blockchain ledger.

Browser Fingerprinting

Browser Fingerprinting is a technique used to track or identify users based on the unique characteristics of their web browser, such as installed fonts, plug-ins, or screen resolution.

Biometric Authentication

Biometric Authentication is a type of authentication that uses unique biological characteristics of an individual, such as fingerprints, facial recognition, or iris scans, to verify their identity.

Bypass Attack

A Bypass Attack is a type of cyber-attack that exploits vulnerabilities in security measures or protocols to bypass access controls or other protections.

Block Cipher

A Block Cipher is a type of encryption that encrypts data in fixed-size blocks, typically using a specific key or algorithm to scramble the data.

Bluejacking

Bluejacking is a type of cyber-attack that uses Bluetooth technology to send unsolicited messages or spam to nearby devices, often used for advertising or social engineering purposes.

Blackout Attack

A Blackout Attack is a type of cyber-attack that targets power grids or other critical infrastructure, often using malware or other tools to cause a widespread blackout or disruption.

Buffer Overflow

A Buffer Overflow is a type of cyber-attack that exploits vulnerabilities in software applications to overflow a buffer or memory space, typically causing the application to crash or execute malicious code.

Bot Traffic

Bot Traffic refers to the traffic generated by bots, often used for web scraping, content indexing, or DDoS attacks.

Backup and Recovery Plan

A Backup and Recovery Plan is a comprehensive plan for protecting data and recovering from data loss or system failures, typically involving regular backups, redundancy, and testing.

Baseline Security

Baseline Security refers to the minimum level of security measures and controls required to protect a system or network from common threats and vulnerabilities.

Behaviour-based Detection

Behaviour-based Detection is a type of cybersecurity threat detection that uses machine learning or artificial intelligence algorithms to analyse and detect anomalous or suspicious behaviour patterns in network traffic or user behaviour.

Bug Bounty Program

A Bug Bounty Program is a program that rewards individuals or security researchers for identifying and reporting security vulnerabilities or weaknesses in software applications or systems.

BIOS Password

A BIOS Password is a password that is required to access or modify the BIOS settings on a computer or device, typically used to prevent unauthorized changes or access.

Browser Extension

A Browser Extension is a software module that extends the functionality of a web browser, typically installed by users to enhance their browsing experience or add new features.

C

Cryptography

Cryptography is the practice of secure communication in the presence of third parties, often achieved through encryption, decryption, and other techniques to protect the confidentiality, integrity, and authenticity of information.

Cyber Attack

A Cyber Attack is an intentional or unintentional attempt to exploit vulnerabilities in computer systems or networks for malicious purposes, such as theft, disruption, or destruction of data or services.

Cyberwarzone

Cyberwarzone can refer to the website Cyberwarzone.com, founded by cybersecurity expert Reza Rafati, which provides news, analysis, and resources related to cyber threats and defence. It can also refer to a segment or area impacted by cyberwar, often including critical infrastructure, government agencies, or military operations.

Cloud Security

Cloud Security refers to the measures and controls used to protect data, applications, and infrastructure in cloud computing environments, often including encryption, access controls, and monitoring.

Cybersecurity Framework

A Cybersecurity Framework is a set of guidelines, best practices, and standards for managing cybersecurity risks and protecting critical infrastructure and assets, often developed by government agencies or industry associations.

Cyber Insurance

Cyber Insurance is a type of insurance policy that provides coverage for losses or damages related to cyber-attacks, data breaches, and other cybersecurity incidents.

Command and Control (C2)

Command and Control (C2) refers to the methods and systems used by attackers to remotely control compromised devices or networks, often used for malicious purposes such as launching DDoS attacks or stealing data.

Certificate Authority (CA)

A Certificate Authority (CA) is a trusted third-party organization that issues and manages digital certificates, often used for secure authentication, encryption, and identification in online transactions.

Content Filtering

Content Filtering is the process of screening and blocking or allowing access to specific websites, applications, or content based on predefined rules or policies, often used to enforce security or compliance requirements.

Cyber Threat Intelligence (CTI)

Cyber Threat Intelligence (CTI) is information about potential or current cyber threats and vulnerabilities, often collected and analysed by security researchers, vendors, or government agencies to improve cybersecurity defences and response.

Cross-Site Scripting (XSS)

Cross-Site Scripting (XSS) is a type of web-based attack that injects malicious scripts or code into a web page or application to steal data or execute unauthorized actions on the victim's browser or device.

Cyber Hygiene

Cyber Hygiene refers to the practices and habits used to maintain good cybersecurity hygiene and protect against common threats, such as strong passwords, software updates, and backups.

Cybersecurity Maturity Model Certification (CMMC)

Cybersecurity Maturity Model Certification (CMMC) is a standard developed by the U.S. Department of Defence (DoD) to assess and certify the cybersecurity posture of contractors and suppliers that handle sensitive DoD information.

Credential Stuffing

Credential Stuffing is a type of cyber-attack that uses stolen or leaked login credentials to gain unauthorized access to other accounts or services, often through automated scripts or tools.

Cyber Espionage

Cyber Espionage is the practice of using cyber-attacks or hacking techniques to gather sensitive information or intelligence from governments, organizations, or individuals, often for political or economic gain.

Container Security

Container Security refers to the measures and controls used to secure containerized applications and environments, often including runtime protection, access controls, and vulnerability management.

Code Injection

Code Injection is a type of attack that exploits vulnerabilities in software applications to inject malicious code or scripts into a target system, often used for privilege escalation, data theft, or remote control.

Cyber Range

A Cyber Range is a virtual or physical environment used for cybersecurity training, testing, or simulation, often including real-world scenarios and exercises to improve skills and readiness.

Cyber Resilience

Cyber Resilience is the ability of an organization or system to withstand and recover from cyber-attacks or disruptions, often achieved through proactive planning, risk management, and incident response.

Cybersecurity Information Sharing Act (CISA)

The Cybersecurity Information Sharing Act (CISA) is a U.S. federal law that promotes the sharing of cybersecurity threat information between the government and private sector entities, often to improve situational awareness and response.

Cybersecurity Operations Center (CSOC)

A Cybersecurity Operations Center (CSOC) is a facility or team responsible for monitoring, detecting, and responding to cyber threats and incidents, often using advanced technologies and techniques to protect against attacks.

Cryptocurrency Security

Cryptocurrency Security refers to the measures and controls used to protect digital assets and transactions in the blockchain ecosystem, often including private key management, multi-factor authentication, and decentralized consensus mechanisms.

Cyber Insurance Policy

A Cyber Insurance Policy is a contractual agreement between an insurer and an insured party that provides coverage for losses or damages related to cyber-attacks or data breaches, often including liability, business interruption, and reputation protection.

Cyber Kill Chain

The Cyber Kill Chain is a model developed by Lockheed Martin that describes the different stages of a cyber-attack, from reconnaissance and weaponization to delivery, exploitation, installation, command and control, and exfiltration.

Cybersecurity Risk Assessment

A Cybersecurity Risk Assessment is a process of identifying, analysing, and evaluating potential risks and threats to an organization's information assets and systems, often using frameworks or methodologies to prioritize and manage risks.

Cybersecurity Incident Response Plan (CIRP)

A Cybersecurity Incident Response Plan (CIRP) is a documented set of procedures and protocols used to detect, analyse, contain, and recover from cybersecurity incidents, often including roles and responsibilities, escalation procedures, and communication plans.

Cybersecurity Information Technology (IT) Audit

A Cybersecurity IT Audit is an independent review of an organization's IT systems, processes, and controls to assess their effectiveness and compliance with cybersecurity standards, regulations, or best practices.

Cybersecurity Operations

Cybersecurity Operations refer to the processes, technologies, and personnel used to manage and monitor cybersecurity risks and threats, often including incident detection, response, and recovery.

Cybersecurity Frameworks and Standards

Cybersecurity Frameworks and Standards are guidelines, best practices, and requirements used to establish and maintain effective cybersecurity programs, often developed by government agencies, industry associations, or international organizations.

Cybersecurity Awareness Training

Cybersecurity Awareness Training is a program of education and training designed to improve employee knowledge and awareness of cybersecurity risks and best practices, often using simulated scenarios and exercises to reinforce learning.

Cybersecurity Governance

Cybersecurity Governance refers to the policies, procedures, and structures used to ensure effective cybersecurity management and oversight, often including risk management, compliance, and accountability frameworks.

Common Vulnerabilities and Exposures (CVE)

Common Vulnerabilities and Exposures (CVE) is a dictionary of publicly known cybersecurity vulnerabilities and exposures, often used to identify and prioritize vulnerabilities for remediation or mitigation.

Cyber Deception

Cyber Deception is the practice of using decoys, honeypots, or other techniques to mislead or divert cyber attackers and enhance situational awareness and response.

Cybersecurity Automation

Cybersecurity Automation refers to the use of automated tools and processes to improve the efficiency, effectiveness, and accuracy of cybersecurity tasks and operations, often including threat detection, response, and remediation.

Cybersecurity Analytics

Cybersecurity Analytics is the use of data analytics and machine learning techniques to identify and analyse cybersecurity threats and incidents, often using advanced algorithms and models to detect anomalous behaviour and patterns.

Cybersecurity Culture

Cybersecurity Culture refers to the values, beliefs, and behaviours that shape an organization's approach to cybersecurity, often including leadership commitment, employee awareness and training, and shared responsibility for security.

Cyber Range

A Cyber Range is a simulated environment used to test and evaluate cybersecurity tools, techniques, and procedures, often including real-world scenarios and simulations to enhance training and readiness.

D

Data Breach

A Data Breach is the unauthorized access, acquisition, or theft of sensitive or confidential data, often resulting in exposure or compromise of personal or business information.

Dark Web

The Dark Web is a part of the internet that is not indexed by search engines and requires special software or authorization to access, often used for illegal or illicit activities such as black markets, cybercrime, or censorship evasion.

Data Loss Prevention (DLP)

Data Loss Prevention (DLP) is the practice of detecting, monitoring, and preventing the unauthorized or accidental disclosure of sensitive or confidential data, often using technologies such as encryption, access controls, and data masking.

Defence in Depth

Defence in Depth is a cybersecurity strategy that involves deploying multiple layers of security controls and measures to protect against different types of threats and attacks, often including network segmentation, access controls, intrusion detection, and incident response.

Digital Forensics

Digital Forensics is the process of collecting, analysing, and preserving digital evidence from computers, mobile devices, or other electronic media for investigative or legal purposes, often involving specialized tools and techniques for data recovery and analysis.

Denial of Service (DoS)

Denial of Service (DoS) is a type of cyber-attack that involves flooding a network or website with traffic or requests, often causing the system to crash or become unavailable to users.

Distributed Denial of Service (DDoS)

Distributed Denial of Service (DDoS) is a type of cyber-attack that involves using multiple compromised devices or systems to flood a network or website with traffic or requests, often causing the system to become unavailable or unusable.

Digital Signature

A Digital Signature is a type of electronic signature that provides proof of the authenticity and integrity of a digital document or message, often using cryptographic techniques to ensure non-repudiation.

Dumpster Diving

Dumpster Diving is a type of physical security breach that involves rummaging through an organization's garbage or recycling bins to find sensitive or confidential information, often used for identity theft or fraud.

Data Classification

Data Classification is the process of categorizing data based on its sensitivity or importance to an organization, often used to determine appropriate security controls and handling procedures.

Digital Certificate

A Digital Certificate is a type of electronic document that verifies the identity of the owner of a public key, often used to secure online transactions and communications.

DNS Spoofing

DNS Spoofing is a type of cyber-attack that involves redirecting or manipulating the Domain Name System (DNS) to redirect users to fake or malicious websites or to intercept communications.

Domain Name System (DNS)

The Domain Name System (DNS) is a protocol used to translate human-readable domain names (such as google.com) into IP addresses (such as 172.217.6.14) used by computers to communicate over a network.

Disaster Recovery

Disaster Recovery is the process of restoring and recovering IT systems and data after a disruptive event or disaster, often involving backup and recovery solutions, redundancy, and business continuity planning.

Data Masking

Data Masking is a technique used to hide or obscure sensitive or confidential data by replacing or obscuring the original data with a substitute, often used to protect data privacy and security.

Digital Rights Management (DRM)

Digital Rights Management (DRM) is a set of technologies and policies used to protect and manage digital content, often including access controls, encryption, and licensing agreements.

Data Encryption

Data Encryption is the process of converting plain text or data into a code or cipher that can only be deciphered with a key or password, often used to protect data confidentiality and privacy.

Digital Identity

Digital Identity is the representation of an individual or entity's online or digital identity, often including personal information, user accounts, credentials, and online activity.

Device Management

Device Management is the process of managing and securing mobile devices, such as smartphones or tablets, used in an organization, often involving policies, controls, and mobile device management (MDM) software.

Digital Watermarking

Digital Watermarking is a technique used to embed a unique and invisible digital signature or identifier into digital media, such as images or videos, for copyright or authentication purposes.

Deep Packet Inspection (DPI)

Deep Packet Inspection (DPI) is a technique used to inspect and analyse network traffic at the packet level to detect and prevent security threats, often used by firewalls, intrusion detection and prevention systems, and network analytics tools.

Data Leakage

Data Leakage is the unauthorized or accidental release of sensitive or confidential data to unauthorized parties, often caused by human error, negligence, or cyber-attacks, such as data breaches or phishing.

Database Security

Database Security is the process of protecting and securing databases and their contents from unauthorized access, modification, or destruction, often involving access controls, encryption, and database activity monitoring.

Denial of Service (DoS)

Denial of Service (DoS) is a type of cyber-attack that involves flooding a network or system with traffic or requests to overload and disrupt its normal operations, often resulting in service disruption or downtime.

Data Loss Prevention (DLP)

Data Loss Prevention (DLP) is a set of policies, procedures, and technologies used to prevent or detect the unauthorized access, use, or transmission of sensitive or confidential data, often involving data classification, access controls, and data encryption.

Dual Factor Authentication (2FA)

Dual Factor Authentication (2FA) is a security process that requires users to provide two different types of authentication factors, such as a password and a biometric, to access a system or application, often used to enhance security and prevent unauthorized access.

Deception Technology

Deception Technology is a set of techniques and technologies used to deceive and mislead attackers and prevent or delay their progress in a network or system, often involving honeypots, decoys, or fake data.

E

Encryption

Encryption is the process of converting plaintext data into an unreadable ciphertext format, often used to protect data confidentiality and privacy.

Endpoint Security

Endpoint Security refers to the protection of devices, such as laptops, mobile phones, or servers, that connect to a network, often including antivirus software, firewalls, and intrusion detection systems.

Exploit

An Exploit is a piece of software or code that takes advantage of a vulnerability or weakness in a system or application to gain unauthorized access or control.

Ethical Hacker

An Ethical Hacker, also known as a White Hat Hacker, is a cybersecurity professional who uses their skills to identify and remediate vulnerabilities and weaknesses in systems or networks, often working on behalf of an organization or with their consent.

Email Spoofing

Email Spoofing is a type of cyber-attack that involves falsifying the sender's email address to appear as if it came from a trusted source, often used for phishing, spamming, or social engineering attacks.

Endpoint Detection and Response (EDR)

Endpoint Detection and Response (EDR) is a security technology that monitors and detects suspicious activity on endpoints, such as malware infections, network anomalies, or unauthorized access, and responds with automated or manual actions to prevent or mitigate the impact of a cyber-attack.

Encryption Key

An Encryption Key is a unique code or password used to encrypt and decrypt data, often used to protect the confidentiality and integrity of data transmissions or storage.

Encryption Algorithm

An Encryption Algorithm is a set of mathematical rules and processes used to encrypt and decrypt data, often involving complex mathematical functions and operations.

Eavesdropping

Eavesdropping is the act of secretly listening in on private or confidential conversations or communications, often used for espionage, surveillance, or unauthorized access.

Enumeration

Enumeration is the process of gathering information about a system or network, often used by attackers to identify potential vulnerabilities or weaknesses.

EDR Agent

An EDR Agent is a software agent installed on an endpoint device that collects and sends data to an EDR solution for analysis and response, often used to detect and prevent cyber-attacks on endpoints.

Egress Filtering

Egress Filtering is a network security technique that monitors and controls outbound network traffic, often used to prevent data exfiltration or unauthorized access.

F

Fuzzing Attack

A Fuzzing Attack is a type of attack where an automated tool or script sends random inputs or data to an application or system to identify vulnerabilities or flaws, often used to identify buffer overflow or injection vulnerabilities.

Firewall

A Firewall is a network security system that monitors and filters incoming and outgoing network traffic, based on predefined security rules and policies, to protect against unauthorized access or malicious activities.

Fileless Malware

Fileless Malware is a type of malware that is designed to operate in memory or within legitimate system processes, rather than as standalone executable files, making it difficult to detect and remove.

Forensic Analysis

Forensic Analysis is the process of collecting, analysing, and interpreting digital evidence from computers, networks, or digital devices, often used for investigating cybercrimes or incidents.

Firmware

Firmware is a type of software that is embedded into hardware devices, providing low-level control over the device's functionality and operations, often used in routers, printers, and other IoT devices.

Fingerprinting

Fingerprinting is the process of identifying or profiling a system or device based on unique characteristics or attributes, such as open ports, operating system versions, or installed applications, often used for reconnaissance or vulnerability scanning.

Full Disk Encryption

Full Disk Encryption is a method of encrypting all data on a disk or device, including the operating system and applications, to protect against unauthorized access or theft of data in the event of loss or theft.

Fraud Detection

Fraud Detection is the process of identifying and preventing fraudulent activities or transactions, often using machine learning or artificial intelligence algorithms to detect unusual or suspicious patterns or behaviour.

File Integrity Monitoring

File Integrity Monitoring is the process of monitoring and detecting changes to critical system files or configurations, often used to detect unauthorized modifications or attacks.

Financial Trojans

Financial Trojans are a type of Trojan malware that is designed to steal financial information or login credentials from a victim's system or device, often through phishing or social engineering techniques.

Federated Identity

Federated Identity is a single sign-on mechanism that allows users to authenticate and access multiple systems or applications, using a single set of login credentials, often used in large organizations or enterprise environments.

Fake WAP

A Fake WAP (Wireless Access Point) is a rogue wireless network that is set up to mimic a legitimate network, often used to capture sensitive information or login credentials from unsuspecting users.

FIDO (Fast Identity Online)

FIDO (Fast Identity Online) is a set of open standards for authentication, using strong multi-factor authentication methods such as biometrics or hardware tokens, to improve security and reduce reliance on passwords.

File Transfer Protocol (FTP)

File Transfer Protocol (FTP) is a standard network protocol used to transfer files between hosts over a TCP-based network, often used for website publishing or file sharing.

Fileless Persistence

Fileless Persistence is a type of persistence technique used by malware to maintain its presence on a compromised system or device, often using registry keys or scheduled tasks to execute commands or payloads.

Flaw

A Flaw is a weakness or vulnerability in a system, application, or network that can be exploited by attackers to gain unauthorized access or control.

False Positive

A False Positive is a security alert or warning that is triggered by legitimate activity or behaviour, rather than by a genuine security threat or attack.

Firmware Update

A Firmware Update is a process of updating or upgrading the firmware on a hardware device, often used to fix security vulnerabilities or bugs.

Formjacking

Formjacking is a type of cyber-attack that steals payment card data or personal information by intercepting or modifying data entered on a website's forms, often using malicious JavaScript code.

G

Gray Hat Hacker

A Gray Hat Hacker is a hacker who operates between ethical and unethical hacking practices, often using their skills to expose vulnerabilities or perform security research, but may also engage in malicious activities.

Gateway

A Gateway is a device or software program that connects two networks or systems, often used to control and filter traffic, provide security, and enable communication between different types of networks.

Gone Phishing

Gone Phishing is a play on words that refers to falling victim to a phishing attack, where an attacker poses as a legitimate entity to deceive a victim into providing sensitive information or clicking on a malicious link.

Global Threat Landscape

The Global Threat Landscape is the overall state of cybersecurity risks and threats around the world, often used to inform decision-making and strategic planning for organizations and governments.

Greyware

Greyware is a term used to describe software or applications that are potentially unwanted or may pose security risks, such as adware, spyware, or other types of malicious or intrusive software.

Ground Station

A Ground Station is a facility used for receiving and transmitting satellite or drone signals, often used for communication, navigation, and remote sensing applications, but also vulnerable to cyber-attacks.

Gaming Malware

Gaming Malware is a type of malware that specifically targets gamers by exploiting vulnerabilities in popular gaming software or platforms, often used to steal login credentials or in-game assets.

Grooming

Grooming is a type of online predatory behaviour where an adult attempts to build trust and emotional connections with a child in order to exploit or abuse them, often through messaging or social media platforms.

GSM (Global System for Mobile Communications)

GSM (Global System for Mobile Communications) is a standard for mobile communication networks that uses digital modulation for voice and data transmission, but also vulnerable to interception, eavesdropping, and other types of attacks.

Ghostware

Ghostware is a type of malware that is designed to avoid detection by security software or tools, often used for espionage, data theft, or cyber espionage.

Geofencing

Geofencing is a location-based technology that creates a virtual boundary around a specific geographic area, often used for tracking, monitoring, or restricting access to certain areas or resources.

Google Dorking

Google Dorking is a technique used by hackers and security researchers to find sensitive or confidential information by using advanced search queries or operators on the Google search engine.

GPU (Graphics Processing Unit)

GPU (Graphics Processing Unit) is a specialized processor used for rendering high-quality images, graphics, or videos, but also vulnerable to attacks such as side-channel attacks or memory corruption.

GPG (GNU Privacy Guard)

GPG, or GNU Privacy Guard, is a free and open-source encryption software used for securing email communication and files, often used as an alternative to proprietary encryption software.

Group Policy Object (GPO)

Group Policy Object (GPO) is a feature in Microsoft Windows that allows administrators to define and enforce system and security settings for users and computers in a domain or network environment.

GEO Blocking

GEO Blocking is a technique used to restrict access to a website, service, or content based on the geographic location of the user, often used for legal, regulatory, or security reasons, but also vulnerable to circumvention and evasion techniques.

H

Header Manipulation

Header Manipulation is a type of cyber-attack that involves modifying the header of a network packet to bypass security controls, intercept data, or execute malicious code.

Honeypot

A Honeypot is a decoy system or network used to detect, deflect, or counteract cyber-attacks by attracting and analysing attacker behaviour or malware.

HTTP Response Splitting

HTTP Response Splitting is a type of web application attack that allows an attacker to inject and manipulate HTTP headers to modify server responses, bypass security controls, or execute malicious code.

Hashing

Hashing is a cryptographic technique that transforms data of arbitrary size into a fixed-size output, often used for data integrity, digital signatures, or password storage.

Hardening

Hardening is the process of configuring, securing, or protecting a system, network, or application to reduce its susceptibility to cyber-attacks, often using security best practices, policies, or tools.

Hardware Security Module (HSM)

A Hardware Security Module (HSM) is a tamper-resistant device used to secure and manage cryptographic keys, often used for authentication, encryption, or digital signing.

Human error

Human error refers to mistakes or oversights made by humans that can lead to security incidents or breaches, often caused by lack of training, awareness, or attention to security best practices.

HTTP (Hypertext Transfer Protocol)

HTTP is a protocol used for transferring data over the internet, often used for web browsing, email, and other applications, but also vulnerable to security threats such as eavesdropping, interception, and manipulation.

HTTPS

HTTPS (Hyper Text Transfer Protocol Secure) is a protocol used for secure communication over the internet, often used to protect sensitive information such as passwords, credit card details, and personal data. HTTPS uses SSL/TLS encryption to ensure data confidentiality and integrity between the client and the server.

Hybrid Cloud

A Hybrid Cloud is a computing environment that combines both public and private cloud infrastructures, often used to balance the advantages of both models, such as scalability, flexibility, and security.

I

Incident Response Plan

An Incident Response Plan is a documented, structured approach for responding to and managing cybersecurity incidents and breaches, often including procedures for identification, containment, eradication, and recovery.

IP Spoofing

IP Spoofing is a technique used to disguise the true source of an IP packet by modifying its header information, often used by attackers to bypass access controls or launch DoS attacks.

Insider Threat

An Insider Threat is a security risk or threat that comes from within an organization, often caused by employees, contractors, or partners who intentionally or unintentionally misuse or abuse their privileges or access.

Intrusion Detection System (IDS)

An Intrusion Detection System (IDS) is a security tool or device used to monitor and analyse network traffic or system events for signs of unauthorized or malicious activity, often including alerting or blocking capabilities.

Internet of Things (IoT)

The Internet of Things (IoT) refers to a network of physical devices, vehicles, home appliances, and other items embedded with sensors, software, and connectivity, enabling them to collect and exchange data over the internet.

IoT Security

IoT Security is the practice of securing Internet of Things (IoT) devices and networks from cyber threats and vulnerabilities, often including security controls, policies, and standards for data protection, access control, and authentication.

Identity and Access Management (IAM)

Identity and Access Management (IAM) is a framework or set of processes used to manage and control user identities and access rights to resources or systems, often including user provisioning, authentication, authorization, and audit.

Incident Response Retainer

An Incident Response Retainer is a contract between an organization and a cybersecurity firm, ensuring that the firm will provide emergency incident response services in the event of a cyber cyber-attack or breach.

Injection Attack

An Injection Attack is a type of cyber-attack where an attacker inserts malicious code or commands into a web application's input fields, potentially allowing the attacker to access or manipulate sensitive data.

J

JSON Web Token (JWT)

JSON Web Token (JWT) is a type of token used for authentication and authorization purposes in web applications, often used as a secure means of transmitting data between parties.

JavaScript Hijacking

JavaScript Hijacking is a type of cyber-attack that exploits vulnerabilities in web applications to execute unauthorized JavaScript code, often used for stealing data or executing malicious actions.

Jailbreaking

Jailbreaking refers to the process of removing software restrictions on mobile devices to allow for customization or the installation of unauthorized apps.

JavaScript Injection

JavaScript Injection is a type of attack that exploits vulnerabilities in web applications to inject malicious code or scripts that can steal sensitive data or compromise the system.

Juice Jacking

Juice Jacking is a type of cyber-attack that involves infecting a public charging station or cable with malware that can steal data from mobile devices when they are plugged in.

Java Security

Java Security refers to the security measures and best practices for using the Java programming language, often including secure coding practices, vulnerability management, and access control mechanisms.

K

Keylogger

A Keylogger is a type of software or hardware device that records every keystroke made on a computer or mobile device, often used by attackers to steal sensitive information such as passwords or credit card numbers.

Kernel

A Kernel is the core component of an operating system that controls system resources and manages hardware and software interactions, often targeted by attackers to gain privileged access to a system.

Kerberos

Kerberos is a network authentication protocol used to verify the identities of users and services in a networked environment, often used in enterprise environments to provide secure authentication and access control.

Kill Chain

The Kill Chain is a framework used in cybersecurity to describe the various stages of a cyber-attack, from the initial reconnaissance to the exfiltration of stolen data. While commonly referred to as the Cyber Kill Chain, it is sometimes simply called the Kill Chain within the industry.

Kali Linux

Kali Linux is a Linux-based operating system designed for penetration testing and ethical hacking, featuring a suite of security tools for testing, auditing, and evaluating the security of computer systems and networks.

Key Exchange

Key Exchange is a process in which two or more parties agree on a shared secret key to establish a secure communication channel, often using encryption algorithms and protocols such as Diffie-Hellman key exchange or RSA key exchange.

L

Lateral Movement

Lateral Movement is the process of spreading or expanding an attack across a network or system by exploiting vulnerabilities or gaining access to new systems or devices, often used by attackers to escalate privileges and access sensitive data.

Log Analysis

Log Analysis is the process of reviewing and analysing log data generated by systems, applications, or network devices to detect security incidents, anomalies, or performance issues, often used for security monitoring, incident response, and compliance.

Least Privilege

Least Privilege is the principle of providing users or systems with only the minimal level of access and permissions required to perform their tasks, often used as a security best practice to limit the impact of security incidents or breaches.

Logic Bomb

A Logic Bomb is a type of malicious code that is programmed to execute a specific action or payload when triggered by a specific event or condition, often used for sabotage, espionage, or financial gain.

Load Balancer

A Load Balancer is a hardware or software device used to distribute network traffic across multiple servers or resources to improve performance, availability, and scalability, often used in web applications, cloud computing, and data centers.

LDAP Injection

LDAP Injection is a type of injection attack that targets LDAP (Lightweight Directory Access Protocol) servers or applications by inserting malicious input data to execute unauthorized commands or operations, often used by attackers to gain unauthorized access or extract sensitive information.

Layer 2

Layer 2, also known as the Data Link Layer, is the second layer of the OSI networking model that manages data communication between adjacent network devices, often involving the use of protocols such as Ethernet or Wi-Fi.

Live Forensics

Live Forensics is the process of collecting and analysing digital evidence from a live or active system, often used in incident response or investigations to preserve volatile data and identify ongoing attacks or threats.

Local Area Network (LAN)

A Local Area Network (LAN) is a network of interconnected devices within a limited geographic area, often used in homes, schools, or businesses to facilitate communication, file sharing, and resource sharing.

M

Malware

Malware, short for malicious software, is a type of software designed to harm, exploit, or damage computers, networks, and devices, often used by attackers for various purposes, such as theft, espionage, or disruption.

Man-in-the-Middle Attack (MITM)

A MITM attack is a type of cyber-attack where an attacker intercepts communication between two parties to eavesdrop, modify, or manipulate the communication, often used to steal sensitive information, such as login credentials or financial data.

Mobile Device Management (MDM)

MDM is a security solution used to manage, monitor, and secure mobile devices, such as smartphones and tablets, often used in enterprise environments to enforce security policies, manage device access, and prevent data loss or theft.

Metadata

Metadata is data that provides information about other data, such as the author, date, or format of a file, often used to organize, search, or manage large datasets, but also contains sensitive information that can be exploited by attackers.

Multi-Factor Authentication (MFA)

Multi-Factor Authentication (MFA) is a security mechanism that requires users to provide two or more factors of authentication to verify their identity, such as a password and a fingerprint. It is used to strengthen security and prevent unauthorized access to systems or data.

Malware Analysis

Malware analysis is the process of dissecting and analysing malicious software to understand its behaviour, purpose, and origin, often used by security researchers, incident responders, and malware analysts to detect and mitigate threats.

Machine Learning

Machine Learning is a subfield of artificial intelligence that enables systems and applications to automatically learn and improve from experience without being explicitly programmed, often used in cybersecurity for threat detection, anomaly detection, and behaviour analysis.

Managed Detection and Response (MDR)

Managed Detection and Response (MDR) is a cybersecurity service that provides continuous monitoring, threat detection, and incident response capabilities for organizations, often using advanced technologies such as machine learning and behavioural analytics.

Managed Security Services (MSS)

Managed Security Services (MSS) is a comprehensive approach to managing and securing an organization's IT infrastructure, often provided by third-party vendors, including services such as firewall management, intrusion detection and prevention, and security information and event management.

Managed Vulnerability Scanning

Managed Vulnerability Scanning is a process of identifying and prioritizing security vulnerabilities and weaknesses in an organization's IT systems and infrastructure, often using automated tools and technologies, and providing reports and recommendations for remediation.

Memory Forensics

Memory Forensics is a branch of digital forensics that focuses on the analysis and extraction of data from a computer's volatile memory, also known as RAM. It involves the capture and analysis of information about the system's processes, network connections, and other critical information that can be used to reconstruct system events and identify potential security breaches. Memory Forensics is a critical tool in the investigation of advanced cyber-attacks and malware infections, as it provides insights into system behaviour that cannot be obtained through traditional file-based forensics.

N

Network Segmentation

Network Segmentation is the process of dividing a computer network into smaller subnetworks or segments, often used to improve security, manageability, and performance.

NIST (National Institute of Standards and Technology)

The National Institute of Standards and Technology (NIST) is a United States government agency that develops and promotes measurement, standards, and technology to enhance productivity, safety, and security.

NIST Cybersecurity Framework

The NIST Cybersecurity Framework is a set of guidelines, best practices, and standards developed by the National Institute of Standards and Technology (NIST) to improve cybersecurity risk management and resilience across critical infrastructure sectors.

Netcat

Netcat is a command-line networking tool used to establish connections, send or receive data over TCP or UDP protocols, often used for testing and debugging network applications, but also by attackers for remote access or data exfiltration.

Nmap

Nmap is a free and open-source network scanner used to discover hosts and services on a network, identify vulnerabilities and misconfigurations, and perform security assessments and penetration testing.

Network Address Translation (NAT)

Network Address Translation (NAT) is a technique used to map one or more private IP addresses to a public IP address, often used to provide internet connectivity to private networks, but also to hide the internal network topology and reduce the attack surface.

Nonce

A Nonce is a random or pseudo-random number used only once in a cryptographic protocol to prevent replay attacks, often used in digital signatures, key exchange, or message authentication.

Network Tap

A Network Tap is a hardware device used to monitor network traffic by copying data from a network cable, often used for troubleshooting, network analysis, and intrusion detection or prevention.

NAC (Network Access Control)

NAC (Network Access Control) is a security solution used to enforce access policies and authentication requirements for devices attempting to connect to a network, often used to prevent unauthorized access, enforce compliance, and improve visibility and control.

Network Sniffer

A Network Sniffer is a tool used to capture and analyse network traffic, often used for troubleshooting, network performance optimization, and security analysis or intrusion detection.

NTLM (NT LAN Manager)

NTLM (NT LAN Manager) is a suite of authentication protocols used in Windows environments to authenticate users and computers, often used in conjunction with Active Directory and Kerberos.

Nessus

Nessus is a proprietary vulnerability scanner used to identify security vulnerabilities, misconfigurations, and compliance issues in computer systems and networks, often used by security professionals for security assessments and penetration testing.

Network Protocol

A Network Protocol is a set of rules and standards used to enable communication between devices on a network, often including specifications for data formats, timing, error handling, and authentication.

Network Security

Network Security is the practice of protecting computer networks and their infrastructure from unauthorized access, use, disclosure, disruption, modification, or destruction, often using a combination of technologies, policies, and procedures.

Network Architecture

Network Architecture is the design and implementation of a computer network, often including the physical and logical layout of devices, protocols, security mechanisms, and performance optimization strategies.

Network Topology

Network Topology is the physical or logical arrangement of devices on a computer network, often including the pattern of interconnections, communication protocols, and network segmentation strategies.

Network Administrator

A Network Administrator is a professional responsible for managing and maintaining computer networks, often including tasks such as installation, configuration, maintenance, troubleshooting, and security management.

NAT Traversal

NAT Traversal is the process of establishing communication between two devices that are behind a Network Address Translation (NAT) device, often used in peer-to-peer or VoIP applications to enable direct communication.

Network Forensics

Network Forensics is the process of collecting, analysing, and preserving network traffic and data for the purpose of investigating and identifying security incidents, often used in incident response, legal or regulatory compliance, or threat intelligence.

Next-Generation Firewall (NGFW)

A Next-Generation Firewall (NGFW) is a firewall that incorporates advanced features such as intrusion prevention, application awareness, and deep packet inspection, often used for enhanced network security.

Noob

Noob (also spelled "n00b" or "newb") is a term used to describe someone who is inexperienced or new to a particular activity or community, often used in online gaming and internet forums to refer to novice players or users.

NTP (Network Time Protocol)

NTP, or Network Time Protocol, is a networking protocol used to synchronize clocks between devices on a network, often used to ensure accurate timekeeping and logging.

Null Byte Injection

Null Byte Injection is a type of injection attack that targets the null byte character in software code, often used to bypass input validation and execute malicious code.

Node.js Security

Node.js Security refers to the practice of securing Node.js applications and systems from security threats and vulnerabilities, often using secure coding practices, testing, and monitoring.

Near Field Communication (NFC)

Near Field Communication, or NFC, is a technology that enables wireless communication and data exchange between devices in close proximity, often used for mobile payments, access control, and other applications.

Non-Repudiation

Non-Repudiation is a security concept that ensures that a user or entity cannot deny or dispute the authenticity or integrity of a message or transaction, often achieved using digital signatures, timestamps, and other cryptographic techniques.

NFT (Non-Fungible Token)

A Non-Fungible Token (NFT) is a unique digital asset that is verified on a blockchain network, often used for buying, selling, and trading collectibles, artwork, and other digital assets that have distinct value or characteristics.

O

OAuth

OAuth is an open-standard authorization protocol that allows third-party applications to access user data from online services without having to store the user's credentials.

Obfuscation

Obfuscation is the practice of deliberately making code, data, or information difficult to understand or read, often used by attackers to conceal malware or hide sensitive information.

OSI Model (Open Systems Interconnection Model)

The OSI Model is a conceptual framework used to describe the communication functions of a networking system, consisting of seven layers that define how data is transmitted and received.

Onion Routing

Onion Routing is a technique used to anonymize internet traffic by routing it through a series of servers, encrypting the data at each hop, and stripping off a layer of encryption at each server until it reaches its destination.

OpenVPN

OpenVPN is an open-source virtual private network (VPN) technology that creates secure connections over the internet, often used to encrypt and secure remote access to private networks.

Operating System

An Operating System (OS) is a collection of software that manages computer hardware and provides common services for computer programs, often targeted by attackers to gain control of a system.

Out-of-Band Authentication

Out-of-Band Authentication is a security mechanism that uses a separate communication channel, such as a phone call or text message, to verify the identity of a user or device.

OTP (One-Time Password)

A One-Time Password (OTP) is a temporary password that is valid for only one login session or transaction, often used for two-factor authentication or as a secondary authentication factor.

Online Identity

An Online Identity is the collection of digital information and data that represents a person or organization on the internet, often used as a target for cyber-attacks or identity theft.

Outdated Software

Outdated Software is software that has not been updated to fix security vulnerabilities or bugs, often targeted by attackers to gain access to systems or data.

Onion Network

The Onion Network is a network of servers used to provide anonymous and private access to the internet, often used by activists, journalists, and whistleblowers to evade surveillance or censorship.

Offensive Security

Offensive Security is the practice of using hacking techniques and tools to identify and exploit vulnerabilities in computer systems and networks, often used as a defensive mechanism to improve security posture.

Overprivileged Users

Overprivileged Users are users with unnecessary or excessive privileges or permissions on a system, often targeted by attackers to gain access to sensitive data or resources.

Obscure Web Attacks

Obscure Web Attacks are sophisticated or unconventional web-based attacks that exploit vulnerabilities in web applications or protocols, often used to steal data or take control of systems.

Off-Path Attack

An Off-Path Attack is a type of network attack that does not require the attacker to be on the same network path as the victim, often used to intercept or modify network traffic.

Over-the-Air (OTA) Updates

Over-the-Air (OTA) Updates are wireless updates for firmware or software that are delivered over the air, often used to fix security vulnerabilities or bugs in mobile devices or Internet of Things (IoT) devices.

Orphaned Accounts

Orphaned Accounts are user accounts that are no longer needed or have been abandoned, often left active and unmonitored, creating security risks for organizations.

On-premises Security

On-premises Security refers to security measures and technologies implemented in-house, within an organization's physical premises or network, often used to protect against cyber-attacks.

Open Source Intelligence (OSINT)

Open Source Intelligence (OSINT) is the collection and analysis of publicly available information and data from open sources, often used in cybersecurity investigations and threat intelligence.

Orchestration

Orchestration is the automated coordination and management of systems, applications, and services, often used to optimize and streamline IT operations and security.

P

Patch

A patch is a piece of software designed to fix security vulnerabilities or bugs in a program, often provided by the software vendor or developer to improve security and performance.

Payload

A payload is a piece of code or data that is carried by a network packet or malware, often used in cyber-attacks to deliver a malicious payload such as a virus or ransomware.

Payload Encryption

Payload Encryption is the process of encrypting data or code within a computer network or storage system, often used to protect sensitive information from unauthorized access or interception.

Penetration Testing

Penetration testing, also known as pen testing or ethical hacking, is the process of simulating an attack on a computer system, application, or network to identify security vulnerabilities and weaknesses.

Phishing

Phishing is a type of social engineering attack where an attacker uses deception to obtain sensitive information such as login credentials, financial information, or personal data from a victim, often using email or other messaging platforms.

Ping of Death

Ping of Death is a type of Denial of Service (DoS) attack that sends oversized or malformed packets to a computer or network device to cause it to crash or become unresponsive.

Plaintext

Plaintext refers to data that is not encrypted and can be read by anyone who has access to it, often used in reference to sensitive data such as passwords or credit card information that should be protected.

Port

A port is a virtual communication channel used by network protocols to identify specific services or applications running on a computer or network device, often used in firewall configurations to control access to specific ports.

Privilege Escalation

Privilege escalation is the process of gaining elevated privileges or permissions on a computer system or network. This process is often used by attackers to gain access to sensitive data or resources.

Protocol

A protocol is a set of rules and standards that govern the communication and exchange of data between computers or network devices, often used to ensure compatibility and interoperability between different systems and applications.

Proxy Server

A proxy server is an intermediary server that acts as a gateway between a user and the internet, often used to improve security, performance, and privacy by filtering or caching web traffic and masking the user's IP address.

Public Key Infrastructure (PKI)

Public Key Infrastructure (PKI) is a system that uses digital certificates and public key cryptography to provide secure communication and authentication over the internet, often used to secure online transactions, email communication, and network access.

Password Manager

A Password Manager is a software application or service that helps users store, manage, and organize their passwords and other sensitive information in a secure and encrypted manner. Password Managers are used to reduce the risk of password-related security incidents and improve password hygiene.

Physical Security

Physical Security is the protection of physical assets, resources, and personnel from unauthorized access, theft, damage, or destruction, often used to ensure the safety and security of buildings, facilities, and infrastructure.

Packet

A Packet is a unit of data that is transmitted over a computer network, often used to transfer information between devices or to establish communication between network nodes.

Packet Sniffing

Packet Sniffing is the process of intercepting and analysing network traffic to extract information, often used by attackers to steal sensitive data or to detect vulnerabilities in network security.

Patch Management

Patch Management is the process of monitoring, evaluating, testing, and deploying software patches and updates to computer systems and applications to prevent security vulnerabilities and maintain system performance.

Point-to-Point Tunnelling Protocol (PPTP)

Point-to-Point Tunnelling Protocol (PPTP) is a protocol used for creating Virtual Private Networks (VPNs), often used for remote access and secure communication between networks and devices.

Post-Quantum Cryptography

Post-Quantum Cryptography is a type of cryptography designed to resist attacks by quantum computers, often used to secure sensitive data and communications in the future quantum computing era.

Privacy Policy

A Privacy Policy is a legal document or statement that describes how an organization collects, uses, and manages personal information and data, often required by data protection regulations such as GDPR or CCPA.

Persistence

Persistence in cybersecurity refers to an attacker's ability to maintain unauthorized access to a system even after a system restart or shutdown, often achieved by installing malware or modifying (system) settings.

Package

In the context of cybersecurity, a package refers to a collection of software files and resources that are bundled together for distribution or installation, often used to deliver updates, security patches, or new features to software applications.

PIP

PIP, or the Python Package Installer, is a tool used for installing and managing Python packages. It is used to download and install packages from the Python Package Index (PyPI) and other repositories, making it easy to manage dependencies and keep Python libraries up to date.

Q

Quantum Cryptography

Quantum Cryptography is a method of encrypting and transmitting data using the principles of quantum physics. This method provides a higher level of security than traditional encryption methods.

Query Language

Query Language is a programming language used to communicate with databases, allowing users to retrieve and manipulate data stored within them.

Quarantine

Quarantine is a security measure used to isolate potentially malicious files or software to prevent them from infecting other systems or networks.

Quality of Service (QoS)

Quality of Service (QoS) is a set of technologies and techniques used to manage network traffic and ensure that certain types of traffic receive priority treatment, such as real-time data or voice traffic.

Quick Response (QR) Code

Quick Response (QR) Code is a type of two-dimensional barcode that can be scanned using a smartphone or other device to quickly access information or a website.

Query String

Query String is a part of a URL that contains data to be passed to a web server, often used for filtering or sorting data or for tracking user activity.

Queue

Queue is a data structure used to store and organize tasks or requests in a first-in, first-out (FIFO) order.

Quantum Key Distribution

Quantum Key Distribution is a method of secure communication that uses the principles of quantum mechanics to establish a shared encryption key between two parties.

Quorum-Based Consensus Algorithm

Quorum-Based Consensus Algorithm is a type of consensus algorithm used in distributed computing systems that requires a certain percentage or quorum of nodes to agree on a decision or transaction before it is executed.

Qubes OS

Qubes OS is a security-focused operating system that uses virtualization to isolate applications and protect the system from attacks

R

Radio Frequency Identification (RFID)
Radio Frequency Identification (RFID) is a wireless technology used for the identification of objects or people, based on electromagnetic fields. It consists of an RFID tag and an RFID reader, which communicates with each other via radio waves.

Rainbow Table
A Rainbow Table is a precomputed table used for reversing cryptographic hash functions, to find the original plaintext input. It is often used by attackers to crack passwords.

RADIUS (Remote Authentication Dial-In User Service)
RADIUS (Remote Authentication Dial-In User Service) is a network protocol used for remote user authentication and authorization. It is commonly used in enterprise environments, where users need to access network resources from remote locations.

Ransomware
Ransomware is a type of malware that encrypts the victim's files and demands a ransom payment in exchange for the decryption key. It is often distributed via phishing emails or exploit kits and can cause significant damage to individuals and organizations.

Ransomware-as-a-Service (RaaS)
Ransomware-as-a-Service (RaaS) is a criminal business model in which ransomware developers rent or sell their software to other criminals, who then use it to launch attacks on their targets. It has led to an increase in the number of ransomware attacks and has made it easier for non-technical criminals to get involved in cybercrime.

Real-Time Monitoring
Real-Time Monitoring is a process of collecting and analysing data in real-time, to detect and respond to security threats as they happen. It is used in various security solutions, such as intrusion detection systems and security information and event management (SIEM) systems.

Real-Time Threat Detection
Real-Time Threat Detection is a capability of security solutions to detect and respond to security threats in real-time, using various techniques such as behavioural analysis, machine learning, and artificial intelligence. It is essential for organizations to protect against advanced and persistent threats.

Recovery Time Objective (RTO)
Recovery Time Objective (RTO) is the maximum acceptable downtime for a system or application, after a disruption or disaster. It is a critical metric in disaster recovery planning and helps organizations to minimize the impact of downtime on their operations.

Red Team
A Red Team is a group of security professionals who simulate real-world attacks against an organization's security defences, to identify vulnerabilities and weaknesses. It is often used in conjunction with a Blue Team, which is responsible for defending against the attacks.

Redaction
Redaction is the process of removing or obscuring sensitive information from a document or file, to protect the privacy and security of individuals or organizations. It is commonly used in legal and government documents, but also in various industries to protect sensitive data.

Redundancy
Redundancy is the duplication of critical components or systems, to provide a backup in case of failure. It is an essential component of high availability and disaster recovery planning, to ensure that systems and applications remain available and operational.

Reflection Attack
A Reflection Attack is a type of DDoS attack that exploits vulnerable network services to generate large volumes of traffic and overwhelm the target's network or infrastructure. It is often used in conjunction with amplification techniques, to increase the volume of attack traffic.

Regulated Data

Regulated Data is data that is subject to legal or regulatory requirements, such as personally identifiable information, financial data, or healthcare information. Organizations must take appropriate measures to protect this data from unauthorized access or disclosure.

Regulatory Compliance

Regulatory Compliance refers to the process of ensuring that an organization follows all relevant laws, regulations, and standards that apply to its operations. Compliance is important for mitigating legal and financial risks and maintaining the trust of customers and stakeholders.

Relay Attack

A Relay Attack is a type of cyber-attack where an attacker intercepts communication between two parties and relays it to another party without the knowledge of the original parties. This type of attack is commonly used to bypass authentication measures and gain unauthorized access to systems or data.

Reliability

Reliability is a measure of the dependability and consistency of a system or component. In cybersecurity, reliability is important for ensuring that systems and networks are available and functioning properly to prevent downtime, data loss, or other negative impacts.

Remote Access Trojan (RAT)

A Remote Access Trojan (RAT) is a type of malware that allows an attacker to take control of a victim's computer or device remotely. RATs are often used for unauthorized access, data theft, and other malicious activities.

Remote Code Execution (RCE)

Remote Code Execution (RCE) is a type of vulnerability that allows an attacker to execute arbitrary code on a remote system or application. This type of vulnerability can be used to take control of systems, steal data, or carry out other malicious activities.

Remote Desktop Protocol (RDP)

Remote Desktop Protocol (RDP) is a protocol used to remotely access and control a computer or device. RDP is commonly used for remote support, remote work, and other purposes, but can also be a potential security risk if not properly secured.

Remote Wipe

Remote Wipe is a security feature that allows a user to erase the data on a lost or stolen device remotely. This feature can protect sensitive data from falling into the wrong hands.

Replay Attack

A Replay Attack is a type of network attack where an attacker intercepts and retransmits data that was previously captured in an attempt to bypass authentication mechanisms and gain unauthorized access.

Risk Assessment

Risk Assessment is the process of identifying, analysing, and evaluating potential risks to an organization's assets and infrastructure, including information and technology systems. This process is critical in developing an effective risk management plan.

Risk Management

Risk Management is the process of identifying, assessing, and prioritizing risks, and taking steps to minimize, monitor, and control those risks. This is essential in ensuring the continuity of business operations and the protection of assets.

Risk Mitigation

Risk Mitigation involves taking actions to reduce the likelihood or impact of potential risks to an organization. This can include implementing security controls and procedures, improving processes, and increasing awareness and training.

Risk Register

A Risk Register is a document that records all identified risks, their potential impact, and the steps being taken to manage them. This provides a comprehensive view of an organization's risk profile and helps in making informed decisions.

Robocall

A Robocall is an automated phone call that delivers a pre-recorded message. This can be used for legitimate purposes, but is also commonly used for fraudulent and malicious activities, such as phishing scams.

Role-Based Access Control

Role-Based Access Control is a security model that restricts access to resources based on the roles and responsibilities of individual users within an organization. This provides granular control over access rights and helps in preventing unauthorized access.

Rogue Access Point

A Rogue Access Point is an unauthorized wireless access point that has been installed on a network. This can allow attackers to gain unauthorized access to the network and potentially compromise sensitive data.

Rogue Antivirus

Rogue Antivirus is a type of malicious software that is disguised as an antivirus program but in reality is designed to harm a computer system or steal personal information.

Rogue Certificate

A Rogue Certificate is a digital certificate that is issued by a Certificate Authority (CA) to a malicious entity that is impersonating a legitimate organization, allowing the malicious entity to carry out attacks undetected.

Rogue Code

Rogue Code refers to any malicious code that is designed to harm a computer system, steal sensitive information, or carry out other malicious activities.

Rogue Device

A Rogue Device is any unauthorized device that is connected to a network or system without proper approval, which can lead to security vulnerabilities and breaches.

Rogue DHCP Attack

A Rogue DHCP (Dynamic Host Configuration Protocol) is a type of attack where a malicious actor sets up a fake DHCP server on a network to distribute false IP addresses, potentially leading to denial-of-service attacks or information theft.

Rogue DHCP Server

A Rogue DHCP Server is a fake DHCP server that is set up by a malicious actor to distribute false IP addresses and potentially carry out attacks on a network.

Rogue Gateway

A Rogue Gateway is an unauthorized gateway device that is set up on a network without proper approval, creating potential security vulnerabilities and enabling unauthorized access.

Rogue Program

A Rogue Program is a type of malware that is disguised as a legitimate program but is designed to harm a computer system or steal sensitive information.

Rogue Scanner

A Rogue Scanner is a type of malware that is designed to look like a legitimate security program, but is actually designed to scam users by presenting false reports of malware infections and charging money for removal.

Rogue Software

Rogue Software refers to any type of malicious software that is disguised as legitimate software, and is designed to harm a computer system or steal sensitive information.

Rogue Wireless Network

A Rogue Wireless Network is an unauthorized wireless network that is set up by a malicious actor without proper approval, creating potential security vulnerabilities and enabling unauthorized access.

Root Certificate

A Root Certificate is a digital certificate that is issued by a trusted Certificate Authority (CA) and is used to verify the authenticity of other digital certificates.

Root Password

A Root Password is a password that is used to gain administrative access to a computer system or network, allowing the user to perform critical functions and make changes to the system configuration.

S

SSL (Secure Sockets Layer)

SSL is a protocol that provides secure communication between two computers over the internet, commonly used for securing online transactions, email, and other sensitive data.

Sandbox

A sandbox is an isolated environment where programs and applications can be executed securely without affecting the system or other programs. This is commonly used in security testing.

SQL Injection

SQL Injection is a type of attack where an attacker injects malicious SQL code into a web application's input box, which can compromise the database and steal sensitive information.

Social Engineering

Social Engineering is the art of manipulating people to divulge sensitive information, usually through deception and impersonation. This is commonly used in phishing attacks and identity theft.

Sniffing

Sniffing is a technique used by attackers to intercept and monitor network traffic, potentially allowing them to capture sensitive information such as usernames and passwords.

Spoofing

Spoofing is the act of impersonating someone or something else in order to gain unauthorized access to a system or network. This can be done through email spoofing, IP spoofing, and other techniques.

Spear Phishing

Spear phishing is a targeted form of phishing that is customized for a specific individual or organization. This is done by researching the target's interests, job role, and relationships to create a convincing message.

Session Hijacking

Session hijacking is a type of attack where an attacker steals the session ID of an authenticated user to gain unauthorized access to a web application.

Security Information and Event Management (SIEM)

SIEM is a software solution that collects, aggregates, and analyses security data from various sources in order to detect and respond to security threats.

Security Operations Center (SOC)

A Security Operations Center (SOC) is a centralized unit responsible for monitoring, detecting, analysing, and responding to security incidents in an organization's IT infrastructure.

The SOC typically comprises a team of security analysts and engineers who use various tools and techniques to protect the organization's assets and data from cyber threats.

Security Testing

Security Testing is a type of software testing that is performed to identify vulnerabilities and weaknesses in an application or system's security posture. This testing is designed to detect security flaws and provide recommendations for remediation. Common types of security testing include penetration testing, vulnerability scanning, and code review.

Script Kiddie

A Script Kiddie is an unskilled hacker who relies on pre-written software tools and scripts to launch attacks on networks and computer systems. These individuals lack the technical expertise to create their own tools or write custom scripts, and instead, use off-the-shelf programs to exploit known vulnerabilities.

Software-Defined Network (SDN)

A Software-Defined Network (SDN) is a network architecture that uses software to manage network traffic and resources instead of traditional hardware-based solutions. SDN allows for greater flexibility and agility in managing network resources and allows for more efficient allocation of resources to meet the needs of the organization.

Stateful Packet Inspection (SPI)

Stateful Packet Inspection (SPI) is a type of firewall technology that examines the state of network connections to identify and block unauthorized access attempts. SPI firewalls keep track of the state of network connections and can detect and block malicious traffic based on predefined rules.

Steganography

Steganography is the practice of hiding secret messages or data within another file or message to avoid detection. This technique involves embedding the data within an image, video, or audio file without changing the file's appearance or functionality. Steganography is often used in conjunction with encryption to provide an extra layer of security.

System Hardening

System hardening is the process of securing computer systems by reducing vulnerabilities and eliminating unnecessary functions or features. This involves configuring the system according to established security policies and guidelines, and implementing various security measures such as access control, patch management, and antivirus software.

Security Controls

Security controls are measures put in place to protect information and systems from unauthorized access, use, disclosure, disruption, modification, or destruction. These controls may be technical, administrative, or physical in nature, and are designed to reduce or eliminate security risks.

Security Policy

A security policy is a document that outlines an organization's approach to information security. It defines the rules, procedures, and guidelines that must be followed in order to ensure the confidentiality, integrity, and availability of information assets. A security policy typically covers areas such as access control, data protection, incident response, and risk management.

Security Audit

A security audit is a systematic evaluation of an organization's information security policies, procedures, and practices. It is typically conducted to identify weaknesses and vulnerabilities in the organization's security posture, and to recommend measures to improve security. A security audit may be conducted internally by the organization's own staff, or by an external auditor or consultant.

Security Token

A Security Token is a physical device or application that generates unique codes or passwords for secure authentication, often used to add an extra layer of security to online accounts and transactions.

Stuxnet

Stuxnet is a computer worm that was discovered in 2010 and believed to have been developed by the US and Israel to sabotage Iran's nuclear program. It is considered one of the most sophisticated and dangerous cyber weapons ever developed, capable of causing physical damage to industrial control systems.

T

TCP/IP

TCP/IP is a suite of communication protocols that enable data to be exchanged between interconnected devices over the internet and other computer networks.

Takedown

Takedown is the act of removing a website or other online content from the internet, often due to a violation of laws or policies.

Tailgating

Tailgating is the practice of following closely behind another person to gain unauthorized access to a restricted area, often used as a method of social engineering to bypass physical security controls.

TACACS+ (Terminal Access Controller Access-Control System Plus)

TACACS+ is a security protocol that provides centralized authentication, authorization, and accounting services for remote access devices.

Threat Hunting

Threat hunting is a proactive approach to identifying and mitigating threats to an organization's security infrastructure by actively searching for and analysing suspicious activities or behaviour.

Threat Intelligence

Threat intelligence is the process of collecting and analysing information about potential or current cyber threats to identify risks and enhance an organization's security posture.

Threat Model

A threat model is a systematic approach to identifying and assessing potential security threats to a system or application and developing measures to mitigate those risks.

Threat Vector

A threat vector is the means by which a cyberattack or other security threat can gain access to a system or network, such as through phishing emails, infected websites, or unsecured devices.

TLS (Transport Layer Security)

TLS is a cryptographic protocol that provides secure communication over the internet and other computer networks, commonly used to secure data transmission for online transactions and other sensitive information.

Tokenization

Tokenization is the process of replacing sensitive data with a non-sensitive equivalent, such as a randomly generated number, to reduce the risk of data breaches or unauthorized access.

Tor Network

The Tor network is a decentralized network of servers and nodes designed to provide anonymous internet access and protect the privacy and security of users.

Traceroute

Traceroute is a command-line tool used to trace the path that network packets take between a source and destination device, often used to troubleshoot network connectivity issues.

Trap and Trace

Trap and trace is a legal process that allows law enforcement agencies to monitor and record internet traffic to identify and investigate criminal activity.

Trojan Horse

A Trojan horse is a type of malware that appears to be legitimate software but is designed to harm a computer system or network by allowing unauthorized access or stealing sensitive data.

Trust Model

A trust model is a framework for establishing and managing trust relationships between entities in a system, often used in the design of secure computer systems and networks.

Trust Zone

A trust zone is a secure area of a computer system or network that is designated as a trusted environment for running critical or sensitive applications.

Two-Factor Authentication (2FA)

Two-factor authentication is a security process that requires users to provide two forms of identification, such as a password and a security token or biometric authentication, to access a system or application.

Temporal Key Integrity Protocol (TKIP)

Temporal Key Integrity Protocol is a wireless security protocol used to secure data transmission over Wi-Fi networks, providing stronger encryption and protection against key attacks.

Third-Party Access

Third-party access refers to the practice of granting access to a computer system or network to individuals or organizations that are not part of the organization that owns the system or network.

Tunnelling

Tunnelling is a technique used to encapsulate one network protocol within another, allowing data to be transmitted securely over a public network such as the internet.

Transcript

A transcript is a written or typed copy of a spoken conversation or presentation, often used in legal and academic settings. In cybersecurity, transcripts of communications may be reviewed as part of incident response or forensic investigations. Transcripts of training sessions and simulations may be used to assess the knowledge and skills of (security) personnel.

U

UDP (User Datagram Protocol)

User Datagram Protocol (UDP) is a transport protocol that operates at the Transport Layer of the OSI Model. UDP is used to send datagrams, which are self-contained units of data, over a network.

Unified Threat Management (UTM)

Unified Threat Management (UTM) is an approach to security management that combines multiple security features into a single platform or device to provide comprehensive protection against various types of threats.

URL (Uniform Resource Locator)

A Uniform Resource Locator (URL) is a unique address that identifies the location of a resource on the Internet. URLs are used to access web pages, files, and other resources on the World Wide Web.

User Account Control (UAC)

User Account Control (UAC) is a security feature in Windows operating systems that prompts users for permission or confirmation before allowing certain actions or changes that could potentially affect the system's security or stability.

User Activity Monitoring (UAM)

User Activity Monitoring (UAM) is a security practice that involves monitoring and analysing user activity on a network or system to detect and prevent security breaches or unauthorized access.

User Behaviour Analytics (UBA)

User Behavior Analytics (UBA) is a type of security analytics that uses machine learning algorithms and statistical analysis to identify abnormal user behaviour that may indicate a security threat.

User Interface (UI)

User Interface (UI) refers to the design and layout of the visual and interactive elements that users interact with when using software or a website. UI design plays an important role in ensuring the usability and accessibility of a system.

User-Agent

User-Agent is a string of text that identifies the browser, operating system, and other relevant information about the user's device when accessing a website or service on the Internet.

USB Device Security

USB Device Security refers to the measures taken to protect a computer system from security threats posed by USB devices such as flash drives, external hard drives, and other portable storage devices.

Unicode Encoding

Unicode Encoding is a system that assigns a unique code point to every character in every language. It allows different computers and software applications to exchange and display text correctly.

Unsecured Network

An Unsecured Network is a network that is not protected by security measures such as firewalls, encryption, or access control. It is vulnerable to attacks and unauthorized access.

UPnP (Universal Plug and Play)

UPnP (Universal Plug and Play) is a networking protocol that allows devices to automatically discover and communicate with each other on a network. It is commonly used for media streaming and home automation.

URL Spoofing

URL Spoofing is a technique used by attackers to disguise a malicious website as a legitimate one. It involves using a similar-looking domain name or URL to trick users into visiting the fake site.

USB Rubber Ducky

USB Rubber Ducky is a type of programmable USB device that can simulate keyboard input to automate tasks or execute commands on a computer system.

Utility Computing

Utility Computing is a model of cloud computing where computing resources such as processing power, storage, and bandwidth are provided as a service on a pay-per-use basis.

Unified Endpoint Management (UEM)

Unified Endpoint Management (UEM) is a cybersecurity solution that allows organizations to manage and secure all their endpoint devices, including mobile devices and laptops, from a single console.

Untrusted Networks

Untrusted Networks are networks that are not secure and are considered risky for transmitting sensitive data. They are often public Wi-Fi networks or other networks that are open to the public.

Uptime

Uptime is the amount of time that a system or service is available and operational. It is a measure of the reliability and stability of a system.

Update

An update refers to a software patch or a newer version of software that is released to improve its functionality, performance, or security.

V

Virus

A computer virus is a type of malicious software that is designed to spread from one computer to another, and has the ability to self-replicate. It can cause damage to the computer system by corrupting files, stealing personal information, or disrupting normal computer operations.

It can be spread through email attachments, infected websites, or infected software.

Vulnerability

A vulnerability is a weakness in a system that can be exploited by attackers to gain unauthorized access to the system or to perform other malicious actions. Vulnerabilities can exist in software, hardware, processes or network configurations. They can be discovered by security researchers, or by attackers who exploit them for their own gain.

Virtual Private Network (VPN)

A Virtual Private Network (VPN) is a technology that allows users to create a secure and encrypted connection between their computer or mobile device and a private network over the internet. It provides a secure way for remote workers to access company resources, and for individuals to browse the internet anonymously.

Virtualization

Virtualization is the process of creating a virtual version of a computer system, including its hardware, operating system, and applications. It allows multiple virtual machines to run on a single physical machine, and enables users to access different operating systems and applications without the need for multiple physical machines.

Voice over Internet Protocol (VoIP)

Voice over Internet Protocol (VoIP) is a technology that allows users to make voice calls over the internet. It uses the internet to transmit voice data in packets, rather than through traditional telephone lines.

VoIP is used by businesses and individuals for cost-effective communication and collaboration.

Virtual Machine (VM)

A virtual machine (VM) is a software-based emulation of a computer system. It allows users to run multiple operating systems on a single physical machine, and to allocate resources such as memory and processing power to each virtual machine as needed. VMs are commonly used in cloud computing and for testing software.

Virus Signature

A virus signature is a unique pattern of code that identifies a specific virus or malware. Virus signatures are used by antivirus software to detect and remove known threats from computer systems.

VLAN (Virtual Local Area Network)

A Virtual Local Area Network (VLAN) is a logical network that groups devices together based on their function or location, rather than their physical connections. VLANs allow network administrators to segment network traffic and improve network performance, security, and management.

Vulnerability Assessment

A Vulnerability Assessment is the process of identifying and evaluating vulnerabilities in a system or network to determine the likelihood of an attack. The goal of a vulnerability assessment is to identify security weaknesses that an attacker could exploit, prioritize them based on risk, and recommend appropriate measures to mitigate those risks.

Virus Scanner

A Virus Scanner is a program that scans files and folders on a computer system for viruses and other malware. Virus scanners use a database of known virus signatures and heuristics to detect malicious code in files and to remove or quarantine infected files.

Virtual Firewall

A Virtual Firewall is a firewall implemented as software on a virtual machine or cloud instance rather than as a physical appliance. Virtual firewalls provide the same security capabilities as physical firewalls and are often used in cloud environments to protect virtual networks.

Voice Biometrics

Voice Biometrics is a security technology that uses voiceprint analysis to identify individuals. Voice biometric systems capture and analyse the unique physical and behavioural characteristics of a person's voice to confirm their identity.

Vulnerability Scanning

Vulnerability Scanning is the process of identifying vulnerabilities in a system or network using automated tools. Vulnerability scanners scan for known vulnerabilities in software and operating systems and generate reports that list the vulnerabilities and recommended actions to remediate them.

VPN Concentrator

A VPN Concentrator is a device that provides secure remote access to a private network by creating and managing VPN connections. VPN concentrators can handle multiple VPN connections simultaneously and provide encryption and authentication services.

Virtual Desktop Infrastructure (VDI)

Virtual Desktop Infrastructure (VDI) is a technology that allows multiple virtual desktops to run on a single physical machine. VDI enables users to access virtual desktops and applications from anywhere, on any device, while maintaining security and control over sensitive data.

Vulnerability Exploitation

Vulnerability Exploitation is the process of taking advantage of a vulnerability in a system or network to gain unauthorized access, steal data, or disrupt operations. Attackers use various tools and techniques to exploit vulnerabilities, including malware, social engineering, and network scanning.

Virtual Patching

Virtual Patching is a technique that involves the use of security policies and rule sets to prevent vulnerabilities from being exploited in a software system or application. Rather than waiting for a vendor to release an official patch for a vulnerability, virtual patching provides an immediate temporary solution to protect against potential threats.

Voice Phishing (Vishing)

Voice Phishing or Vishing is a type of phishing attack that is conducted through voice communication channels, such as phone calls or VoIP calls. The attacker typically poses as a trusted individual or organization and attempts to persuade the victim to reveal sensitive information, such as login credentials or financial details.

Virtual Private Cloud (VPC)

A Virtual Private Cloud or VPC is a cloud computing service that allows users to create isolated virtual networks within a public cloud environment. VPCs provide enhanced security and control over network configurations and allow users to run their applications and services in a private, dedicated environment.

Virtualization Sprawl

Virtualization Sprawl is a phenomenon that occurs when virtual machines (VMs) are created and deployed without proper management and oversight. This can lead to an uncontrolled proliferation of VMs across an organization's infrastructure. This results in wasted resources, increased maintenance costs, and potential security risks.

W

WAF (Web Application Firewall)

Web Application Firewall (WAF) is a security tool designed to protect web applications by monitoring and filtering HTTP traffic between a web application and the internet.

WAP (Wireless Access Point)

A Wireless Access Point (WAP) is a hardware device that allows wireless devices to connect to a wired network using Wi-Fi.

WEP (Wired Equivalent Privacy)

Wired Equivalent Privacy (WEP) is a security protocol for wireless networks. It provides weak security and is no longer recommended for use.

Web Security

Web Security refers to the process of securing websites, web applications, and web services from various online threats such as malware, hacking, phishing, and other cyber-attacks.

Wi-Fi Protected Access (WPA)

Wi-Fi Protected Access (WPA) is a security protocol for wireless networks. It provides better security than WEP and is currently the recommended security protocol for wireless networks.

Worm

A worm is a type of malware that spreads through computer networks by exploiting vulnerabilities in software or using social engineering techniques to trick users into executing malicious code.

Wi-Fi

Wi-Fi is a wireless networking technology that allows devices to connect to the internet and other devices without the need for cables or wires.

Whaling

Whaling is a type of phishing attack that targets high-profile individuals such as executives and senior managers to gain access to sensitive information or to carry out financial fraud.

White Hat Hacker

A White Hat Hacker is a computer security professional who uses their skills to identify vulnerabilities and weaknesses in systems and networks in order to improve their security.

Windows Registry

The Windows Registry is a database used by the Microsoft Windows operating system to store configuration settings and other system-related information. It can be accessed and modified using the Windows Registry Editor.

Wi-Fi Direct

Wi-Fi Direct is a technology that allows two devices to connect to each other without a wireless access point. It uses Wi-Fi Protected Setup (WPS) or Near Field Communication (NFC) for device discovery and peer-to-peer connection.

Weak Password

A weak password is a password that can be easily guessed or cracked by attackers. It is important to use strong passwords, which include a mix of uppercase and lowercase letters, numbers, and special characters, and to avoid using common words or personal information.

Wireless Network

A wireless network is a network that allows devices to connect to the internet or each other without the use of physical cables. It uses radio waves to transmit data between devices.

Watering Hole Attack

A watering hole attack is a type of cyber-attack that targets a specific group of users by infecting websites that they are likely to visit. The attacker compromises a website and installs malware, which is then downloaded by the visitors of the website.

Wireless Sniffing

Wireless sniffing is the process of capturing and analysing wireless network traffic. This is often done by attackers to intercept sensitive information, such as usernames and passwords.

Web-Based Attack

A web-based attack is a type of cyber-attack that targets vulnerabilities in web applications. This can include injecting malicious code into web pages, exploiting vulnerabilities in the underlying web server, or stealing sensitive information from web applications.

Wireless Penetration Testing

Wireless penetration testing is the process of assessing the security of a wireless network by simulating an attack. This is done by identifying vulnerabilities in the network and exploiting them to gain unauthorized access.

WORM (Write Once Read Many)

WORM is a type of storage device that allows data to be written only once and then read many times. This is often used for archiving data that needs to be preserved for a long time.

Wiping

Wiping is the process of securely erasing data from a storage device, such as a hard drive or a flash drive. This is often done to protect sensitive information from falling into the wrong hands.

Wireless Intrusion Detection System (WIDS)

Wireless Intrusion Detection System (WIDS) is a type of security system designed to detect and alert network administrators of unauthorized access attempts to wireless networks. WIDS can detect rogue access points, spoofed MAC addresses, and other wireless attacks.

Wireless Intrusion Detection and Prevention System (WIDPS)

Wireless Intrusion Detection and Prevention System (WIDPS) is a type of security system designed to detect and prevent unauthorized access attempts to wireless networks. WIDPS combines the features of WIDS and Wireless Intrusion Prevention System (WIPS) to not only detect but also prevent wireless attacks.

Wireless Intrusion Prevention System (WIPS)

Wireless Intrusion Prevention System (WIPS) is a type of security system designed to prevent unauthorized access attempts to wireless networks. WIPS can detect rogue access points, spoofed MAC addresses, and other wireless attacks, and then take appropriate action to block them.

Web Shell

Web shell is a type of malicious script that hackers use to take control of a web server or a web application. Once installed, web shells allow attackers to execute arbitrary commands on the web server, which can result in data theft, system compromise, and other malicious activities.

Wildcard Mask

Wildcard Mask is a term used in networking to define a range of IP addresses. It is used in conjunction with subnet masks to determine which IP addresses are allowed or blocked by network access control lists (ACLs).

Wireless LAN (WLAN)

Wireless LAN (WLAN) is a type of local area network (LAN) that uses wireless communication to connect devices. WLANs are commonly used in homes, offices, and public places, such as airports and coffee shops, to provide internet access to users without the need for cables.

Web Server

Web Server is a computer program that delivers web content, such as web pages and web applications, to clients over the internet. Web servers use various protocols, such as HTTP and HTTPS, to communicate with clients and provide them with the requested content.

Workload

Workload is a term used to describe the amount of processing power, memory, storage, and other resources required to run a specific application or workload. In IT, workload is often used to determine the size and capacity of infrastructure, such as servers and storage systems.

Web Crawler

Web Crawler is a type of software that automatically browses the internet and collects information from web pages. Web crawlers are commonly used by search engines, such as Google and Bing, to index web pages and build their search databases.

Wireless Key Logger

Wireless Key Logger is a type of hardware or software device that captures keystrokes entered on a wireless keyboard. Wireless key loggers are commonly used by attackers to steal sensitive information, such as passwords and credit card numbers, from unsuspecting users.

Wireless Bridge

A wireless bridge is a networking device that connects two or more network segments together wirelessly. It is often used to extend the range of a wireless network or to connect two physically separated networks.

Wireless Fidelity (Wi-Fi)

Wi-Fi is a wireless networking technology that allows devices to connect to the internet and communicate with each other wirelessly. It is a widely used technology for connecting to the internet, particularly in homes and businesses.

Web Application

A web application is a software application that runs on a web server and is accessed through a web browser. It allows users to interact with the application through a web interface, rather than through a desktop application.

Wi-Fi Analyzer

A Wi-Fi analyser is a tool used to analyse and optimize wireless network performance. It allows users to see which wireless networks are available in the area, as well as their signal strength, channel usage, and other parameters.

War Dialling

War dialling is the practice of dialling a large number of phone numbers in an attempt to find a computer or modem connected to a network. It is often used to identify vulnerable systems that can be exploited for unauthorized access.

Wi-Fi Pineapple

The Wi-Fi Pineapple is a wireless networking device used for penetration testing and hacking. It is designed to mimic a legitimate wireless access point and capture sensitive information from unsuspecting users.

WAF Bypass

A WAF (Web Application Firewall) bypass is a technique used to circumvent the security measures put in place by a WAF. It can be used to exploit vulnerabilities in web applications and gain unauthorized access to sensitive information.

Web Scraping

Web scraping is the process of automatically extracting data from websites. It is often used for data mining or research purposes, but can also be used for malicious purposes such as stealing data or intellectual property.

Web Cookies

Web cookies are small text files that are stored on a user's computer when they visit a website. They are often used to track user behaviour and preferences, and can be used for targeted advertising.

Web Application Security Scanner (WASS)

A web application security scanner is a tool used to identify vulnerabilities in web applications. It automates the process of scanning web applications for common security issues, such as SQL injection and cross-site scripting (XSS) vulnerabilities.

X

X.509 Certificate

An X.509 certificate is a digital document that uses a standard format to verify the identity of a user, device, or organization. It is used for authentication and encryption purposes in various online transactions and communications.

Xen Hypervisor

Xen Hypervisor is an open-source software that allows multiple operating systems to run on a single host machine. It creates a virtual machine environment that isolates each operating system and provides them with dedicated resources, making it an efficient solution for virtualization.

XSRF (Cross-Site Request Forgery)

XSRF, also known as Cross-Site Request Forgery, is a type of cyber-attack in which an attacker exploits a website's trust in a user's identity to perform unauthorized actions on their behalf.
It is a serious security threat that can compromise user accounts and sensitive information.

XML External Entity (XXE)

XML External Entity (XXE) is a vulnerability that occurs when an XML parser processes external entities within an XML document. Attackers can exploit this vulnerability to execute malicious code and gain unauthorized access to sensitive information.

XML Injection

XML Injection is a type of cyber-attack in which an attacker injects malicious code into an XML input field, which can then be executed by the application that processes the input. This can result in unauthorized access to sensitive data, system compromise, and other security breaches.

XOR Encryption

XOR Encryption is a simple encryption technique that uses the XOR (exclusive OR) operation to encrypt and decrypt data. It is commonly used in computer security as a basic encryption method.

XSS (Cross-Site Scripting)

XSS (Cross-Site Scripting) is a type of cyber-attack in which an attacker injects malicious code into a web page viewed by other users. The code is then executed by the user's web browser, allowing the attacker to steal sensitive information, perform unauthorized actions, or spread malware.

Y

Yara

Yara is an open-source tool used to create custom malware signatures and detect patterns in files and processes.

YubiKey

YubiKey is a hardware authentication device used for two-factor authentication and password less login.

YARA-L

YARA-L is a variant of YARA that incorporates machine learning algorithms for more accurate detection of malware.

YARA Rules

YARA Rules are a set of guidelines used to create and customize signatures for detecting malware.

YAML

YAML (Yet Another Markup Language) is a human-readable data serialization format used for configuration files.

Yara-Rules-Generator

Yara-Rules-Generator is a tool used to generate YARA rules based on malware samples.

YOLO

YOLO, an acronym for "you only live once," is a term often used in the context of living life to the fullest. However, in the field of cybersecurity, YOLO has taken on a different meaning. Cybersecurity experts believe that mistakes will inevitably be made, but it's important to learn from them and take steps to prevent similar mistakes from happening again. In this sense, YOLO serves as a reminder that cybersecurity is an ongoing process of continuous improvement and learning.

Youtube Scam

Youtube Scam is a type of online scam that leverages the popularity of Youtube to deceive users into clicking on malicious links or downloading harmful software. These scams may take various forms, such as fake video downloads, click-bait videos, or phishing scams that steal users' login credentials.

Your Call Is Important To Us Scam

Your Call Is Important To Us scam is a type of social engineering attack that targets individuals through phone calls, pretending to be a legitimate organization such as a bank, government agency, or customer service representative.

Z

Zigbee

Zigbee is a wireless communication protocol widely used in Internet of Things (IoT) devices. It provides low-power, low-cost, and low-data-rate networking that is suitable for various applications, including home automation, industrial automation, and medical devices.

Zero-Day

Zero-Day refers to a software vulnerability that is unknown to the software vendor and has not yet been patched. Attackers can exploit zero-day vulnerabilities to launch targeted attacks that can compromise user data and systems.

Zero Trust

Zero Trust is a security model that requires strict identity verification for all users, devices, and applications attempting to access a network. It assumes that every device, user, and application is a potential threat and employs multiple layers of security to protect against data breaches and cyber-attacks.

Zone Transfer

Zone Transfer is a process in which a DNS server shares its zone information with another DNS server. It is used to improve the speed and reliability of DNS queries and updates.

Zoo

The Malware Zoo is a repository of various malware samples that are commonly used by cybersecurity researchers and analysts to study the behaviour of malware and develop effective strategies to detect and mitigate them.

The samples are collected from various sources and are categorized based on their behaviour, such as trojans, worms, viruses, and more.

Zombie

In the context of cybersecurity, a zombie is a computer or device that has been infected with malware and is being controlled remotely by an attacker. These devices can be used to launch cyber-attacks, such as Distributed Denial of Service (DDoS) attacks, without the knowledge of the device owner. The term "zombie" comes from the fact that the infected device is essentially "dead" to the user and is under the control of the attacker

Z-Wave

Z-Wave is a wireless communication protocol used in smart home automation systems. It allows devices such as lights, locks, and thermostats to communicate with each other and with a central hub.

Made in the USA
Las Vegas, NV
13 May 2025

a38efdb3-d2b1-48f2-b505-eaadad6c9c2fR01